ENVIRONMENTAL CONCEPT

The book is written according to the syllabus of "Environmental Studies" for 3-year B.A. /B.Sc. /B.Com. /B.Mus. Part-II (General and Honours Courses of studies) under the University of Calcutta.

ENVIRONMENTAL CONCEPT

Dr Ajit Kumar Bera, Ph.D., F.M.I.N.C.A.

2000 Millinium Medal of Honours (U.S.A.)
Director, Institute of Environmental Analysis and Social Development (India)
Member, Asian Environmental Council
Corresponding Member, Environment and Health (England)

New Central Book Agency (P) Ltd

LONDON
HYDERABAD ERNAKULUM BHUBNESWAR
DELHI KOLKATA PUNE GUWAHATI

NCBA

REGD OFFICE

8/1 Chintamoni Das Lane, Kolkata 700009, India
e mail : ncbapvtltd@eth.net

OVERSEAS

NCBA (UK) Ltd. 149 Park Avenue North, Northampton, NN3 2HY, UK
e mail : ncbauk@yahoo.com

EXPORT

NCBA Exports Pvt. Ltd. 212 Shahpur Jat, New Delhi 110049
e mail : ncbaexports@ncbapvtltd.com

BRANCHES

2/27 Ansari Road, 1st Floor
Daryaganj, **New Delhi** 110 00 2
e mail : ncbadel@ncbapvtltd.com

House No 3-1-315, 1st Floor
Nimboliadda, Kachiguda, **Hyderabad**
email : ncbahydb@ncbapvtltd.com

Shop Nos 3& 4, Vinayak Towers
681/B Budhwar Peth, Appa Balwant Chowk
Pune 411 002
email : ncbapune@ncbapvtltd.com

GSS Shopping Complex, 1st Floor
Opposite College Post Office,
Convent Road, **Ernakulam** 682 035
0484-4021054/53

Shop No -15, Bharati Towers, Ground Floor
Forest Park
Bhubaneswar 751 001
email : ncbabub@ncbapvtltd.com

Radhamayee Complex (Second Floor)
Opp. SBI, Panbazar, Jaswanta Road
Guwahati - 781 001
email : ncbaguwahati@ncbapvtltd.com

ENVIRONMENTAL CONCEPT. Dr Ajit Kumar Bera

First Published: April 2001
Reprinted: May 2013
Reprinted: 2018

PUBLISHER
New Central Book Agency (P) Ltd
8/1, Chintamoni Das Lane, Kolkata 700 009

TYPESETTER
Barun Sasmol, 3 Garanhatta Street, Kolkata 700 006

PRINTER
New Central Book Agency (P) Ltd
Web-Offset Division, Dhulagarh, Sankrail, Howrah
COVER DESIGNER
Ankit, 6A Atalbehari Bose Lane, Kolkata 700 009
COVER PRINTER
Biswanath Studio, 3 Garanhatta Street, Kolkata 700 006
PROJECT SUPERVISOR
Usha Ranjan Bhowmik
PROOF CHECKING
Subas Maitra
PROJECT TEAM
Jaydeep Ghosh, Bikash Mukherjee, Arun Kabri and Prabhat Jas

ISBN: 978 81 7381 406 8

Price: ₹ 165.00

Preface

Environment, today, is under constant threat. Man's own activities have led to ecological crisis and have disturbed the balance of nature. Deforestation, population explosion, industrialisation, urbanization and intensive agriculture have caused tremendous damage to our environment. Man has destroyed many of the ecosystems, generated chemical and radioactive pollution, produced non-biodegradable matter like plastics, endangered plant of the rivers and oceans with sewage and industrial wastes. The possibility of green house effect is warning the globe and damaged ozone layer has also affected the life on earth to a greater extent. Man's expanding population is the biggest challenge to the quality of the environment. The developments in industrial and agricultural sectors to provide food and other basic amenities to the increasing population have further deteriorated the environment-uncontrolled mechanisation, over exploitation of natural resources and extensive use of chemical fertilizers and pesticides have brought about many changes in different components of the environment.

The title of this book **'Environmental Concept'**, is a precise indication of its contents and focus of attention. The main aim of this book is to help in acquiring and understanding various fundamental concepts of environment. It deals with key issues like environmental issues of global and national concern, environmental policies, lawful control of water, air, land and noise pollution and preservation of ecological balance.

Proper preservation of environment, is, therefore, essential to make the masses aware of the changes in the quality of our environment and strategies to prevent the situation from worsening further. With this objective of arousing general awarness among the students, The University of Calcutta has introduced the subject of Environmental Studies in the general Three-Year Degree Course curricula. The syllabus has been framed by The University of Calcutta thoroughly. The book has been divided into ten chapters together with one hundred broad questions and over one hundred and fifty short questions. My research studies in Environmental Studies that had been carried over a decade, attendance in different symposiums, publication and paper works, have no doubt helped greatly in answering the questions and problems faced in different chapters.

I am grateful to Mr. Amitabha Sen, Director, New Central Book Agency (P) Ltd. and his team for bringing out the book in such a short time.

25th December, 2000
Calcutta

Dr. Ajit Kumar Bera

UNIVERSITY OF CALCUTTA

Notification No. CSR/36/2000

Full Marks [50 + (Lecture-40)]

ENVIRONMENT

		Lecture Periods
1.	**FUNDAMENTAL OF ENVIRONMENT** Definition and basic concepts, Needs for environment studies, Changes in environment, Natural and man-made disasters, Nature vs. Nurture, Land use patterns, Economic development and environment, Heredity and environment, Environmental hazards and risks.	6
2.	**NATURE AND NATURAL PROCESSES** Components of the earth; Natural cycles-carbon, Nitrogen and Oxygen.	3
3.	**ECOSYSTEM** Ecology and concept of ecosystem, Ecosystems of the world-environmental interactions with plants and animals, Forest ecology, Importance of forests, Conservation of forests.	5
4.	**POPULATION AND ENVIRONMENT** Human population distribution, Human Society and Environment Population growth and natural resources, population, education; Impact of economic development on environment in India in particular.	3
5.	**LAND AND WATER USE OF THE EARTH** Land use for various purposes, Water requirement for human activities.	2
6.	**AIR POLLUTION** Roles of individual gases, 'Green House' gases and global warning ozone hole Air pollution effects, noise and odour pollution.	4
7.	**ENERGY SOURCE** Conventional and Non-conventional sources of energy.	2
8.	**ENVIRONMENT AND PUBLIC HEALTH** Major water, food and air borne diseases of mantcivic sense and environment and personal Hygiene issues, Health hazards in agricultural pest control, Heavy metal toxicity.	6
9.	**WASTE MANAGEMENT** Treatment of waste water, solid waste management, management of persistent organic pollute, Water Pollution management.	4
10.	**ENVIRONMENTAL POLICIES** History of environmental institutions and instruments, environment politicses at the national and state level, Human rights issues relating to environment, Women and environment, Green Bench, National environment related movements.	5

The above will come into effect from the academic session 2000-2001.

Contents

List of Figures

Figures		Pages

Chapter 1

FUNDAMENTALS OF ENVIRONMENT

INTRODUCTION

In the short time span since the industrial revolution (since about 1760), the face of the earth has changed in many areas. In some cases, the change has been irreversible. Man has been conscious of his environment, its impact and influence for a long time, since man and environment are always in close interaction. In the present scenario, humanity is forced to investigate the environmental consequences of its developmental actions — on a local, national and global scale. In the 19th and 20th centuries, unprecedented technological and economic progress generated a material boon and the euphoria resulted in a recession of the environmental and ecological awareness. There was a time when change was called progress. However, the present generation, who have inherited the benefits of the past progress, are also inheritors of the grave environmental mistakes of the past. The key word today is sustainable development, which is defined as "the ability to meet the needs of the present without compromising the ability of future generations to meet their own needs". If this concept is put into practice, the gains of the past will be retained and future progress will be attained. Sustainable development has become a somewhat over-used phrase — it calls for a balanced use of resources.

The global concern for environment may be expressed as a three-dimensional problem. The three dimensions are :

(i) environmental pollution

(ii) ecological decay and destruction, and

(iii) resource depletion.

In 1972, the UN Conference on Human Environment was held in Stockholm. Discussions held here first drew attention to environment and the related issues of pollution, ecological decay and resource depletion.

It was obvious that the problems had to be dealt with dedication as well as expertise. The first step to achieve this was the setting up of UNEP — the United Nations Environmental Programme — in order to frame fresh guidelines for integrating environmental concern in overall development and the lending policy of development banks, and rapid growth of a large international body of EAGs, or Environmental Advocacy Groups. These groups are non-governmental bodies and are, hence, more or less free from charge of dictating terms. In order to gain legitimacy in the countries where they function, they collaborate with like-minded local people.

The shrinking of forests, increase of deserts, the alarming rate of air, water and land pollution, ruthless and indiscriminate use and exhaustion of natural resources, depletion of endangered species — these are the main problems which every nation is facing today or will face in the years to come. Therefore, what is most important is consciousness about the importance of our environment and the preventive measures to be adopted so that Mother Earth can provide the future generations a safe, benevolent and bountiful home.

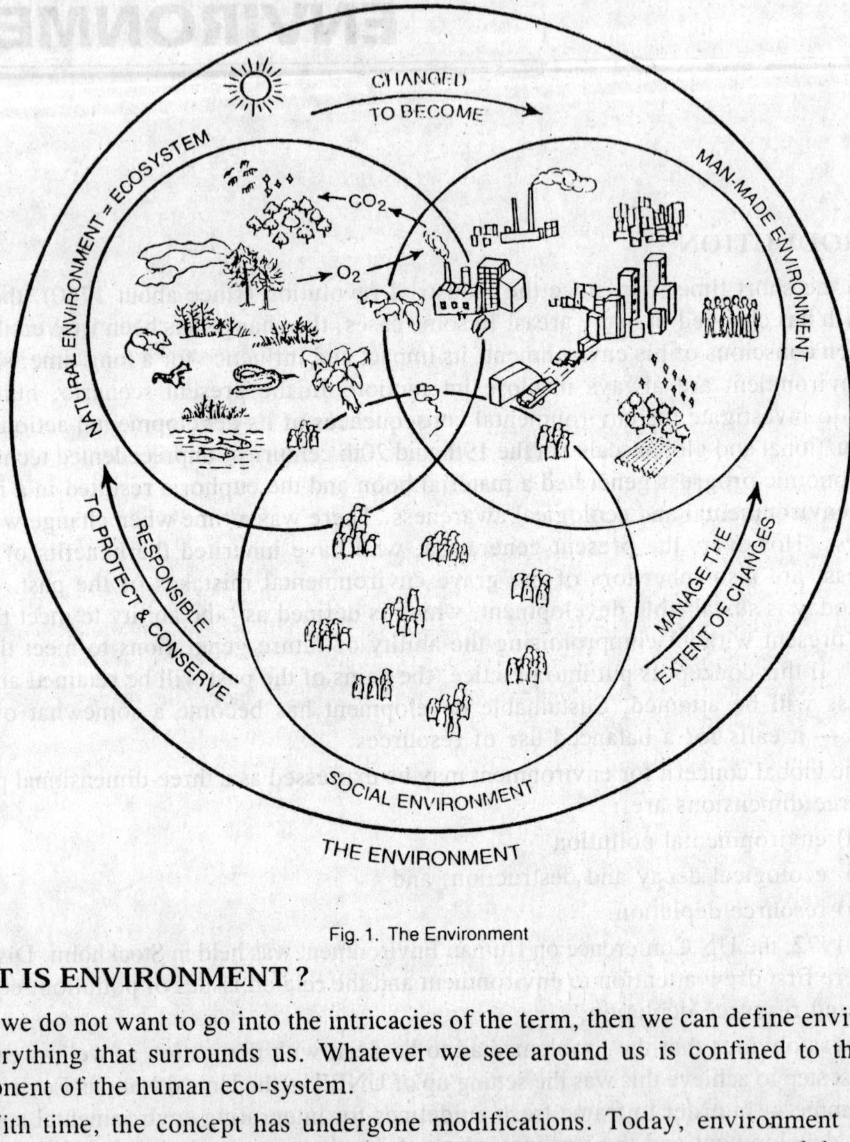

Fig. 1. The Environment

WHAT IS ENVIRONMENT ?

If we do not want to go into the intricacies of the term, then we can define environment as everything that surrounds us. Whatever we see around us is confined to the living component of the human eco-system.

With time, the concept has undergone modifications. Today, environment means a single system of the interacting living and non-living natural components of the earth.

But the earth is not the only planet of the solar family, which again belongs to our home Galaxy — the Milky Way. There are about 100 billion such galaxies floating in the vast universe, each containing about 100 billion stars!! In this universe, not a single event can be said to be isolated, and no object is independent of the rest. Since every thing is interrelated with every other thing, logic demands that the entire universe is our environment. But, for practical reasons, environmental study deals only with the system of interaction between non-living and living components of the globe.

In 1977, the first international conference on Environmental Education was held in Tiflis (capital city of Georgia Republic). The programme was organised by UNESCO and

UNEP, and here it was noted that "the environment includes a complex of natural, built and social components in the life of humanity".

DEFINITION OF THE TERM "ENVIRONMENT"

A list has been prepared of the various ways in which the term "environment" has been defined by national and international organisations, as well as individuals. The definitions are :

- **Environment** — "The physical, chemical and biotic conditions surrounding an organism." — P. N. Arora and M. C. Arora, Dictionary of Environment.
- **Environment** — "The surroundings of any organism including the physical world and other organisms." — P. H. Collin, Dictionary of Ecology and the Environment.
- **Environment** — "The complete range of external conditions, physical and biological, in which an organism lives. Environment includes social, cultural, and (for humans) economic and political considerations, as well as the more usually understood features such as soil, climate and food supply." — M. Allby, Dictionary of Ecology.
- **Environment** — "In Biogeography, the sum of physical, chemical and biological conditions experienced by an organism, including climate, soil, water, light, neighbouring vegetation, individuals of its own sort, and members of other species." — J. Smith, Dictionary of Geography.
- **Environment** — ".....that which surrounds, the sum total of the conditions of the surroundings within which an organism, or group, or an object, exists (including the natural condition, the natural as modified by human activity, and the artificial." — A. N. Clark, Dictionary of Geography.
- **Environment** — "Surrounding conditions, esp. circumstance of life of person or society." — J. B. Sykes, The Concise Oxford Dictionary.
- **Environment** — "All the surroundings but could be differentiated as natural environment and the artificial environment." — W. D. Sawyer, Applied Biogeography.
- **Environment** — "The sum of the biological, chemical and physical properties of the surroundings in which a particular organism lives." — J. Coombs, Dictionary of Biotechnology.
- **Environment** — "...... refers to the sum total of conditions which surround man at a given point in space and time." — C. C. Park, Environment.
- **Environment** — "The term 'Environment' means the entire range of external influence acting on an organism, both the physical and biological, and other organisms, i.e. forces of nature surrounding an individual." — Encyclopaedia Britannica.
- **Environment** — "The environment includes a complex of natural, built and social components in the life of humanity." — UNESCO and UNEP.
- **Environment** — "Environment means man's total environmental system including not only the biosphere, but also his interactions with his natural and man-made surroundings." — United States Council on Environmental Quality, U.S.A.
- **Environment** — "The term Environment includes water, air and land and human beings, other living creatures, plants, micro-organisms and property." — Section 2(a) of the India Environmental Protection Act, 1986.
- **Environment** — "...... means sum total of all conditions and influences that affect the development of life of all organisms." — T. N. Khoshoo, Secretary, Department of Environment, Government of India.

Studying the definitions, we can conclude that the environment has two principal components :

(i) The lithosphere, the hydrosphere and the atmosphere constitute the non-living environment. They provide habitat and media for the organisms to live, as well as the materials for their maintenance.

(ii) The living beings, plants and animals, including man, constitute the living or biotic environment. The interactions between the organisms arise due to their primary needs of life, mainly food, reproduction and maintenance.

Therefore, **"the environment consists of life and life-support systems (air, water, soils, sediments and topography) around us."**

Basic Concept of Environment

The term environment has been derived from a French word *'environner'*, which means 'to surround'. It brings within its domâin a sum total of all the external conditions and influences that affect life on this planet. In this context, the question arises whether it is really possible to separate the two — the organisms and the forces that affect them.

We all know that man is different from all other organisms. He has been blessed with a mind that has made him more of a rational and social being. He is not merely a biotic organism. Due to his socio-cultural instincts and super intelligence, his creations have introduced the manners of his interventions with nature, by which he has created the cultural landscape, which again varies with time and space.

To be on the safe side, the environment can be defined as an inseparable whole. It consists of interacting systems comprising the abiotic (physical) and biotic (biological) elements. The biotic and abiotic elements taken together make up a system that is inseparable, mutually interacting and mutually influencing in nature.

Since we have introduced the term "system" in our attempt to define "environment", we should have a clear idea about what a system is. A system may be defined as a complex of elements that are intimately related with one another and also interact upon one another. A system can also have sub-systems within it. If anything goes wrong with any one of the sub-systems, then it will affect the functioning of the entire system. If the environment is considered to be a system, then the biotic and abiotic elements constitute the inseparable, mutually interacting and mutually influencing sub-systems.

In this way, the term "ecosystem" came into operation. It includes both living organisms (plants and animals, including man) and non-living factors (soil, rocks, climate, water bodies, landforms etc.) of the environment in which the living organisms exist. From this, it is evident that the ecosystem is an all-encompassing environmental system. The positive and negative feedbacks maintain this system in a state of dynamic equilibrium, by controlling the flow of energy and matter between the inorganic and organic realms.

The term 'ecosystem' helps in understanding the environment as a system, which consists of not only the biotic and abiotic elements, but also the energy which makes the system function in this form. Therefore, the basic constituents of the ecosystem or the system of environment are the living organisms, the non-living surroundings and the energy.

Environment is an all-comprehensive term. If we add a prefix to the term environment, then its meaning gets restricted.

In this way, the following types of environments have been recognized :

- **Physical Environment**

This consists of only non-living or abiotic elements surrounding an individual organism or a species. Physical space, soil, land, water, air, climate etc. come under this category.

- **Biological Environment**

  This consists of only living or biotic elements surrounding an individual organism or a species, including the concerned organism itself.

- **Cultural Environment**

  It consists of all human artifacts, such as housing, clothings, tools etc. It may include human activities, human settlements, variety of living conditions of human beings etc.

- **Perceptual Environment**

  This is an inadequate concept which focuses upon one's perception. For instance, the same forest is perceived differently by different organisms. Man sees, smells and realises the forest in a much different way from a bird.

- **Conceptual Environment**

  This highlights the superiority of human in comparison to other organisms, and, thus, introduces the concept of human environment.

- **Human Environment**

  This consists of continuing interaction between different organisms and their surroundings, especially man and his surroundings. Man — being the superior among all animals — has developed the capacity that enables him to modify his environment to suit his needs. No natural or unaltered environment can be found in the world any more. Man has successfully altered the landscape by clearing forests, irrigating arid deserts, ploughing grasslands etc. In this way, man has made hostile and non-productive environments livable for himself, i.e. creating a comfortable habitat where man is the most dominating organism and is influencing both directly and indirectly all other organisms living there.

- **Operational Environment**

  This consist of both perceivable and non-perceivable elements which influence the organisms. For instance, viruses cannot be perceived without the help of electron microscopes, but they influence human life by causing diseases.

- **Total Environment**

  In any situation, the total environment consists of all forces and materials, even including those elements that do not influence behaviour in a specific situation. For instance, we all know that we live within the magnetic field of the earth. This magnetism is only shown by the compass. Otherwise, it has no impact on us in any known way.

  The various types of environment as discussed here has proved how widely the term "environment" can be used.

Principal Characteristics of Environment

The principal characteristics of the environment has been listed below :

(i) At any given point of time, the environment of any area is the sum total of all biotic elements and the abiotic elements around them.

(ii) The three basic components that constitute the structure of the environment are biome, habitat and energy.

(iii) The elements of the environment are systematically organised and interact with one another to maintain the integrity of the system.

Thus, the environment is a perfectly functioning system.

(iv) The input of solar energy is responsible for the functioning of the system.

(v) The environment is an open system since there is a continuous inflow and outflow of matter and energy.

(vi) The productivity of the environment is determined by the availability and amount of energy.

Components of the Environment

The three basic components of environment are :

(I) abiotic (physical or inorganic) components,

(II) biotic (organic) components, and the

(III) energy components.

Again, the abiotic components of the environment consist of :

(a) the lithosphere — the chief reservoir of mineral nutrients,

(b) the atmosphere — the chief reservoir of gases essential for organic life, and

(c) the hydrosphere — the chief reservoir of liquid water.

The biotic component of environment include all kinds of organic life, ranging from microorganisms to plants and animals, including man.

Energy is the third component of environment, which is indispensable for the generation and sustenance of all forms of organic life. The sun is the main source of energy in the environment. Geo-thermal energy is yet another type of energy. Since photosynthesis is essential for the existence of organic life, we find that life is confined to only those regions where solar energy can be captured for photosynthesis. This forms a narrow belt of life, that extends from about 180-210 m below sea level to almost 6 km (snow-line in mountain ranges). This is known as the Biosphere, which can be said to be a thin film (1/1000th) when we consider the earth's radius (6,370 kms).

What is Environmental Studies ?

There are several fields of study associated with the environment. With time, man realized the growing importance of maintaining his environment, and subjects such as ecology, environmental engineering, environmental sciences, environmental studies etc. gained popularity.

There is a fundamental difference between environmental science and environmental studies. The former lays emphasis on scientific qualities and issues of environmental interest, while environmental studies focus on questions related to environmental ethics and aesthetics.

The concern for preserving the environment is a relatively new phenomenon. There was a time when man would derive the maximum benefit from his surroundings, without thinking of the consequences. It was only since the 1950s that nations of the world started conservation and wise utilization of their natural resources — such as water, soil, fuel, flora and fauna. It has been accepted that nature is a treasure-house that provides us with food, water, energy, medicine and various other amenities. No wonder the prevention and protection of the environment has become so crucial.

Developed countries have made considerable progress in the field of protection and conservation of the environment on a long-term basis. However, the developing nations were quite late in understanding the gravity of the situation, and, hence, they are lagging behind.

Necessity of Environmental Studies

The natural resources of the earth — which include air, water, soil, flora and faum —

represent our environment. For the benefit of the present and future generations, these priceless resources should be safeguarded, by means of careful planning and management.

At the end of the 20th century, we are realising the acute environmental crisis as an impact of indiscriminate and ignorant utilisation of natural resources. The rise in population and demand for space and basic amenities have led to overutilization of the available resources. In order to create an awareness among the masses about the importance of proper utilization and conservation of the resources, environmental education has become a must.

What is Environmental Education ?

Environmental education is the process in order to create awareness and sensitivity to the total environment by developing appropriate attitudes and acquiring adequate knowledge and skills with the purpose of solving environmental problems.

Objectives of Environmental Education

The following may be suggested as the objectives of any environmental education programme —

a) to develop proper attitudes and skills for understanding and appreciating the interdependence of man and his environment,

b) to use natural resources carefully and adequately,

c) to formulate a new behavioural code with the aim of improving the overall quality of life for the future generations.

Principal Regions Covered Under Environmental Education

(1) Planning, management and conservation of natural resources
(2) Natural hazard management
(3) Population control
(4) Ecosystem, ecology and biosphere
(5) Illiteracy, poverty and useful employment
(6) Health and sanitation
(7) Social ills
(8) World economy
(9) World policy and law
(10) Consumption of energy and its management
(11) Development of environment
(12) Importance of oceans
(13) Meaningful dialogue between the nations of the world
(14) Moral leadership and guidance among the masses.

The main target of an environmental education programme of any country should be the youth. The young people today are losing faith in the formal education system. In order to evoke interest and participation, the education should be imparted through popular media such as television, films, journals, newspapers etc. Scientists, educationists and environmentalists should come together and help the mass media to promote environmental awareness.

Changes in the Environment

Almost everybody is fascinated by the notion of change. Right from the day they are born, till the moment they breathe their last, human beings experience a variety of change. They are all familiar with the sunshine and sunset and passage of day into night, as well as the change of the seasons. We all notice that the weather in one year is never quite similar to the weather in previous years. Let us take for example the Monsoon Rains in West Bengal. A few years ago, the rains arrived in Bengal by early June and October was sunny and pleasant. Now, the rains arrive much later, and the festivities of October are marred by the showers.

Environmental change is studied by scientists from environmental, geographical and geological disciplines. The work of those scientists have delved into the intricacies of the past environments and finally confirms that environmental change is real, various and complex.

What is Environmental Change ?

Environmental factors are, naturally, variable. For instance, air temperature varies on a diurnal and annual basis. In order to measure sustained temperature changes, we take average values for days, months, seasons, years, and even longer periods.

Then, the similar averages are compared when it is found that the mean temperature for one year is greater than that in the previous year; we know that a change has occurred.

It must be kept in mind that average values should not be treated as some sort of norm. Average values for all the principle atmospheric variables over a period of thirty years are used to defined "climatic norms". This term is often misleading, since it tries to establish that the climatic norms are somehow permanent. However, current thinking suggests that the climate is ever changing. The climatic norms of one generation may be another generation's climatic extremes. Thus, we may conclude from this argument that — change is the norm, constancy the exception.

In this context, scientists have found that environmental variables display three basic types of changes :

(i) a discontinuity, which is an abrupt and permanent change in the average value,

(ii) a trend, which is a smooth increase or decrease (not necessarily linear in nature) in the average, and

(iii) a function, which is a regular or irregular change characterized by at least two maxima (or minima) and one minimum (or maximum).

Causes of Environmental Change

(i) **Ecospheric Influences**

The ecosphere is the first source of environmental change, since the interactions between the atmosphere, biosphere, hydrosphere, pedosphere and toposphere produce environmental cycles, trends and steady states.

Directional changes or trends occur when a threshold within the ecosphere is crossed, just as what happened when the Antarctic ice expanded during the Late Eocene atmospheric cooling. The ice-sheet has lasted ever since through, recently (December 2000) an area of 20,000 sq. miles (51,000 sq. kms) has been satellite-observed as melted! This has caused grave concern to the environmentalists.

(ii) **Cosmic Influences**

The sun is the most important source of power of the ecosphere. Steady state changes about periodic and quasi-periodic fluctuations are promoted by solar influences. A number of ecospheric processes are finely adjusted to solar cycles. Also some ecospheric processes are attuned to various astronomical pulses, such as orbital changes in the sun and the planets, the solar system's passage around our galaxy, Milky Way, and the Milk Way's interactions with the neighbouring galaxies. The bombardment by asteroids and comets may also instigate and encourage biospheric trends.

(iii) **Geological Influences**

Cycles, steady states and trends in the ecosphere are also produced by geological forces, and the ultimate seat of change lies in the core and mantle process.

The core and mantle processes act through the agency of the lithosphere. The mechanism of plate-tectonics influences sea-level change, volcanic and mountain building activities, continental drift and true polar wander.

Geological changes have caused long-term bio-diversity trends, since it is largely dependent on relative fragmentation of land-masses.

Evidence of Environmental Change

The environment records its own history. This has made the task of environmental reconstruction possible. Although the record is incomplete, at least it gives us a hint of the way things were. All history, whether human or environmental, is a matter of imperfect record. Therefore, it depends on us — how well we perform our job and interpret the past. It is up to us to gather the shreds of evidence, assess their significance, and then weave together to form a finished picture, which will tell us about the bygone days. But, there is no way of knowing whether the interpretation is accurate.

There are various evidence of environmental change. The principal categories of evidence are : geochemical, biological and physical.

(i) **Geo-chemical Evidence**

The conditions in air, water and soil influence and exert some control over the mineralogy, elemental composition, and isotopic composition of sediments and soils. Because of this, scientists have made use of geochemical data as a guide to past environmental states.

The main lines of geo-chemical evidence and interpretation have been listed in the table below :

Table : Geo-chemical Evidence of Environmental Changes

Type of Evidence	Examples of Evidence	Environmental Factors (changes) Indicated
Mineralogy		
Mineral Ratios	Magnesium/calcium ratio	Salinity and composition of sea water
Clay minerals	Kaolinite, smectite, geothite	precipitation
Duricrusts	Alcretes, ferricretes, calcretes	rainfall
Elemental Composition		
Substitute elements	Strontium and magnesium substitution in marine shells	temperature
Trace elements	Boron, rubidium, strontium and gallium	salinity
Isotopes		
Cosmogenic nuclide	Berryllium-10, carbon-14	Solar modulation of cosmic radiation
Carbon isotope ratio ($^{13}C/^{12}C$ or $\delta^{13}C$)	Carbone isotope ratios in soil carbonates and in organisms	continental biomass or variations in the density and extent of vegetation
Oxygen isotope ratio ($^{18}O/^{16}O$ or $\delta^{18}O$)	Proxy temperature records from foraminifera in deep-sea cores	temperature

(ii) **Biological Evidence**

Almost all plants and animals are sensitive to climatic conditions. The greater the sensitivity, the more suitable they are as indicative of the past climates.

The biological evidences can be further categorised into botanical and zoological evidences, as shown in the table below —

Table : Biological Evidence of Environmental Change

Type of Evidence	Examples of Evidence	Paleo-Environmental Factors Indicated
Botanical		
Macro-fossil plants	Seeds, fruits, twigs, leaves, trunks, wood fragments	Temperature, rainfall, flora
Micro-fossil plants	Pollen grains, spores, leaf hairs and epidermis, diatom and desmid skeletons	Temperature, rainfall, flora
Floral lists	Compilations of plants present in particular places	Regional climate
Tree — growth rings	Ring width, ring-width variability, width of early wood, variations in cell-size	Water availability, frost temperature, growing season
Leaf physiognomy	Leaf shape, size leaf-margin form	Climate
Zoological		
Mammals	Faunal composition, population structure, size of individuals	Climate, habitat, community structure
Amphibians and reptiles	Species distribution	Warmth, presence of water
Insects	Species distribution	Temperature, rainfall, habitat
Molluscs	Species Distribution	Climate, Ecology, Salinity
Corals	Species distribution	Temperature, Salinity
Cladocerous and Ostracods	Abundance in lake cores	Climate, water conditions, producing in lakes

(iii) **Physical Evidence**

The following table shows the variety in physical evidence that denote environmental changes —

Table : Physical Evidence of Environmental Changes

Type of Evidence	Examples of Evidence (changes) Indicated	Paleo-Environmental Factors
Erosional Landforms	Glacial : glacial troughs (U-shaped valleys), hanging valleys, fjords, rock drumlins, rock basins, melt water channels, cirques	Ice-movement, snow line (cirques)
	Periglacial : permafrost horizons, rock glaciers, pingoes, ice-wedges	Frigid climate

Type of Evidence	Examples of Evidence	Paleo-Environmental Factors (changes) Indicated
	Tropical : Tors and inselbergs	Torrid climate
	Fluvial : Palaeochannels and river terraces	Stream discharge
Sediment textures, structures properties	Alluvial deposits, dunes, tsunamites, tempestites	Water and air current directions, air current velocities, storms, floods, tsunamis
Terrestrial soils and sediments	Till plains, fluvio-glacial features, periglacial features	Frigid climates
	Palaeosols (buried soil profile)	Vegetation type, climate, atmospheric composition
Lacustrine sediments	Ancient shorelines, lake sediments	Lake levels — rainfall, evaporation, soil moisture
Marine sediments	Deep-sea cores	Surface and deep-water temperature, salinity
Glaciers	Advances, retreats	Temperature, duration of melting season, cloudiness, sunshine, snow-fall

What is Environmental Hazard ?

It is indeed difficult to define an environmental hazard. During all these years, considerable attention has been given to 'natural hazards'. Burton and Kates (1964a) defined natural hazards as 'those elements of the physical environment harmful to Man and caused by forces extraneous to him'. Traditionally, natural hazards were believed to be 'Acts of God'. However, this perspective has not been very helpful since it implies that human beings have no part to play in creating these hazards and have even less hope of mitigating them. With time, the ideas of cause and effect have changed, and with that has changed the concept of hazard. Human influence — both deliberate and inadvertent — has spread rapidly over the world. Therefore, it is becoming increasingly difficult to distinguish between Acts of God and Acts of Man !

Natural Hazards result from the conflict of geo-physical processes with people. They lie at the interface between the natural events system and the human use system. In this interpretation of natural hazards, human beings play a central role — firstly, by virtue of location, since hazards exist only when people and their possessions get in the way of natural processes, and, secondly, through perception, since wherever humans settle and use land, they place value judgements on natural processes as part of a general environmental appraisal.

Natural and Man-made Disasters

Almost everyday, the media tells us about various disasters striking a blow on societies and individuals across the globe. Some are caused by nature's whims, while some result from man's interference with natural systems, or carelessness.

Natural Disaster : Landslides

When landslides occur, great amounts of material move at tremendous velocity and are deposited on otherwise undisturbed ground.

A combination of the following causes result in landslides :

(1) **Slow erosion** caused by alternate freezing and thawing water, and wind action gradually wear away supporting materials.

(2) **Water** after heavy rains affect marginally stable slopes, by liquefying the materials.

(3) **Advancing glaciers** often displace supporting material along the valley walls, and, consequently, the slopes above are robbed of their ice-support.

(4) **Earthquakes** commonly cause landslides in the form of ground failure and avalanche.

(5) **Engineering defects** make the upslope materials unstable and susceptible to slides.

Effects of Landslides

Landslides result in unbelievable loss of life and property. Where the slope is relatively gradual, the foundation material can lose its shearing strength and an entire village may shift downslope. Buildings are tilted and depressions are formed.

The peril of landslides is ever present in the mountainous countries of the world, such as Nepal, Tibet, Norway, Northern Italy, Switzerland and the mountainous regions of North and South America.

The Himalayan regions of India, as well as the Western Ghats, are susceptible to landslides. In West Bengal itself, the monsoon rains bring disaster to the Darjeeling Himalayas. Indiscriminate construction along unstable slopes, rapid deforestation and growing population pressure have disrupted the lithology of the area.

Man-Made Disasters

Over the years, man has constantly tried to befriend Nature. Yet, he continues to be dominated by the whims of Nature. Whenever he has tried to interfere with the existing systems of the earth, he has invited disaster. Also, he has disturbed the normal functioning of the planet and caused several catastrophes because of his own deficiencies.

Industrial accidents are probably a common form of a man-made disaster.

Bhopal Gas Tragedy : An Industrial Accident

The Bhopal Gas Tragedy occurred on 2/3 December 1984, in Bhopal, the capital city of Madhya Pradesh. The accidental release of methyl isocyanate (MIC) and related products from the pesticide manufacturing plants claimed 2,500 lives and caused acute health problems to 20,000-50,000 residents of the city.

The accident assumed the severe proportion due to the following reasons —

(a) poor decision of industrial location

(b) poor technology

(c) poor maintenance procedures

(d) poor safety management

(e) slow response to emergency.

From this incident, it was evident that if development has to be sustainable in nature, industrialization has to be more systematic.

Nature Versus Nurture

Our environment is constantly undergoing changes that are affecting our lives directly and indirectly. Therefore, several questions haunt the mind of the common man. Where lies the motor of change in communities and ecosystems ? Can we find it within the biosphere ? Does it lie in the environment ? Or, is it a combination of both the biosphere and the environment ?

Let us look for an appropriate answer.

Autogenic Community Change

Communities and ecosystems have the capacity to change themselves by the process of autogenic succession.

The classical conception of autogenic sussession says that it is a unidirectional sequence of community, and related ecosystem, changes that follow the opening up of a new habitat. **The sequence of events occur even when the physical environment is not changing.**

Allogenic Community Change

Many community and ecosystem changes are caused by fluctuations in the physical environment. A number of environmental factors disrupt the interactions between individuals and species and thereby disturb communities and ecosystems. For example, climatic changes affect marine and terrestrial communities.

Nature Versus Nurture

For a long time, human societies have had a major impact on their environment. Their tendency has been to exploit it as if it were an inexhaustible resource. Such practices had time and again led to disaster. In the past, pressures on the environment have been typically localised in nature, and, therefore, caused only local or regional impoverishment. But, today, the growth in global population and economy, widespread industrialisation and the development of international trade and society, altogether have occurred on such a scale that they have caused severe environmental damage. Unsustainable exploitation of the planet's resources are taking place on a global scale.

It is easy to provide examples of such damage and unsustainable exploitation. Between 1950 and the late 1980s, the total area of the world under tropical forest cover was reduced by 50%. If the trend is not checked, there will only be a few pockets of such valuable forests left by the early twenty-first century. This will be accompanied by the extinction of a number of plant and animal species. On the whole, major alterations will occur in the global climatic system.

But this is just a single example. As civilization progresses, we find ourselves pondering over a question —

"Is science a blessing or a curse" ?

Gone are those wonderful days when man roamed amidst such greenery, befriending nature to feed him and clothe him. Instead, modern man today clears forests and makes space for industry, the workaholic being in him is more dependent on time-saving canned food, he seeks refreshment in the air-conditioned comfort of his room. Man's intimacy with nature is almost a forgotten chapter. The opinions and philosophies of man have undergone enormous changes due to pressure of circumstances.

The **Declaration on the Human Environment** agreed at the **United Nations Conference** at **Stockholm in 1972** adopted some principles guiding environmental policy. India was represented by the then Prime Minister, Late Mrs. **Indira Gandhi**.

The principles were —

(i) harm from pollution should be minimised, **but regulations should also consider** social and economic goals;

(ii) the "sovereign right" of a state **not to have its territory polluted as a consequence** of activities in another state **takes precedence over the sovereign right of a state to do what it wants within its boundaries;**

(iii) the international community should set **limits on the use and abuse of "global** commons", such as the high seas and ocea**n** resources, **the atmosphere, outer** space, and Antarctica.

Land Use Pattern

Land can be classified in many ways. Here, we will be discussing four categories only — cropland, pasture, forest and other land.

(1) **Cropland** — This kind of land is used for standard production of grains, vegetable and other plants that are consumed by human beings or fed to animals for human consumption.

If land is to be used naturally, then there must be suitably fertile soil and adequate temperature and rainfall conditions, as needed by the crop.

Land that is not naturally fertile can also be converted to cropland by the application of fertiliser and introduction of irrigation.

The area covered by cropland can either contract or expand, from one year to another. Area under cropland can contract for two reasons —

(i) deliberate decision to reduce overproduction of food and allow some land to return to a natural state, and

(ii) environmental degradation resulting from soil erosion, contamination of soil and water by anthropogenic activities, and leaching of nutrients out of the soil.

Expansion of cropland is caused by the following reasons —

(i) conversion of other land to agricultural land by the application of fertilizer and water,

(ii) attempts by government on private individuals to increase agricultural productivity, and

(iii) clearing of forested land.

(2) **Pasture** — This comprises areas that domestic animals graze on. These are mostly grasslands, such as the productive ones in northern temperate climates. They are particularly useful for cattle and sheep. Goats also feed on bush and vegetation. Excessive animal population can reduce pasture land.

(3) **Forest and Woodland** — They comprise areas covered by trees. The principal types of forests are —

(i) the vast stretches of conifers in subarctic areas,

(ii) mixed hardwood and conifer forests of the temperate regions of North America and Europe, and

(iii) the environmentally fragile tropical rainforests.

Tree-covered areas may expand due to abandonment of cropland or may contract due to conversion to cropland.

(4) **Other Land** — This generally means places without usable vegetation. They are mostly termed as wasteland.

Other land includes Arctic Tundra, arid deserts, steep, rocky mountain-sides, as well as areas covered by human habitations, industry, shopping malls along with their parking lots, roads, airports, and so on.

It is difficult to calculate exactly the amount of "other" land covered by constructed areas. In most countries it is less that 1%.

What is Economic Development ?

When we talk about a country that is developed, it is understood that the country has successfully achieved a high material standard of life. Basing on this criterion, we differentiate between the First World (Developed) countries like USA, and the Third World (Developing) countries like India.

However, the First World development is lopsided since it has over-exploited the valuable and scarce natural resources. The First World accounts for approximately 26% of the world's population, and consumes 80% of the world's commercial energy, 85% of paper, 79% of steel and 86% of other metals. These countries achieve these high levels of material prosperity by utilizing not only environmental resources, but human resources too. In this context we notice a strange phenomenon — material achievement and money value displacing and destroying human values and thus creating an imbalance in our life style.

After the World War II (1939-45), the pattern of development in the developing countries followed the path as shown by the Western World. It laid stress on urban-based economic development. This kind of development did not help in improving the condition of the rural population.

Economic development should not be the one and only objective of a development programme, if it does not involve the participation of the people. If the people are left out, it destroys their initiative and creativity, making them dependent, worthless, selfish and even anti-social.

Therefore, economic development must only be one of the components of development. Human participation must be the king-pin for all-round integrated development.

Economic Development and Environment

Environment and economic development are said to be two sides of the same coin. The degradation of the environment started with the onward march of civilisation and technology. This process of environmental degradation was accelerated with the development of socio-cultural activities. These activities are agriculture, industries, transport, civil construction including roads and railways, buildings etc. With the growing population, the requirement of foodgrains and other consumer goods increased greatly, leading to further environmental degradation.

Environmental degradation can also detract from the pace of economic development by imposing high costs on developing countries through health related expenses and the reduced productivity of resources.

Today, there are seven basic issues related to economic development and conservation of our environment. They are —

(i) the concept of sustainable development,
(ii) population and resources,
(iii) poverty,
(iv) economic development and employment opportunities,
(v) rural development,
(vi) urban development, and
(vii) global economic development through environment-friendly policies.

If we consider economic development on a global scale, we will see that the major portion of the available resources is utilized by a minor section of the world's population. This small section of the population comprises the First World. They claim to be economically and materially advanced and have a high capital income. This modern, Western model of development is characterised by a high-profile, environmentally costly life-style that is essentially exploitative.

The marked differences in life-styles have divided the world's population into two classes — the affluent "haves" and the unfortunate, poor "have-nots".

The developing world, in an effort to blindly imitate the West, is following the environmentally costly, polluting and exploitative style of development. The saddest reality is that, in such countries, only a negligible section of the population, comprising the rich the elite and the 'practically intelligent' — can reach such a life-style. The major portion of the population remains in the dark.

Heredity and Environment

Like begets like — it is an age-old observation that is recognised in almost all human groups. The blood of the parents flows in the veins of the children and they show many traits common with their parents. The difference in heredity is probably the cause of difference in the qualities or traits of individuals or groups, even in different environments.

There is great controversy regarding the question whether heredity influences human behaviour or the environment.

Some say that certain qualities, such as those of health and intelligence, depend largely on heredity, while social qualities of an individual, or a group, such as morals, customs and beliefs depend more directly on the environment.

Heredity contains all the potentialities of life. However, all its actualities are evoked within and under the conditions of environment.

From various evidences, it can be said that heredity is potentiality made actual within an environment. All the qualities of life are contained in the heredity, while all the evocation of qualities depends on the environment. The higher the potentiality, the greater is the demand made on environment. Instead of placing the importance of one of the factors over another, we should try to correlate the two factors. We should accept the coequal importance of heredity and environment as two ultimate determinants of everything that lives.

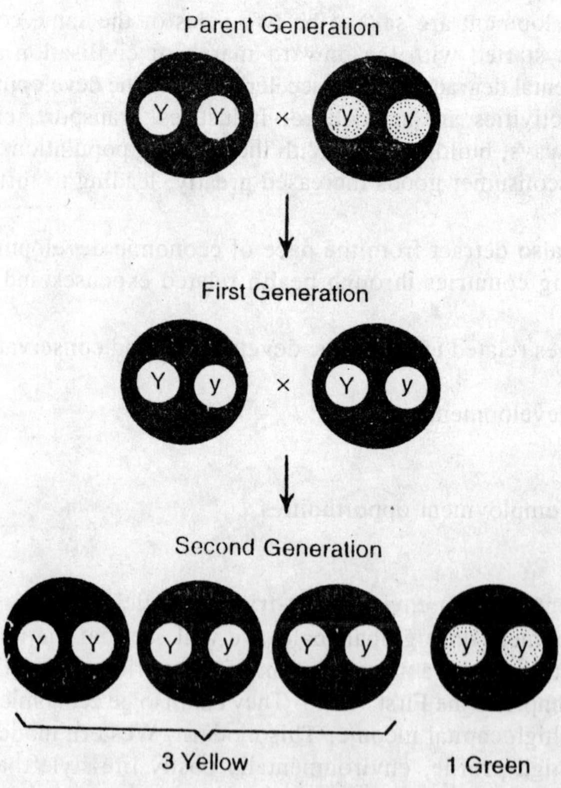

Fig. 2. Mendel crossed a plant having two genes for yellow peas (YY) with a plant having two genes for green peas (yy). Crossing the second generation yielded three yellow pea plants and one green pea plant

Heredity : The Experiments of Gregor Mendel

Gregor Mendel (1822-1884), an Austrian monk and amateur botanist, conducted his famous experiment with pea plants and the results of his experiment explained the complexities of heredity.

Mendel bred several varieties of pea plants. He made detailed observation of their offsprings. As breeding partners, he chose plants that differed by only one observable trait. Yellow plants were crossed with green ones and tall plants with short.

For instance, Mendel crossed a plant having two genes for yellow peas (YY) with a plant having two genes for green peas (yy). When the offsprings of the first generation were studied, it was observed that the peas of each offspring were yellow, but carried one gene for yellow and one gene for green (Yy). The peas were yellow because the gene for yellow is dominant over the recessive gene for green. Crossing the first generation produced three yellow pea plants and one green pea plant (Fig. 2).

Genes : Carriers of Inherited Traits

Genes are units of heredity. They occur in pairs for each trait. Mendel said that the offspring inherited one unit of the pair from each parent.

The genes of higher organisms (excluding bacteria and primitive plants, such as green-blue algae) are located on rope-like bodies called chromosomes, within the nucleus of each and every cell of the organism. Like genes, chromosomes also occur in pairs. The body cells of every plant or animal carry pairs of chromosomes in a number best-suited for its species. Human beings have twenty-three pairs, i.e. a total of forty-six chromosomes, each carrying many times that number of genes.

DNA

Genes are located on chromosomes and each gene carries a set of instructions encoded in its chemical structure. A cell makes the rest of its structural parts and chemical machinery from this coded information carried in genes. This chemical substance, DNA (deoxyribonucleic acid) controls the heredity in every living organism.

In 1951, biologist James Watson, along with British chemist Francis Crick, attempted to explain the structure of DNA. They said that the DNA is a long, two-stranded molecule shaped like a double helix, that could reduplicate itself within minutes. Further research reveals that while DNA directs the making of an organism according to the instructions in it genetic code, another nucleic acid, RNA (ribonucleic acid), "copies" the blueprint from DNA and "carried" the instructions to the cytoplasm of a cell. Thereafter, the instructions are "translated" into the production of proteins, which are the basic building blocks of cells. Therefore DNA is the language of life (Fig. 3).

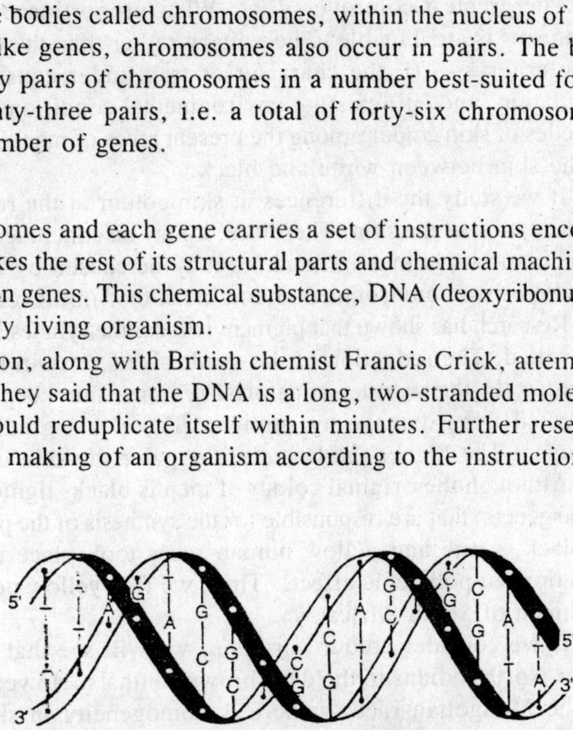

Fig. 3. The DNA molecule consists of two spiral sugar-phosphate strands. The strands are limited by the nitrogenous bases adenine (A), guanine (G), thymine (T), and cytosine (C)

To understand the DNA working the Human Genome Project was launched in 1990. Its work was 'to creats a map of the entire set of genes (genome) in the human cell by decoding the 3 billion units or base pairs (bp) of the human DNA'. The genome is called the ''instruction book of life'. In April 2000, the rough draft of the human genome was completed. Now work is on — on pin-pointing the genes and working out their functions.

Mutation

A mutation is a change in molecular structure on DNA code of a gene that produces an altered gene. Random mutations are usually harmful to an individual because any change in the intricate structure of a gene can impair the delicate balance within an organism, as well as between an organism and its environment.

Influence of Environment and Heredity

Genes function in a cellular environment. In most cases, the changes in structure and position of genes are not related to the environment. Therefore, these changes are mostly detrimental in their effect. Commonly, they are recognised as lethals, or sublethals.

To a great extent, the reactions of organisms are determined not only by their past and present environment, but also by their hereditary construction. From our experiences in everyday life, we can understand the differences in reaction, as those between civilized man and the savage, between a healthy man and a victim of polio. The hereditary constitution as mentioned here is provided by a long, earlier course of evolution and their immediate circumstances of ancestry.

The greatest controversy is : What proportion of the differences between different organisms is attributable to hereditary rather than the environment. This depends on three basic criteria — (i) the character or trait under consideration, (ii) genetic nature of the population, and (iii) existing environmental conditions. For example, we can consider the varieties of skin colour among the present races of man. There is a wide range of pigmentation of the skin between white and black.

If we study the differences in skin colour at the root, we will say that it is due to the pigmentation of the skin. Therefore, it may be concluded that it depends on genes. However, skin colour variations in mankind may be caused by differences in exposure to sunlight, i.e. there is an environmental condition that influences skin colour.

Research has shown that pigment reduces the synthesis of vitamin D, which is enzymatically controlled. The reduction of the synthesis of vitamin D by the skin is beneficial in higher latitudes. In the warmer equatorial regions, this keeps the body cool and keeps the skin protected from damage by sunlight. There is a gradient of skin colour correlated with latitudes. The higher the latitude, the paler the skin colour.

Although the original colour of man is black, lighter colour of skin arose by mutations of the gene(s) that are responsible for the synthesis of the pigment. Therefore, the differentiation of black, white and yellow human races took place almost half a million years ago by mutations of polygenic effects. Thus, we find yellow people in East Asia who resemble the Bushmen of South Africa.

If we consider colour variation, we will see that India shows a variety — from the fairer North Indians to the dark brown santhals. However, in isolated pockets — as shown by the Mongolian race — there is homogeneity in skin colour. This was because their isolation from the races carrying black pigment gave no scope for selective change and adaptation. Colour variation is present only where there is selective change and distribution.

Hazards and Risk

Definition of Hazard

Natural hazards are defined as "those elements of the physical environment harmful to Man and caused by forces extraneous to him". Traditionally, natural hazards have also been looked upon as "Acts of God". However, this perspective has not been popular since it suggests that humans have no part to play in creating those hazards and have even less hope of alleviating them.

The term 'environmental hazards' brings within its domain both natural and human dimensions. The extent to which hazards are 'voluntary' or 'involuntary' is of prime importance. Basing on the great width of possible hazard identification, Kates (1978) defined environmental hazard as — "the threat potential posed to man or nature by events originating in, or transmitted by, the natural or built environment". Under this definition can be included both long-term environmental deterioration (soil acidification, accumulate of greenhouse gases) and all social hazards, both involuntary and communal (crime, terrorism), as well as voluntary and personal hazards (drug abuse, trekking etc.)

The working definition of environmental hazards is as follows :

Extreme geophysical events and significant technological accidents, characterised by concentrated releases of energy or materials, which pose an unexpected threat to endanger human life and is capable of causing extensive damage to goods and the environment.

Definition of Risk

Risk is usually defined by multiplication of the two terms — 'probability' of events, and the 'magnitude' of specific consequences, assuming that society should be indifferent toward a low-consequence/high-probability risk, as well as a high-consequence/low-probability risk, with identical expected values.

Public response to risk is obviously determined by voluntariness, personal ability to influence the risk, familiarity with the hazard, and the catastrophic potential. Therefore, while technical assessment of risk is vital for decisions about competing designs or materials, it often fails to inform society choices of technology.

Definition of Disaster

The term 'disaster' is used in a wide variety of ways, depending upon its various components — physical, demographic, epidemiological, social, economic and political. In order to obtain a satisfactory definition some measure of magnitude must be employed. This must be in connection with the population at risk and to some index of the usual demographic experience of that population. In addition, the definition must do justice to the different elements that arise from disasters, such as the physical effects of immediate impacts, short and long-term demographic effects, social disruption, psychological effects, economic effects, political effects etc

Demographers have defined a demographic crisis or disaster as an excess of deaths (or illness) over normal expectations in a restricted time-space frame-work that is usually sufficient to denote a population crisis. In this demographic equation, there are three crucial variables —

(i) the size of the population effected;

(ii) the actual excess mortality rate; and

(iii) the duration of the crisis.

Again, geographers and other social scientists tend to define disasters more in environmental and behavioural terms. For instance, Sjoberg (1962) defined disaster as a '........ severe, relatively sudden, and frequently unexpected disruption of normal structural arrangements within a social system, or subsystem, resulting from a force, "natural" or "social", "internal" to a system or "external" to it, over which the system has no firm control'.

We may conclude from the above definitions that disasters have a characteristic unexpected or unforseen nature, always exceeding the normal expectation of the community. They are high-magnitude events in physical and demographic terms when compared to some normal period of human experience. They have immense impact on environment, society and human psychology and cause damage to existing facilities and societal structures.

QUESTIONS FOR EXAMINATION

A. Essay-Type Questions

1. Why is environmental study necessary ?
   Ans. Pp. 6-8
2. Give a brief account of the components of environment.
   Ans. Pp. 4-6
3. What are the basic components of environment ?
   Ans. Pp. 1-6
4. Describe the different types of man-made and natural disasters of environment.
   Ans. Pp. 11-12
5. Explain with examples the natural changes of environment.
   Ans. Pp. 8-12
6. Describe Nature versus Nurture.
   Ans. Pp. 12-13
7. How do environmental hazards influence man ? Suggest some remedial measures.
   Ans. Pp. 18-19
8. Describe the principal characteristics of environment.
   Ans. Pp. 4-6
9. Describe the components of land use pattern.
   Ans. Pp. 14-15
10. Explain 'the economic development and environment'.
    Ans. Pp. 14-16
11. Describe the influence of heredity and environment on a living being.
    Ans. Pp. 16-18
12. Analyse the environmental hazards and risks.
    Ans. Pp. 18-19

B. Short Answer-Type Questions

1. Define environment.
   Ans. Page 4
2. What is environment ?
   Ans. Page 2
3. What is biotic component ?
   Ans. Page 5
4. What is abiotic component ?
   Ans. Page 4
5. What is physical environment ?
   Ans. Page 4
6. What is social or cultural environment ?
   Ans. Page 5
7. What is biological environment ?
   Ans. Page 5

8. What is Human environment ?
   Ans. Page 5
9. What is Conceptual environment ?
   Ans. Page 5
10. What is environmental study ?
    Ans. Page 6
11. What are the needs of environmental study ?
    Ans. Page 6
12. What is environmental education ?
    Ans. Page 7
13. What are the objectives of environmental education ?
    Ans. Page 7
14. What is environmental change ?
    Ans. Page 8
15. What is Environmental Hazard ?
    Ans. Page 18
16. What is economic development ?
    Ans. Page 14
17. What is DNA ?
    Ans. Page 17
18. Define Hazard.
    Ans. Page 18
19. Define Risk.
    Ans. Page 19
20. Define Disaster.
    Ans. Page 19.

Chapter 2

NATURE AND NATURAL PROCESSES

INTRODUCTION

The globe has been divided into seven continents and five oceans.

In descending order of magnitude, the continents are — Asia, Africa, North America, South America, Antarctica, Europe and Australaia/Oceania.

Similarly, the oceans are — Pacific, Atlantic, Indian, Antarctic and Arctic.

The distribution of land (28%) and sea (72%) is not symmetrical. Land dominates the northern hemisphere, especially between 20° North and 70° North latitudes. On the other hand, sea dominates the southern hemisphere, especially between 50° South and 60° South latitudes.

Principal Constituents of the Earth

The principal constituents of the earth can be considered in four broad groups —

(1) the **lithosphere,** which is the outer skin of the earth made up of rocks and minerals,

(2) the **atmosphere**, which is the gas or vapour envelope around the earth,

(3) the **hydrosphere,** which is the liquid portion of the earth, including the water vapour of the atmosphere, the water present in oceans, seas, rivers and lakes, and the water present in rocks, and,

(4) the **biosphere,** which is the world of living organisms that dwell on land, in water and in the air that we breath.

Origin of the Earth and the Universe

From the very beginning, man has been curious to know how the earth and the universe came into being. Due to this common interest, all the early civilizations developed their own explanations and versions of the origin of the earth and nature of the universe.

COSMOLOGY is the field of study, which deals with the evolution of ideas regarding the origin of the earth, its relation to the solar system, and how the solar system is related to the universe.

Man had to wait until the invention of the telescope, when he could peer into space and explore the universe. However, this could be done at a limited scale. After two or three hundred years, more powerful telescopes were developed. In the meantime, there had been new developments in the fields of mathematics and physics. These enable man to explore space more adequately.

There are two rival theories explaining the origin of the universe :

(a) **The superdense or "BIG BANG" theory**

This theory was put forward by Ryle. He suggested that a vast explosion of superdense matter created the universe. This explosion produced the galaxies of stars which are scattered throughout the space. The stars are also flying away from each other, at the amazing speed of 600 million km/hour.

(b) **The steady state or continuous creation theory**

This theory was elaborated by Hoyle, Bondi and Gold. They rejected the Big Bang Theory. Instead, they put forward the idea that matter is being continuously created. New galaxies are born and compensate for the ones which are receding beyond man's ken.

The Earth in the Solar System

The sun is one of the 100 billion stars belonging to the MILKY WAY galaxy. The solar family of nine major planets and at least a thousand tiny planets known as asteroids, is dwarfed and dominated by the SUN. The sun contains over 99.87% of the total mass in the solar system. In spite of their comparative smallness and the enormous distances of empty space that separate the planets from the sun as well as from one another, the sun keeps its planets under rigid control. Every planet revolves around the sun continuously, in their own specific elliptical orbits. These planets are held near the sun by the pull of gravity. They are kept from being drawn into the sun by the tremendous speed with which they revolve through space. The lesser the distance from the sun, the faster they move.

The Earth is the only planet in the solar system known to support living creatures. This is because the Earth's composition and distance from the sun have provided exactly the necessary conditions for the evolution to an advanced form of life.

The **Geocentric Theory** refers to the ancient and medieval times when it was thought that the earth was the centre of the universe.

This traditional belief was demolished by Copernicus. He said that the earth was one among the many planets in a sun-centered system. This is the **Heliocentric Theory**. Today, it is no longer a theory but an established fact.

During the past two hundred years, a number of theories have been advanced regarding the origin of the earth :

(i) **The Nebular Theory** of Kant and Laplace. In the 18th century, they said that the solar system originated from a hot, rotating, gaseous mass which contracted while cooling and thrown off rings of matter which condensed to form planets.

(ii) **The Planetesimal Hypothesis** put forward by the Americans — Chamberlin and Moulton. They supposed that the planets originated through the coalescence, by gravitational attraction, of planetesimals or fragments of solar material.

(iii) **The Tidal Theory** of Jeans says that a wandering star came near the sun and produced a tidal distortion in the sun. This resulted in a cigar-shaped filament of solar matter being pulled away from the sun. In due course, this materialized into concentration of planets.

(iv) **The Twin-sun Theory** put forward by Hoyle, according to which the solar system was derived from the sun's former twin which exploded and shattered. Following the explosion, some of the materials became concentrated into planets due to gravitational attraction.

The Mystery Beneath the Crust

When we look upwards, we can see into space for millions of kilometers. But, when we try to penetrate downward (by boring) we can only reach down to a land depth of about 4.3 km (14,000 feet). Thus, till today, man has only been able to scratch the surface of the planet, but has only penetrated up to such a minute depth — which is even less than 0.001% of the distance from the surface to the centre of the earth.

The **Mohole Project** was taken up by American scientists with the aim of improving our knowledge of the sub-crust. The scientists planned to drill a hole, about 10 km deep, from the surface, through the crust to the material below. However, the project turned out to be so expensive that it was eventually abandoned after the early work.

Later, much deep sea drilling was done and cores of ocean crust from sites of structural interest were obtained (D.S.D.P. or Deep Sea Drilling Project, and the I.P.O.D. or International Phase of Ocean Drilling Programmes). Valuable information was obtained regarding the behaviour of the earth's crust and the rocks beneath.

We do not know exactly what lies beneath and what kind of conditions prevail in the earth's interior. The geologists have intelligently interpreted the various kinds of evidence and tried to tell us about the composition, structure and nature of the earth.

Composition and Structure of the Earth

The earth can be compared to an onion, because it is made up of a series of "shell" or onion-like layers. These layers (lithosphere) are composed of different materials. There are differences in views regarding the number of layers, their constitution and thickness.

The following is the generally accepted interpretation of the composition and structure of the earth :

(a) **The Crust :** This is the outer layer of the earth. It is composed of crystalline rocks with sedimentary rock clippings. The depth of the crust is about 20 to 30 miles (32.2 to 48.3 km). The specific gravity of the rocks vary between 2.0 and 3.0. The crust, or outer

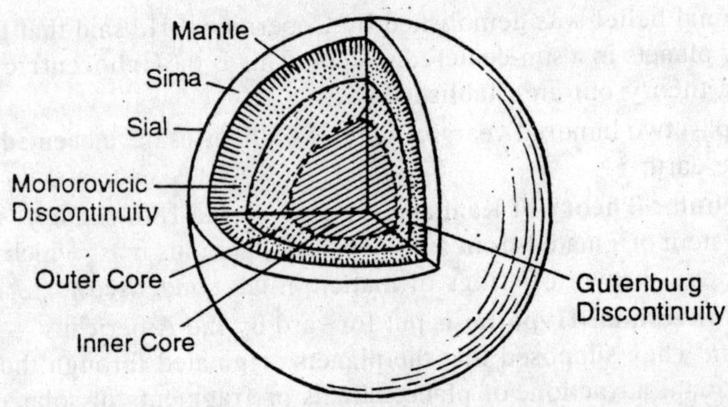

Fig. 4(a). Structure of the Earth

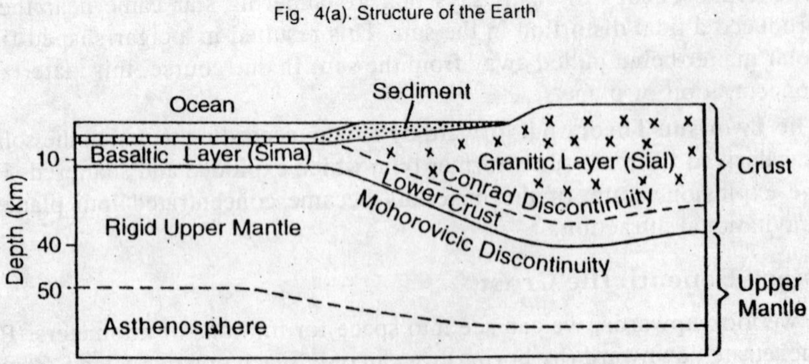

Fig. 4(b). Schematic Section of the Lithosphere

zone is separated from the zone underneath by a distinct break. This discontinuity is the MOHOROVICIC DISCONTINUITY.

The crust is distinguished into 2 layers —

(i) **Sial** — This is the outer layer. It is made up of sedimentary and granitic rocks. The name comes from silica (Si) and alumina (Al).

(ii) **Sima** — This is the underlying layer. It is made up of dense basaltic rocks. The name comes from silica (Si) and magnesia (Ma).

(b) **The Mantle** : This is the middle layer which is composed of ultrabasic rocks. it is said that the mantle consists of the mineral olivine. Olivine is a heavy silicate of magnesium and iron. The specific gravity of the rocks here vary between 3.0 and 5.0. The mantle extends downward to a depth of about 1,800 miles (3,000 km). The mantle is separated from the core (or centre) of the earth by the **Gutenberg Discontinuity**.

If the mantle is further subdivided, we will find an interesting layer near its outer margin. This is the **Asthenosphere** or **Low Velocity Layer**. The asthenosphere is found at depths of between 50 km 250 km. It supposedly contains partially molten material.

(c) **The Core** — It occurs at depths below 2,900 km.

From various evidences found so far, the core may be divided into 2 zones —

(i) an outer core which exists in a liquid or plastic state; and

(ii) an inner core which is most probably solid.

It is assumed that the core is composed of a nickel-iron mixture. Hence, it is known as NIFE.

We know that both temperature and pressure increase with depth, as one penetrates below the earth's surface. Therefore, although the earth's outer crust is solid, the material at the earth's centre will exist in a molten or gaseous state.

Composition of the Atmosphere

Air is not a chemical compound. It is a mechanical mixture of gases. Four gases — nitrogen, oxygen, argon and carbon dioxide — make up 99.98% of the air by volume.

In general, the atmosphere can be said to be composed of —

(a) gases

(b) water vapour

(c) dust particles.

Average Composition of Dry Air (below 25 Km)

COMPONENT	SYMBOL	VOLUME % (DRY AIR)
Nitrogen	N_2	78.08
Oxygen	O_2	20.94
Argon	Ar	0.93
Carbon dioxide	CO_2	0.03 (very variable)
Neon	Ne	0.0018
Helium	He	0.0005
Ozone	O_3	0.00006
Hydrogen	H	0.00005
Krypton	Kr	Trace
Xenon	Xe	Trace
Methane	CH_4	Trace

(a) From the table we see that the principal gases comprising dry air at sea level are nitrogen, oxygen, argon, carbon dioxide, neon, helium, ozone, hydrogen, krypton, xenon and methane.

Out of these gases, there are some that are so inert chemically that they are never found in any chemical compound. These gases are argon, neon, helium, krypton and xenon.

(b) Besides these gases, **water vapour**, which varies with time and space, is a vital constituent of the atmosphere.

(c) **Aerosols** are present in the atmosphere in significant quantities. Suspended particles of dust, sea-salt, organic matter, smoke etc. are collectively called aerosoles.

Principal Gases in the Atmosphere and their Functions

(1) **Oxygen (O_2)** —

(i) All living organisms inhale O_2. No life is possible without this gas.

(ii) It can combine with all other elements and thus can form different compounds.

(iii) It is indispensable for combustion.

(2) **Nitrogen (N_2)** —

(i) Its main function in the atmosphere is to dilute oxygen and regulate combustion.

(ii) Indirectly, it aids oxidation of different kinds.

(3) **Carbon dioxide (CO_2)** —

(i) Plants inhale this gas.

(ii) Green plants utilize CO_2 in photosynthesis and prepare their own food.

(iii) It is of great climatic significance because it efficiently absorbs heat from the upper atmosphere.

(iv) It influences the flow of energy through the atmosphere because CO_2 returns almost half of the absorbed heat back to the earth.

During the past century, large scale fossil fuel burning has increased the concentration of CO_2 in the air. Ultimately, this has resulted in the warming of the lower atmosphere.

(4) **Ozone (O_3)** — This triatomic form of oxygen is the most efficient absorber of the scorching ultra-violet radiation from the sun. The ozonosphere protects us from the ill-effects of excessive quantities of UV rays.

The composition of the atmosphere varies with height, latitude and time.

The light gases, especially helium and hydrogen, are found in abundance in the upper atmosphere. Water vapour constitutes almost 4% of the atmosphere by volume, only near the surface. Above 10–12 km, it is nearly absent. Ozone is found mainly between 15–35 km, in the Troposphere.

Ozone and water vapour are also the two gases whose concentrations in the atmosphere vary with latitude and season.

Ozone content is low over the Equator (0°). It is high over latitudes north of 50°N, that too mostly during the spring season.

Layers of the Atmosphere

The Earth's atmosphere can be separated into shells, where each layer between the shells is marked by unique temperature gradient and physical characteristics.

Table : Major Regions of the Atmosphere

Region	Altitude range (km)	Temperature range (°C)	Important Chemical Species
Troposphere	0-11	15 to –56	N_2, O_2, CO_2, H_2O
Stratosphere	11-50	–56 to –2	O_3
Mesosphere	50-85	–2 to –92	O_2^+, O^+, NO^+
Thermosphere	85-800	–92 to 1,200	O_2^+, O^+, NO^+
Exosphere	800 above		H^+, He^+

It can be seen from the table that the atmosphere may be broadly divided into four distinct regions. The atmosphere extends up to 800 km with temperature varying from a minimum of –2°C to a maximum of 1,200°C.

The characteristics of the four layers have been discussed below :

(i) **Troposphere** : Almost 70% of the mass of the atmosphere is contained in this layer.

It is more or less homogeneous in composition where there is no air pollution. The water content here also depends on the hydrological cycle.

The troposphere is a region of turbulence. This is because of the global energy flow that arises from imbalances of heating and cooling rates between the equator and the poles. The air is far from uniform, depending on density and temperature.

In the troposphere, temperature decreases uniformly with increasing altitude. Near the ground level, the air is heated by radiation from the earth.

At the top of the troposphere is the tropopause. This is the cold layer (–56°C) which marks temperature invertion, i.e. transition from negative to positive lapse rates.

(ii) **Stratosphere** : This is the quiescent layer marked by a positive lapse rate. The temperature increases with increase in altitude. At the upper limit of the stratosphere it is –2°C.

This region has the maximum concentration of Ozone. The gas absorbs ultraviolet radiation of the sun, raising the temperature and causing a positive lapse rate. The importance of ozone lies in the fact that it acts as a protective shield for life on earth and from the detrimental effects of the scorching ultraviolet rays. It also supplies the heat for dividing the earth into a quiescent stratosphere and turbulent troposphere.

Since mixing in the stratosphere is very slow, the molecules or particles here persist for a long time. Therefore, once the pollutants are able to reach the stratosphere, they pose long-term global hazards, compared to their impact in the more dense troposphere.

(iii) **Mesosphere** : This layer has been so named because of its situation in the middle of the five layers that is divided according to the thermal conditions of the atmosphere. The mesosphere stretches at altitudes between 50 and 80 km. It is also known as upper Troposphere since, due to the absence of ultraviolet absorbing species, temperature falls with increasing altitude, i.e. negative lapse rate prevails, basically similar to what happens in the troposphere.

During summer, the temperature of the mesopause over Arctic region can drop to as low as –100°C. The upper part of this layer remains colder while the lower part is warm. Due to this, there arises a connective motion of air. A significant feature of this layer is the formation of noctilucent cloud or an ice-cloud, formed by the deposition of a very small amount of water vapour on the nickel containing cosmic dust (by depositing, it means here the process by which water vapour turns into ice-crystals directly on the condensation nuclei). The noctilucent cloud is silver-white and light blue in colour. It is cirrus-like in shape and appears over higher latitudes before sunset and disappears after sunset.

A series of intense photochemical reactions, i.e. dissociations and recombinations of different elements of the atmosphere, take place in the mesosphere under the action of the sun's ultraviolet radiation.

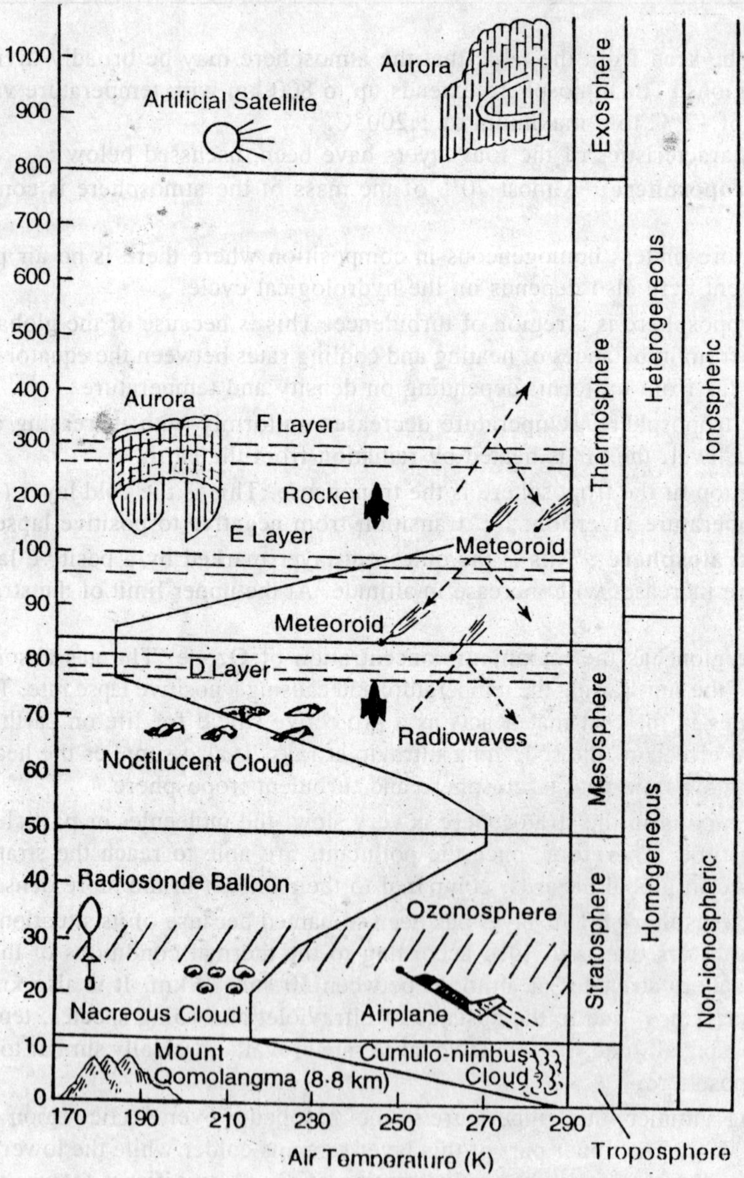

Fig. 5. Layers of the Atmosphere

In the layer below the mesosphere, the air is homogeneously mixed since both horizontal and vertical motions are present. For this reason, the atmosphere up to 90 km is termed as the homogeneous atmosphere.

(iv) **Thermosphere :** This layer that extents from the mesopause up to about 800 km is noted for two striking features —

(a) Temperature rises with increasing altitude i.e. positive lapse rate prevails here. Satellite data shows that at 200 km temperature stays around 700°C, and at 300 km it exceeds 1,000°C. The high temperature results from the heat released by the dissociation of oxygen and nitrogen molecules and atoms. The dissociation is caused by the sun's ultraviolet radiation with wavelengths shorter than 0.175 microns, that can absorb the gases in the layer.

(b) The air is highly ionized. The gases present here, especially nitric oxide and oxygen, split into atoms and undergo ionization, following absorption of solar radiation in the far ultraviolet region.

Over higher latitudes, the resplendent aurora appears in the Thermosphere. It is the outcome of the collision of some of the charged particles thrown out of the sun with the molecules and atoms of gases in the thermosphere, under the action of the earth's magnetic field.

(v) **Exosphere :** This is the outermost layer of the atmosphere, and also the transition zone between the earth's atmosphere and interplanetary space. The air is inconceivably thin and almost completely ionized. It consists of helium and hydrogen, the lightest constituents of air.

Basing on its electric properties, the atmosphere can be divided into two layers —

(a) The non-ionosphere is the section of the atmosphere up to 60 km. Here, the constituents remain in neutral state.

(b) The Ionosphere is the section of the atmosphere between 60 and 2,000 km. The ultraviolet radiation from the sun ionizes the air and produces ions and free electrons. The air thus becomes a mixture of charged particles and non-ionized neutral particles. These free electrons act as mirror and reflect certain types of radio-waves.

The Hydrosphere

The hydrosphere for the most part fills the depression of the rock sphere, but because of its penetrative qualities some water is found in the rocks and much exists in the troposphere in the form of water vapour. The oceans, which cover about 72% of the surface, contain the great bulk of the water. The average depth of the oceans is about three kilometers (containing 350,000 plant species and 11 million animal species). The general level of the ocean floor — so-called deep-sea trenches — parallel some of the continental margins and island areas.

The Biosphere

If we try and glance over the surface of our earth, we will see life everywhere on land and in the oceans. On land, life exists from sea-level to an altitude of 3,000 meters, abundant evidence of life is found in the upper 100 meters of the oceans. Life also extents up to a depth of 10,000 metres beneath the oceans, as well as in the upper reaches of the atmosphere and high mountains, up to an altitude of almost 10,000 meters. The biologically inhabited part of the hydrosphere, lithosphere and atmosphere together constitute the biosphere.

What is the Biosphere ?

Biosphere is the component part of the earth that includes all forms of organic life which require food for continuing all life activities. Thus, the sphere of living matter, along with the layer of water, air and soil surrounding it on the surface of the earth is termed the "biosphere".

Why do we need to study the Biosphere ?

One should study the Biosphere with a definite purpose in mind. The various ways in which the study of this subject may help us have been summarized as follows :

(i) Identification and assessment of the impact of man's actions upon the biosphere and conversely to those of the biosphere on man.

(ii) Analysis and comparison of the functioning of the natural, modified and managed ecosystems on a global scale.

(iii) Development of ways and means to monitor and measure both quantitative and qualitative altertions in the environment in order to establish scientific criteria that will provide a base for rational management of natural resources and also establish standards of environment quality.

(iv) Promotion of development and application of computer simulation and other approaches which will help the predictions of likely future trends, allowing mankind to direct its action for long-term best interests.

(v) Development of study material for environmental education at all levels and stimulating global awareness about environmental problems with the help of the public media.

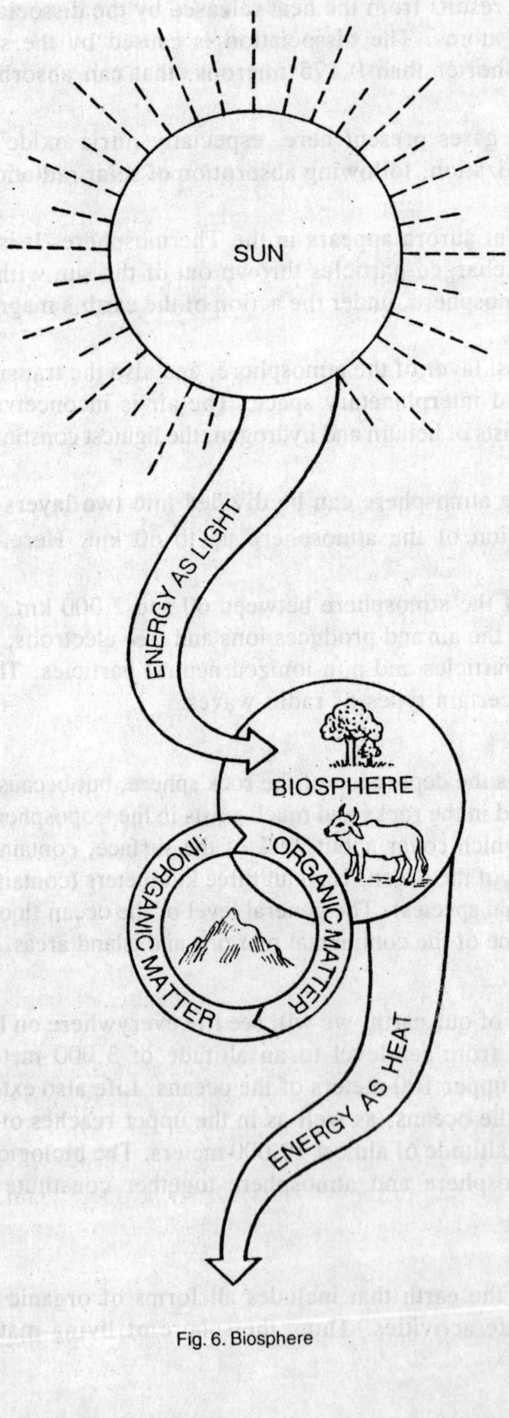

Fig. 6. Biosphere

Subject Matter of Study of the Biosphere

The study of the biosphere includes :

(i) Ecological effects of increasing human population and activities on tropical and subtropical ecosystems.

(ii) Ecological effects of various land use and management practices on Mediterranean and temperate forest ecosystems.

(iii) Impact of man's activities, especially irrigation practices, on the sensitive arid and semi-arid regions.

(iv) Impact of man's activities on the value and resources of water-bodies and wetlands.

(v) Human activities and related environmental problems affecting the society.

(vi) Genetic and demographic changes resulting from changing environmental conditions.

Dynamics of the Biosphere

Unlike inorganic life, organic life, i.e. plants, animals etc., need food to continue their existence. The principal food that the organic life needs is carbon, which maintains life by providing heat. The atmosphere happens to be the original sources of carbon. Plants and other forms of vegetable life can take carbon directly from the atmosphere. However, animals get the required carbon from the vegetables and the animals (feeding on the vegetable matter) that they consume.

The Process of Photosynthesis

The process of photosynthesis forms the primary pathway by which plants withdraw carbon from the carbon dioxide pool and utilize it to build essential carbohydrates and other organic compounds.

In order to understand the relationships between different organisms in the universe, we should understand the energy flow in the earth as a whole. To do so, we must consider here the first and second laws of thermodynamics.

The first law states that energy can be neither created nor destroyed; it is transferred or transformed into different forms.

The second law states that during energy transformation, energy changes from a concentrated to a dispersed condition.

These laws explain the production of living tissues and the succession of living plant tissue. Solar energy is utilized and combined with essential materials in the process of photosynthesis, as shown in the following reaction :

$$CO_2 + H_2O + \text{Minerals} + \text{Sunlight} \longrightarrow \text{Organic matter} + O_2 + \text{Heat}$$

Photosynthesis is critical to life on earth, since it removes carbon dioxide from the atmosphere and substitutes oxygen. Human cannot live as they do in an oxygen-deficient atmosphere.

When the organic life does not have the amount of food it requires, or it cannot assimilate the food due to some defects in its "food-manufacturing machinery", it leads to its "death". The death is followed by disintegration and, finally, the matter is returned to the atmosphere, its original home.

Thus the "Cycle of Life" between the atmosphere and the organic forms is completed.

Energy Flow in the Ecosystems

In any ecosystem, energy in the form of food passes through a number of stages, or Tropic levels, thus forming a Food Chain.

Energy from sunlight is taken up by autotrophs (food-producing plants), which, in turn, produce carbohydrate, or the food substance, by photosynthesis. These autotrophs again provide sustenance to the herbivores, and the carbon stored in the carbohydrates manufactured by the autotrophs are transferred to the animals. The herbivores are eaten by the carnivores, and the carbon continues its journey further along the food-chain. By the complex biochemical process called respiration, plants and animals extract necessary energy from the organic compounds.

Division of Organic Life

We can divide Biosphere, or the organic life, into three principal classes. This division is based mainly on the degree of the freedom of movement and the possession of some organs that are specially developed. The classes are :

(1) Plant Life

(2) Animal Life

(3) Human Life.

Unlike animals and humans, plants are fixed to the ground where it was formed by its roots. On the other hand the intellect of man is far more developed than that of any animal.

However, none of these forms of life remain confined to any particular region or locality. Animals and humans have their own organs of locomotion that carry them from one place to another. But in the case of plants, various agents, such as water, wind, birds or man may take the seeds from place to place. If the environment is favourable the seeds may germinate in a new region. This is how plant life spreads.

Bio-Geo Chemical Cycles

The energy required for the maintenance of living organisms comes from sunlight. However, only this is not sufficient. The materials needed for the existence of living things are provided by the Earth.

Bio-geo chemical cycle involve the cyclic movement of material or nutrient. The term is so since the cycling of elements involve biological organism (bio), geological environment (geo) and the chemical changes.

General Characteristic Features of Bio-Geochemical Cycles

The significant features characteristic of bio-geochemical cycles are —

(1) A bio-geochemical **pool** is a quantity of any chemical substance, either in a biotic, or in an abiotic component of an ecosystem.

For instance, the atmosphere contains an enormous pool of carbon, in the form of carbon dioxide gas, while the ocean waters contain carbon in the form of dissolved bicarbonate. Carbon is contained by calcareous rocks in the form of particulate carbonate. Living organisms contain carbon as organic matter.

(2) The **flux rate**, i.e., the quantity of material which is passing from one pool to another, per unit time and per unit area or volume of the system.

Turnover rate is the flux rate into or out of a pool, divided by the quantity of nutrient in the pool. This allows the importance of the flux process to be determined in relation to pool size.

Turnover time is the quantity of nutrient in the pool, divided by the flux rate. It indicates the time necessary for the movement of a quantity of nutrient equal to that in the pool.

Classification of Nutrients

According to their importance as structural parts of organic matter, elements essential for life can be classified into three categories. These categories and their constituents are shown in the table —

Table : Necessary Elements for Life

Categories	Elements	Symbols
Major constituents (20-60 atoms %)	Hydrogen	H
	Carbon	C
	Oxygen	O
	Nitrogen	N
	Sodium	Na

Categories	Elements	Symbols
Macronutrients (0.02-2 atoms %)	Magnesium	Mg
	Phosphorus	P
	Sulphur	S
	Chlorine	Cl
	Potassium	K
	Calcium	Ca
	Boron	B
	Silicon	Si
	Vanadium	V
	Manganese	Mn
Micronutrients trace elements (<0.001 atoms %)	Iron	Fe
	Cobalt	Co
	Copper	Cu
	Zinc	Zn
	Molybdenum	Mo
	Iodine	I

However, other workers have identified **major constituents macro-** and **micro-constituents.**

(1) **Major constituents** — are most important in the bio-geochemical process of the earth.

(2) **Macroconutrients** are those elements and compounds that are needed by living organisms in large quantities and are major constituents of protoplasm.

(3) **Micronutrients** are those elements and compounds that are indispensable for the functioning of living systems, but are needed in only small quantities.

Types of Bio-Geochemical Cycles

(1) **Gaseous Nutrient Cycle**, associated mainly with the atmosphere and ocean. Such are carbon, oxygen and nitrogen cycles.

(2) **Sedimentary Nutrient Cycle**, where the lithosphere or sedimentary rock is the nutrient reservoir.

As per syllabus only three gaseous cycles have been discussed — carbon cycle, nitrogen cycle and oxygen cycle.

The Carbon Cycle

The carbon cycle is probably the most important, as well as the simplest of the gaseous cycles. It is said to be the perfect cycle, in which the carbon is returned to the atmosphere almost as fast as it is removed.

The movement of the carbon occurs from the atmospheric reservoir to the producers, then the consumers, and from them to the decomposers, then back to the reservoir.

The two principal components of the carbon cycle are carbon dioxide and organic carbon.

Reservoir : (i) The atmosphere is the gaseous reservoir in the carbon cycle. It has a carbon concentration of 0.03%. Almost 2.5×10^{10} tons of carbon are annually removed by the terrestrial organisms. Marine organisms remove about 1.9×10^{10} tons. If we also consider the removal by fresh organisms, the annual withdrawal of carbon is almost 9×10^{10} tons.

(ii) The sea is the second major reservoir of carbon. When salinity of sea water is 35 gms per kilo, CO_2 content is 47 cc per liter.

Withdrawal of CO_2 from the Atmospheric Reserves

The primary producers or green vegetation play the most significant role in drawing the CO_2 from the atmosphere and/or the hydrosphere, and then helping to build up organic carbon from inorganic sources.

This can be represented by the equation below

$$6CO_2 + 6H_2O \underset{673\ kcal}{\overset{hv}{\rightleftharpoons}} C_6H_{12}O_6 + CO_2$$

This carbon is then carried further in two ways —

(a) by **Food chain** through herbivores and carnivores, and

(b) by **Geologic sources.**

Plants combine a portion of the carbon with oxygen, nitrogen, sulphur and phosphorus. In this way proteins are formed. The proteins then move through the food chain until they reach the decomposers.

The geologic component of the system deals with the deposition of plant material, which is later formed into peat coal and oil.

There are also aquatic organisms that fix CO_2 directly from dissolved salts in the water.

Also, CO_2 is removed from the atmosphere by precipitation.

Return of CO_2 to the Atmospheric Reservoir

A considerable amount of the biologically fixed CO_2 is returned to the atmosphere by the respiratory activity of the producers and consumers.

The most substantial return of CO_2 to the atmosphere is contributed by the respiratory activity of the decomposers that work upon dead and decaying organisms and fecal matter.

Return of CO_2 from the biota also occurs through the non-biological process of combustion. This happens in fire-wood burning, forest fire or accidental building fire, and so on.

Another source is geologic, when burning of fossil fuel gives back the carbon that had been locked in the rock strata over the years. The same is also done by volcanoes, hot springs and fissures in the rocks.

With the advancement of civilization, CO_2 emissions have increased due to industrial and agricultural activities.

The dissolution of sedimentary rocks (formed by calcium carbonate depositions), when available to the aquatic environment, may return the carbon to the atmosphere.

Increase of CO_2 in the Atmosphere

The amount of CO_2 injected into the atmosphere is small in comparison to the total CO_2 in circulation. Yet, this is having a perceptible effect. This is because the atmospheric reservoir is small and large oceanic reservoirs cannot absorb the new CO_2 as fast as it is being produced.

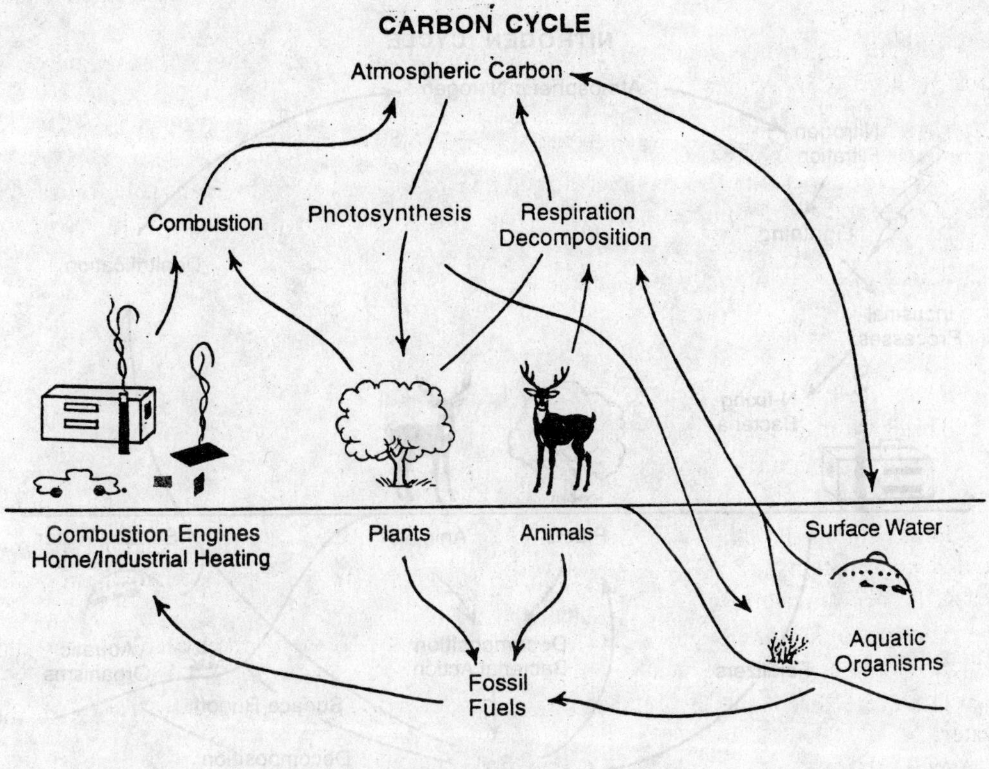

Fig. 7. The Carbon Cycle

There has been a steady rise in the CO_2 content of the atmosphere during the 20th century. The generally accepted value is now 0.055%.

Conclusion

Thus, the carbon cycle is considered to be an important cycle, especially in productivity, pH and alkalinity. There are numerous ways in which carbon is utilized, as well as restored to the atmosphere. The extent to which the system will regulate or adapt itself to the present rise in the volume of release of CO_2 is still a question.

The Nitrogen Cycle

The most abundant element in the atmosphere is nitrogen. In its elemental form it is a colourless and odourless gas which cannot be used by plants or animals. But in combination with oxygen or other elements, nitrogen is available to living organisms as a nutrient.

The nitrogen cycle may be defined as the circular flow of nitrogen from free nitrogen gas in the atmosphere to nitrates in the soil, and, finally, back to atmospheric nitrogen.

Nitrogen Fixation : By this process, nitrogen gas is converted to nitrates. This can be done in many ways :

(i) There are some **Nitrogen-fixing bacteria** that live in the soil or in nodules on the roots of leguminous plants. They can convert nitrogen gas to nitrate. Nitrogen fixation is also done by some types of blue-green algae and fungi.

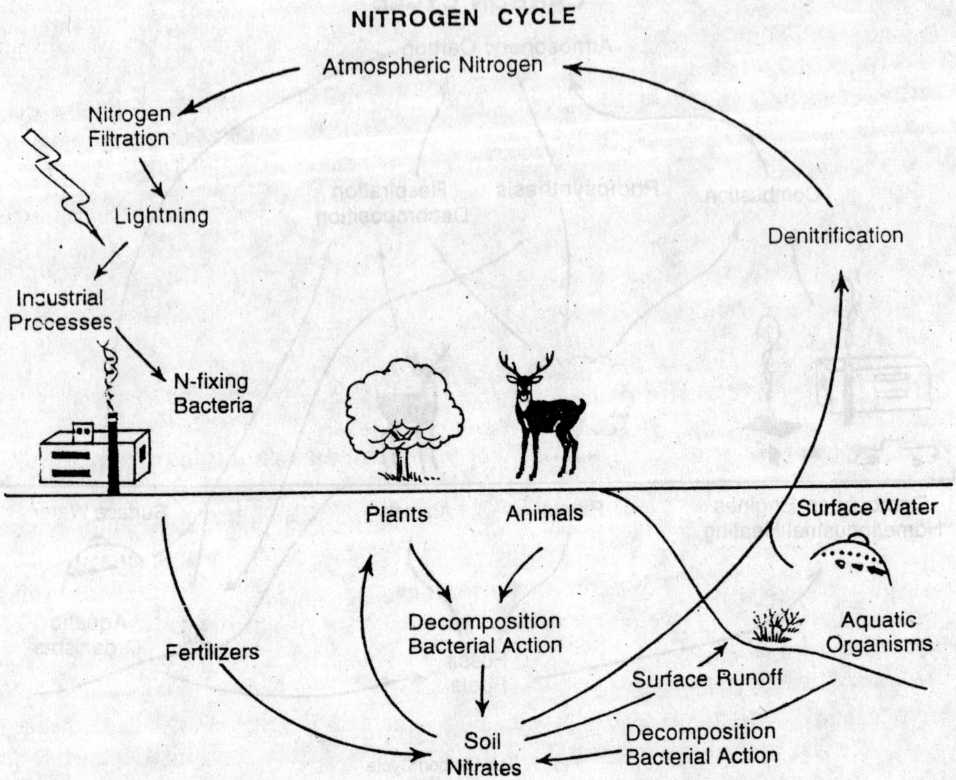

Fig. 8. The Nitrogen Cycle

(ii) Nitrogen fixation also occurs in the atmosphere. This is **natural nitrogen fixation.** It takes place when lightning occurs, because the electrical current that passes through the atmospheric nitrogen converts some of the nitrogen gas to nitrogen compounds. These compounds can be used by plants.

(iii) Nitrates are also released from dead and decaying plants and animals and animal wastes.

Denitrification : At the same time, when nitrates are being produced from nitrogen gas, other nitrates are breaking down and releasing nitrogen gas back to the atmosphere. This process of reversal is called denitrification.

Denitrification occurs

(i) when some forms of bacteria come in contact with nitrates, and also,

(ii) when run-off water carry nitrates into surface water which constantly exchanges nitrogen with the atmosphere.

There are some ecosystems where the process of nitrogen fixation and denitrification are attuned according to the productivity demands of the ecosystems.

The processes are the most rapid in the temperate ecosystems, especially during winter.

The Oxygen Cycle

The element oxygen can be said to be ubiquitous. It is chemically extremely reactive and can combine with a wide range of other elements. For instance, oxygen combines with hydrogen to form water (H_2O); in combination with carbon forms carbon monoxide (CO) and carbon dioxide (CO_2); with sulphur it forms sulphur dioxide (SO_2), and similar other compounds with other elements. Oxygen is an important constituent of organic substances like sugars, cellulose and starches. It is found in almost all minerals and rocks.

The biogeochemical cycling of oxygen is very complex. Two reasons are mainly responsible for this —

(i) **Oxygen has a high degree of chemical reactivity,** and

(ii) **Oxygen is present in a wide range of biotic and abiotic ecosystem components.**

Oxygen in its elemental state is known as free oxygen. There are two main pools of free oxygen —

(i) the **atmosphere** contains about 0.8×10^{15}t (Johnson 1970); and

(ii) the **oceans** contain about 0.2×10^{15}t.

The production and renewal of these two pools are carried out by the two following processes —

(i) **Photodissociation of water vapour in the upper atmosphere,** as a result of which oxygen is released when water molecules are split by light;

(ii) **Photosynthesis,** by which energy is fixed and oxygen is released. Photosynthesis is the major contributor of molecular oxygen.

The ecosystems of the past produced more oxygen than was used in respiration, oxidation of rocks or the decay of organic matter. The presence of fossil fuels represent reduced carbon withdrawn from the bio-geochemical cycles. They prove the lack of oxidation and the decay of some types of ancient ecosystems.

It is usually difficult to assess global biogeochemical cycles. But it is said that the oxygen cycle is a perfect cycle in a state of dynamic equilibrium, in spite of anthropogenic activity that involves fossil fuel burning. The burning of fossil fuel releases annually 2,000 times greater carbon than is stored. As a result, oxygen is rapidly removed from the atmosphere.

In 1970, Machta and Hughes said that between 1910 and 1970, fossil fuel burning has not had any discernible effect on oxygen concentrations. The cycle has maintained a steady state condition probably because it has **negative feedback mechanisms.**

According to Redfield (1958), sulphate-reducing bacteria, which are found in anaerobic environment, may operate in such a way.

These chemosynthetic bacteria are capable of using sulphate ion as a source of oxygen. This can be shown as —

$$\underset{\text{Sulphate ion}}{SO_4^{2-}} + \underset{\text{Carbon}}{2C} \longrightarrow \underset{\text{Carbon dioxide}}{2CO_2} + \underset{\text{Sulphide ion}}{S^{2-}}$$

In this process, free oxygen is not released, but organic matter is decomposed and nutrients are released. The nutrients are phosphates, nitrates and carbon dioxide. Subsequently, carbon dioxide may be fluxed to a situation where it is used in photosynthesis and consequently oxygen is released.

However, it should be kept in mind that these bacteria survive only in anerobic habitats. Therefore, any change in the content of atmospheric oxygen would reflect the abundance of anerobic habitats. As a result, bacteria populations will increase and this would regulate oxygen supply.

An increased concentration of carbon dioxide in the atmosphere may increase photosynthesis and production of molecular oxygen. At the same time, pollution, rampant deforestation

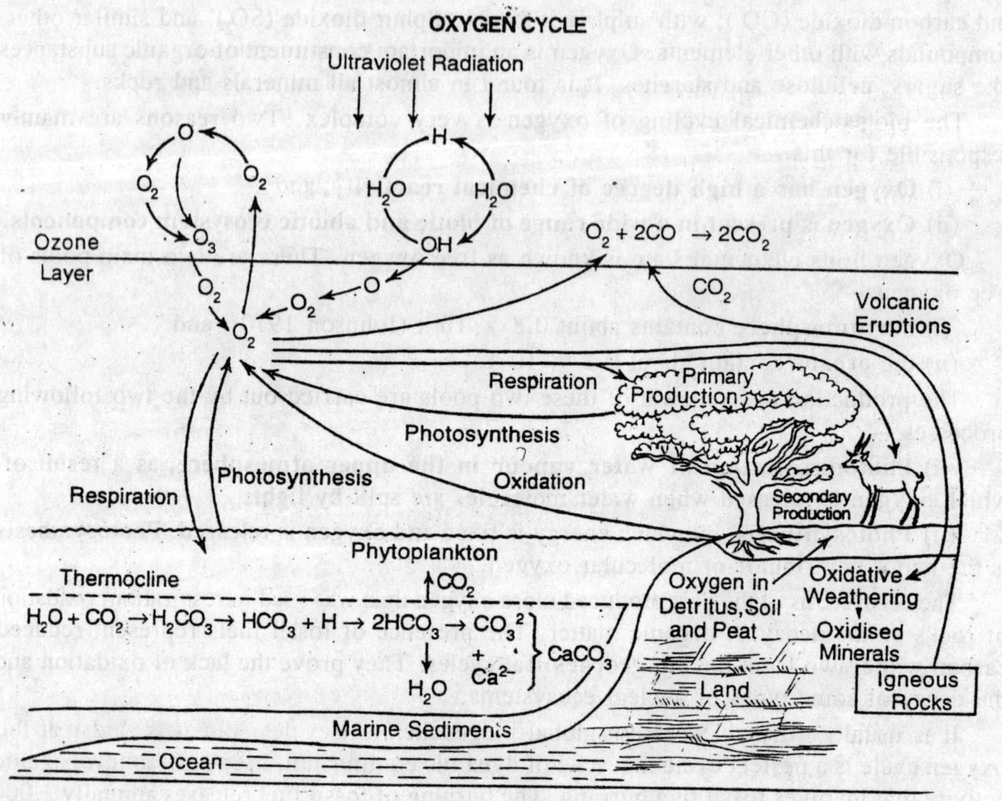

Fig. 9. The Oxygen Cycle

and other anthropogenic activities may reduce photosynthesis. This will lead to an imbalance in both the carbon and oxygen cycles.

QUESTIONS FOR EXAMINATION

A. Essay-Type Questions

1. What are the different hypotheses regarding the origin of the earth ?
   Ans. Pp. 22-23
2. Describe the principal constituents of the earth.
   Ans. Pp. 23-25
3. Analyse the structure and lithology of the earth's form.
   Ans. Pp. 23-24
4. Describe the different layers of the atmosphere.
   Ans. Pp. 26-28
5. Describe the situation and nature of the Biosphere.
   Ans. Pp. 29-31
6. Explain the Nitrogen Cycle.
   Ans. Pp. 35-36
7. Explain the Carbon Cycle.
   Ans. Pp. 33-35
8. Explain the Oxygen Cycle.
   Ans. Pp. 36-38
9. Analyse the processes of Bio-Geochemical Cycle.
   Ans. Pp. 32-33
10. Write an account on the organic life.
    Ans. Pp. 31-32

B. Short Answer-Type Questions

1. What is Atmosphere ?
   Ans. Page 25
2. What is Lithosphere ?
   Ans. Page 24
3. What is Hydrosphere ?
   Ans. Page 29
4. How many principal gases are there in the atmosphere ?
   Ans. Page 26
5. What is Ozone (O_3) ?
   Ans. Page 26
6. What is Biosphere ?
   Ans. Page 29
7. Why do we need to study the Biosphere ?
   Ans. Page 30
8. What is the subject matter of the Biosphere ?
   Ans. Page 30
9. Define dynamics of the Biosphere.
   Ans. Page 29

10. What is the process of photosynthesis ?
    Ans. Page 31
11. What is energy flow ?
    Ans. Page 31
12. What is Bio-Geochemical Cycle ?
    Ans. Page 32
13. Give a few names of the necessary elements for life.
    Ans. Page 32
14. How many types of Bio-Geochemical cycles are there ?
    Ans. Page 33
15. What is Carbon Dioxide (CO_2) ?
    Ans. Page 33
16. What is nitrogen fixation ?
    Ans. Page 35
17. What is the importance of Oxygen ?
    Ans. Page 36
18. What is negative feedback mechanism ?
    Ans. Page 37

Chapter 3

ECOSYSTEM

INTRODUCTION

According to the Oxford Dictionary of Ecology, ecology is defined as —

"the scientific study of the interrelationships among organisms and between organisms, and between them and all aspects, living and non-living, of their environment."

Ernst Heinrich Philipp Haeckel, a German anatomist, zoologist and field naturalist, first coined the word "ecology" in his Generelle Morphologie der Organicmen. It was published in two volumes in 1866. The German word "Ökologie" was derived from the Greek "oikos" meaning 'house' and 'logos' meaning 'discourse'.

The principal aim of an ecologist is to understand how an organism fits into its environment. To any organism, its environment is of supreme importance. The success or failure of an organism as an individual will be determined by its ability to exist in the environment where it lives.

There are several definitions of ecology. According to Haeckel, ecology is 'the domestic side of organic life' and 'the knowledge of the sum of the relations of organisms to the surrounding outer world, to organic and inorganic conditions of existence". This "surrounding outer world" is actually another word for environment.

In 1927, Charles Sutherland Elton, a British zoologist, in his book 'Animal Ecology' wrote that ecology is 'the study of animals and plants in relation to their habits and habitats'. Today, an ecologist would probably use the word 'organisms' instead of 'animal and plants', since we now recognize other categories of organisms (bacteria, fungi and Protista), which are neither in the plant nor in the animal kingdoms.

In recent times, Krebs (1985) has defined ecology as 'the scientific study of the interactions that determine the distribution and abundance of organisms."

Ecology may be compared to an enormous jigsaw puzzle. Each organism has specific requirement for life. The requirements of one interlock with those of many other individuals in the area. Some of these individuals may belong to the same species, but most are very different organisms who have different ways living and interacting.

Let us clarify the concept of ecology as a jigsaw puzzle. An animal catches other animals to satisfy its hunger. It is, thus, a predator, which, in turn, is again hunted or killed by another species of predator. During the lifetime of the animal, it has to find a mate belonging to same species, in order to reproduce. The animal also has to fight 'competitors' for food and in the process will probably catch diseases.

How far the animal will be successful in avoiding the predator, catching its prey and withstanding disease, and so on, will depend on the relationship it has with the organisms around it. The life of the animal will also be affected by the time of the year, weather and the quality of nesting or sleeping sites.

Frequently Used Words in the Study of Ecology

Population : It comprises a group of organisms, all belonging to the same species, occupying a particular area.

Autecology : It is the study of individual organisms and populations. It includes physiological ecology, animal behaviour and population dynamics. Usually it involves the study of only one or two species.

Synecology : It is the study of entire plant and animal communities. It includes the study of terrestrial ecosystems, biological aspects of oceanography and applied problems of human management and alteration of ecosystems.

Community : The term refers to any grouping of populations of different organisms who live together in a particular environment, and essentially a part of the biotic component of the environment. In the environment, the organisms interact by competition, predation, mutualism etc. These interactions give the community a structure.

What is Ecology ?

The field of ecology is quite a complex one. It is the study of the relationships between organisms, or groups of organisms, their distribution and abundance, in an environment.

Definition of Ecology

(1) L. De Vere Burton has defined ecology as —

"The study of relationships between living organisms and the environments in which they live is the science of Ecology."

(2) According to Eugene P. Odum —

"Ecology is the study of the relation of organisms or groups of organisms to their environment, or the science of the interrelations between living organisms and their environment."

Therefore, it may be concluded that **ecology involves the totality of all the reciprocal interactions that take place between living organisms and their environment.**

Classification of Ecology

There are several subdivisions of ecology, but only a few important ones have been discussed here.

Scientists have broadly classified ecology into —

(1) **Autecology,** which involves the study of one species of organism, and

(2) **Synecology,** which is the study of communities or entire ecosystems.

The following are a few specialized branches of ecology —

(1) **Habitat ecology** is the ecological study of various habitats on earth and their effects on the organisms living there.

According to the type of habitat under consideration, ecology is further classified into **fresh water ecology, marine ecology, grassland ecology, desert ecology** etc.

(2) **Community ecology** — is the study of the local distribution of animals in different habitats, the recognition and composition of community units, and succession.

(3) **Human ecology** — also known as population ecology, studies man's relationship with the environment, particularly the impact of human behaviour on the environment and the implications of these effects for man.

(4) **Applied ecology** — which is the application of ecological concepts to human needs and requirements, such as **forest conservation, animal husbandry, agriculture, horticulture, wild-life management** etc.

(5) **Systems ecology** —which is a relatively modern branch of ecology, deals with the analysis and understanding of the function and structure of ecosystems, mainly by using applied mathematics.

Ecosystems of the World

What is Ecosystem ?

The ecosystem is the basic functional unit in ecology, since it comprises all the living organisms in an area in interaction with the physical environment.

The term "ecosystem" was coined by the British ecologist A. G. Tansley in 1935, from **"eco"**, meaning **environment**, and **"system"**, meaning a **complex of coordinated units.**

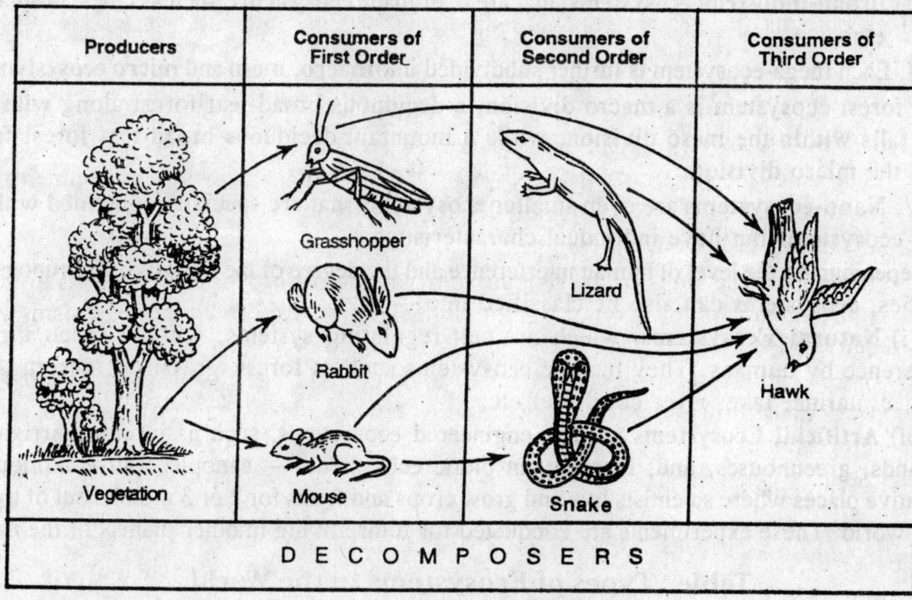

Fig. 10. Food Chain in Terrestrial Ecosystem

Definition of Ecosystem

In 1971, Odum defined ecosystem as any unit that included within it all the organisms (i.e. the community) of a given area interacting with the physical environment, so that a flow of energy results in a clearly defined trophic structure, biotic diversity and material cycles.

In this context, the following terms need to be classified —

(a) The **trophic structure** is the level of nourishment. Plants form the first trophic level, herbivores form the second trophic level and carnivores form the subsequent trophic levels.

(b) **Biotic diversity** refers to the different kinds or types of organisms and their numbers.

(c) **Material cycles** refer to the exchange of materials between living and non-living parts of the system, the transfer of nutrients from one trophic level to another and their recyclization.

Classification of Ecosystems

In 1973, **Ellenberg** said that the world can be classified into different ecosystems in a hierarchical order —

I. The **Biosphere** is largest and all-encompassing ecosystem.

II. **Mega-ecosystems**, under which come the —

(a) **marine ecosystems**, related to saline water environment, such as oceans and seas,

(b) **fresh-water ecosystems**, as in rivers and lakes,

(c) **semi-terrestrial ecosystems**, related to wet soil and air,

(d) **terrestrial ecosystems**, related to aerated soil and air, such as forests, grasslands, deserts,

(e) **urban-industrial ecosystems,** that are man-made ecosystems, such as cities, cropland etc.

III. Each mega-ecosystem is further subdivided into**macro, meso** and **micro ecosystems.**

A forest ecosystem is a macro division, a deciduous broad-leaf forest along with its fauna falls within the meso division, while a mountain deciduous broad-leaf forest falls within the micro division.

IV. **Nano-ecosystems** are even smaller ecosystems that are specially contained within larger ecosystems but have individual characteristics.

Depending on the level of human interference and the degree of the impact of anthropogenic activities, ecosystems can also be classified into —

(i) **Natural Ecosystems,** which are self-regulating systems, without much direct interference by humans. They include ecosystems such as forest, grassland, desert, sea, ocean, estuarine, lake, river coral reef etc.

(ii) **Artificial Ecosystems** or man-engineered ecosystems, such as in cities, irrigated croplands, greenhouses, and, recently, in biotic ecosystems — canopied, air-conditioned, vegetative places where scientists live and grow crops and fruits for 2 or 3 months out of touch of the world. These experiments are conducted for future living in other planets or the man.

Table : Types of Ecosystems in the World

Type of Ecosystem	Location
1. Mountain Ecosystem	eg : The Himalayan region
2. Foot-hill Ecosystem	eg : Terai and Dooars region of India
3. Riverine Ecosystem	eg : The River Ganges
4. Inland Water Ecosystem	eg : Ponds, lakes, wetlands etc.
5. Agricultural Ecosystem	eg : Cultivated lands — food crops,
	plantation and commercial crops etc.
6. Rural Ecosystem	eg : Village community
7. Urban Ecosystem	eg : Towns, cities, municipalities
8. Mining Ecosystem	eg : Mineral-rich areas of Chota Nagpur Plateau, India
9. Forest Ecosystem	eg : Coniferous forests, deciduous forests etc.

Type of Ecosystem	Location
10. Desert Ecosystem	eg : Thar Desert
11. Grassland Ecosystem	eg : Prairies of USA, Pampas of South America etc.
12. Coastal Ecosystem	eg : Konkan coast, Malabar Coast of India
13. Island Ecosystem	eg : Andaman and Nicobar Islands, India
14. Marine Ecosystem	eg : Bays, gulfs and oceans of the world
15. Mangrove Ecosystem	eg : Sunderbans in India and Bangladesh

As per above table, there are various types of ecosystems in different corners of the world. We have mentioned only fifteen ecosystems here, but micro level analysis will give rise to even more ecosystems. Only a few have been discussed in detail.

Characteristics of Forest Ecosystems

Plant Biomass : Because of their size and longevity, trees have formed the most massive and complex ecosystems of the earth. The total amount of plant biomass per hectare is high. More than three-quarters of the total plant bio-mass in a mature forest is contained in trees, and that in the trunks generally exceeds that in the canopy and roots combined. However, the contribution of the component parts of the trees to the total biomass is variable. It depends on the age of the individuals, as well as the stage of development of the forest ecosystem.

Herbivores consume a relatively small, but variable proportion of the annual photosynthetic production. Up to 75% of this may enter the detrital or decomposer food chain, taking the form of litter. This supports a diverse population of soil organisms. The volume of this dead organic material (DOM) can be double that of the fresh leaf tissue.

The type of stratification and degree of structural development of the component plant life forms of the forest ecosystem depends on the amount of tree biomass and, especially, on the density and depth of tree canopy that has been shaped by the particular environmental conditions.

Let us take the example of a tropical rain forest. The multi-layered tree canopies reduce the penetration of sunlight. Consequently, the growth of small non-arboreal forms beneath it is limited.

Animal Biomass : In a forest ecosystem, the most dense animal population are found in the canopy and the soil. The tree-trunks and the canopy provide shelter for roosting, nesting and feeding to a variety of birds, including plant feeders, insect eaters and predators.

Arboreal animals — such as reptiles, and especially monkeys, squirrels, pine martens and sloths — show morphological adaptations, such as prehensile toes and nails.

There is a small number of vertebrates living on the surface. They look for the openness of the forest and feeding opportunities. In temperate forest eco-systems, the ground-dwellers include the polecat, fox, wild cat, wild boar, the red and fallow deer, as well as larger ground-nesting birds, such as blackcock, grouse, capercaillie and turkey (in America).

The upper soil horizons are dominated by burrowing vertebrate and invertebrate animals, as also microscopic decomposers.

The most numerous above-ground animals are the herbivorous, predatory and laprophytic insects. However, their populations fluctuate from year to year and often attain the level of pests causing damage.

The animal bio-mass of forests is small, but extremely varied, and along with it the complex structure and diverse food supply of the plant biomass provides a diversity of microhabitats for the animal population.

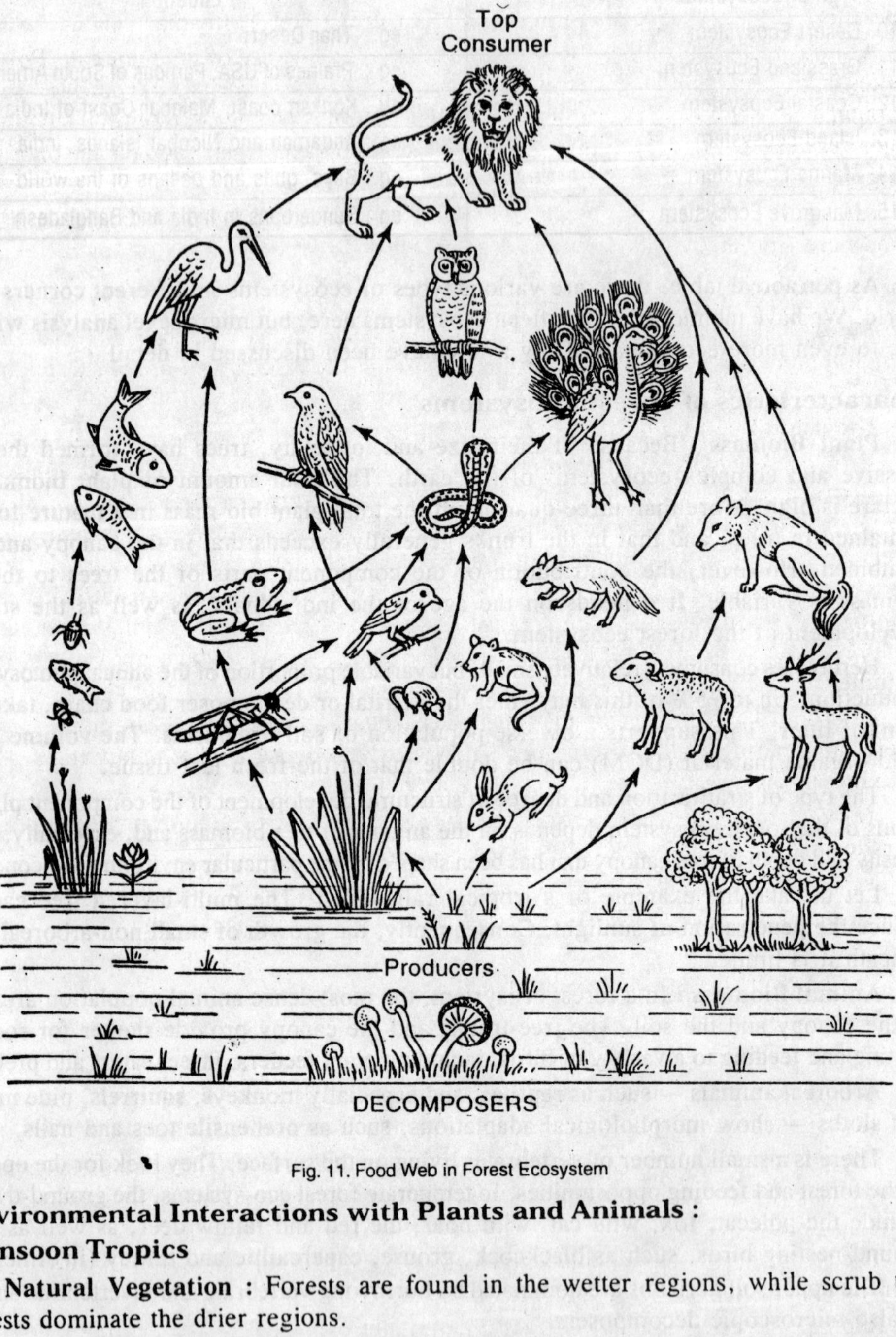

Fig. 11. Food Web in Forest Ecosystem

Environmental Interactions with Plants and Animals : Monsoon Tropics

Natural Vegetation : Forests are found in the wetter regions, while scrub thorn forests dominate the drier regions.

In **Asia**, the Monsoon Rain Forests, in contrast to the Rainy Tropical Forests (selva), have fewer species. The trees are also smaller in girth. The trees are mainly **broadleaved and deciduous** in nature.

The common species are **teak** and **bamboo**. The trees have wide spaces between them, therefore there is little interlocking of crowns. **Mangrove forests** flourish on deltaic and coastal plains.

Scrub thorn forests and **tall, coarse grasses** compose the natural vegetation of **Monsoon Australia.** The **eucalyptus** is indigenous to Australia and Tasmania.

Animal Life : The Monsoon lands of Asia have a variety of wild animals. **Poisonous snakes** from king cobra to vipers, **insects, birds** and different kinds of **reptiles** are found in abundance. Several species of **monkeys** are found in the fringes of cultivated land. The larger vertebrates include the **rhinoceroses, elephants** and **tigers.** Asia is the only habitat of tiger.

Animal life in Australia is not as varied **Kangaroos** are the most famous marsupials found here. **Insects, birds, crocodiles** and **reptiles** are found.

Rainy Tropics

Natural Vegetation : The natural vegetation in the Rainy Tropics is luxuriant because of high temperatures, heavy precipitation and high humidities that prevail throughout the year.

The natural vegetation may be classified into —

(a) **The selva or Rain Forest :** It is a broadleaf evergreen forest. Species do not occur in pure stand. The trunks have little branch structure and stretch (30-45 m) into the air, when they suddenly burst into branches and foliage. The trees compete with each other for light. The crowns of the trees coalesce to form a thick **canopy**. Above the canopy tower are seen the **emergents**, which are the forest giants. An intricate network of **lianas, parasitic plants** and **orchids** weave around the trunks. Sunlight cannot reach the forest floor due to the canopy cover. Hence growth of grass and other vegetative cover is limited.

(b) **Jungle :** They are found along places such as steep slopes, drainage ways etc., where light can reach the forest floor. It is actually a dense thicket of **low trees, shrubs** and **vines**.

(c) **Coastal Types :** These are mainly **mangrove** forest found in mud flats, lagoons, **marshes** and deltaic regions.

The growth of vegetation in the Rainy Tropics is rapid, continuous and uninterrupted.

Animal Life : The native animal life in the Rainy Tropics is as abundant and as varied as the natural vegetation.

The animal life is characterised by —

(a) an abundance and **variety of insects,**

(b) an abundance of **arboreal fauna,**

(c) a few **grazing and carnivorous species**, and

(d) an abundance of **aquatic life**.

The warm, humid climate is just suitable to be the breeding ground of insects. They include brightly coloured **butterflies, mosquitoes, termites, spiders, ants, ticks and gnats.**

The monotony of the selva is compensated by the brilliant colours of the birds, ranging from tiny **humming birds** to gorgeous **parrots.**

Reptiles are camouflaged by their colours and their resemblance to the lianas. They vary from poisonous vipers to gigantic anacondas.

Monkeys, sloths, bats and other arboreal creatures are also found in plenty. They feed on the fruits and nuts of the trees.

Due to the lack of forage, these forests lack in herbivores. As a result, carnivores feeding on herbivores are also uncommon.

Ant-eaters with long tongues, ground cats, wild pigs and lowland gorillas (only in Africa) are the ground types.

Fish, water fowl and crocodiles form the aquatic life. In Africa, **hippopotami** feed on the aquatic plants in the quiet tropical rivers.

Tropical Desert

Natural Vegetation : Desert plants are mainly **xerophytes.** They are species adapted to extreme aridity, harsh temperatures, droughts and high rates of evaporation.

The xerophytes have certain ways to depend themselves against the climatic extremes —

(a) Some of them have long tap roots that can reach the ground water at great depths.

(b) Some xerophytes have roots that have extreme lateral systems, often exceeding the size of the plant.

(c) Leaves are often narrow or modified into thorns to reduce evaporation loss.

(d) Water can be stored inside stems and roots.

(e) Thorny and unpalatable plants discourage grazing animals.

(f) There are a few species that are **ephemeral** in nature and have a very short life-span; they grow only when there is sufficient moisture.

Besides xerophytes, grasses grow here, usually in solitary tufts.

Animal Life : Desert animals are well adapted to subsist on scanty vegetation and minimum of water.

Some animals have camouflaging properties, the colours ranging from pale yellow to red. In the Sahara, desert fox, species of antelope and burrow animals are common. Birds, and even insects, are scarce.

The camel is best suited to the desert environment. Its hump is a device for storing fat. A series of sacs in the walls of the stomach store water. Padded feet and knees protect the animal against the friction of rock and sand. The nostril can be closed during a sand storm.

Polar Region

Natural Vegetation : In the Tundra, conditions for growth are extremely hostile. Periods of growth are short. During the warm season, the ground is saturated with water.

The natural cover of Tundra can be classified into —

(a) **The Bush Tundra**, composed of scrubby alders, birches and willows of very low height;

(b) **The Grass Tundra**, composed of mosses, lichens, sedges, a few flowering plants and low bushes;

(c) **The Desert Tundra**, which consists of small islands of vegetation found in pockets of soil among the bare rocky surface.

Animal Life : The warm-blooded animals of the Tundra region have developed adequate means of conserving body heat in the freezing temperature conditions. All have thick fur or feather cover. Their colours are mostly white since it radiates less heat. The animal have thick layers of fat that provide insulation against heat loss. The fat is also a food reserve during the hostile, barren winter.

Forest Ecology

A forest is a three-dimensional ecological system. It is dominated by trees and other woody vegetation. They exist in constant dynamic interaction with the air-earth matrix of the landscape. The forest is not merely a strand of trees, it is a community of woody and herbaceous plants. In fact, it is a complex ecological system, characterized by a layered structure of functional parts.

Definition of Forest Ecology

Forest ecology deals with the structure, composition and function of forests as landscape ecosystems. It studies the climate, soil and physiography of different areas where the individual trees and other organisms of the forest community occur.

In forest ecology, one has to study —

(i) the forest organisms and how they respond to the physical factors of the environment, and

(ii) the functional relationships of whole ecosystems in forested landscapes.

Economic Importance of Forest

In the modern world, forests have an important place in the general economy of any country. The significance and usefulness of forests date back to those days when man learnt the merits of a settled life. He would use wood for fuel, as well as thatching and making huts; wild fruits and leaves would be consumed as food, and tree barks would be used as clothing. The forests were also hunting grounds and a retreat from enemy attacks.

Forest serve people in many tangible ways. They are an inexhaustible reserve and provide man and industries with numerous raw materials. No wonder forests have been termed as "Green Gold". Forests constitute a perennial economy, unlike minerals that, once mined, cannot be renewed.

Major Forest Products

(1) **Timber**

Forest provides us with both hard woods and soft woods.

Tropical hard woods include sal, teak, ebony, greenheart, mahogany, ironwood, logwood, semul, sissoo etc.

Soft woods include pine, blue pine, fir, spruce, cedar, poplar etc.

There are various industries that are solely dependent on timber. Saw mills, hardboard factories, chip board factories, plywood factories, match industry, window, door and furniture-making industries are a few of them.

Timber is also used to make packing boxes, sports goods, wooden toys, railway sleepers etc.

(2) **Paper Pulp**

90% of the world's paper is manufactured from the soft wood pulp obtained from coniferous trees. Due to this reason paper industries dominate in USA, Canada, Russia, Norway, Sweden and Finland, which account for the greatest concentration of coniferous forests.

(3) **Cellulose**

The cellulose obtained from soft woods is used to manufacture synthetic fibre or rayon. The wood from spruce trees yield finest quality rayon.

(4) **Fuel Wood, Finewood and Charcoal**

Forest provides fuelwood to millions, especially in developing countries, for cooking and heating.

Finewood is also obtained from forests. However, in doing so, forests are fast being depleted.

Minor Forest Produce

Not only wood, forests provide us with a number of minor products that are as essential to the industries. In India, these minor products are used to manufacture valuable articles for export.

(1) **Resin** is obtained mainly from pine trees. This is used to make turpentine, which is mainly used as a solvent for paints and varnish.

White resin is used in manufacturing paper, oils and greases, adhesive tape, laundry soap, linoleum, printing ink etc.

(2) **Lac** is secreted by a particular type of insects (Laccifer Lacca). These insects feed on the saps of host trees, such as kul, sissoo, peepal, palash etc.

Lac is widely used for making paints, bangles, fireworks, sealing wax, electrical insulation material, spirit laguns etc.

(3) **Gums** are extracted from the stems of different trees. They are used in confectionery, medicine, and in the manufacture of pastes, ink and coloured crayons.

(4) **Tanning materials** are also a gift of the forests. They are essential raw material in leather industry. Tanning materials are used to coagulated the protein in hides and skins in order to produce resistant leather.

(5) **Bamboo** is called the poor man's timber. It is used for construction, for making pulp and producing paper and newsprint, and the young bamboo shoots are eaten as a food item.

(6) **Cane** grows in abundance in most forests. They are used mainly for making ropes, bags, strings etc.

Ecological Importance of Forests

A forest is in constant interaction with its environment. The most significant environmental factors are micro climate, soil characteristics, availability of moisture and biological activities.

The forest are not only valued for the direct benefits of forest produce, but also for the indirect benefits.

The ecological importance of forests have been listed here :

(1) Forest helps in ameliorating climatic extremes

Trees shield the ground from direct exposure to the sun. Therefore, the temperature underneath the trees are lower and the ground cooler.

During the day, the leaves utilise sunlight for photosynthesis. Heat is mainly given out at night during respiration. As a result, temperature on the forest floor remains low during the day and higher during the dark hours of night. This reduces loss of water due to evaporation.

(2) Forest tends to increase the rainfall of a locality

Extensive forests condense low clouds. To some extent, this increases precipitation. Therefore, afforestation measures are taken to improve arid regions.

(3) Forest stems wind-velocity

Strong winds cause serious soil erosion if the soil is dry and devoid of vegetation. Therefore wind-breaks and shelter belts are planted to protect crops.

(4) Forest cover checks run-off from the surface and thus reduces soil erosion

Forests guard the soil by putting up a wall of operation to combat the initial forces of erosion. This is done at three levels, — canopy, ground and underground levels :

(i) The canopy, which is often so thick that it reduces the forceful impact caused by raindrops.

(ii) At the ground-level, there is a dense mat of leaf-litter and other vegetable matter. This obstructs the surface flow and checks the velocity of run-off.

(iii) At the underground level, the litter and humus forms an organic blanket. This blanket performs the function of a sieve. The water slowly filters downward through it and then to the underlying soil layer. The numerous root hairs hold capillary and hygroscopic water around them.

Except for a layer of concrete, nothing else will hold the soil as firmly on a sloping surface, as a cover of trees.

Conservation of Forest

With the spread of civilization and the growing demands for forest produce, the world's forest cover is steadily diminishing by burning, clearing and felling trees for fuel, or to make space for settlements, agriculture and industry.

Finally, we have realised that forests should not only be preserved for maintaining timber supplies, but also for checking soil erosion, flood, safeguarding water supplies, and for providing recreational facilities.

We have made a list of ways in which the problems can be overcome :

(1) **Afforestation :** Forests felled for timber supply must essentially be replanted with seedling trees. The new trees may not always be the same as those removed.

Many areas which were not forested previously may also be planted in order to check soil erosion.

(2) **Selective Cutting Practices :** With the aim of better regeneration and survival, the cutting practices should be selective. The weak or diseased species, or the mature species, that are occupying space uselessly, must be removed. By this method, sufficient trees will remain to prevent soil erosion and the species can regenerate at the same time.

(3) **Clear-cutting Practices :** This is an alternative to selective cutting. By this method, all the trees are removed, irrespective of age or type. Initially, this may seem to be wasteful. But, if the area is replanted, erosion can be checked. This method is also cheaper and easier.

(4) **Protection of Forests :** Forests should be efficiently protected from natural hazards such as fires and pests.

In order to protect forests from fires, there should be close system of lookout towers and air patrol, that can give an earliest possible warning. This system is very popular in the USA and Canada.

Forests should be inspected regularly and sprayed with insecticides in order to fight insects and pests. Insects or animals that prey on the unwanted insect can also introduce into the forest.

(5) **Re-use of Waste Paper :** By recycling newsprint and other inferior paper products, timber consumption can be reduced.

Forest Ecosystem

At present, forest and woodland cover almost one-third of the earth's land surface. They are the largest, most complex and most productive of the earth's ecosystems.

The dominant components of forest ecosystems are **trees.** These are **large, woody perennials.** They can be distinguished from smaller, woody shrubs by their height, which is above 3 m. They possess a single main stem (trunk). They also have a distinct crown of leaf-bearing branches.

On the other hand, shrubs are less than 3 m in height. They have several basal stems and lack a well-defined crown.

Size of Trees

The height and girth of trees are achieved by a very considerable expenditure of energy. This is used in the formation of strengthening, conducting and storage tissues.

Three types of tissue constitute the tree trunk

(i) **The inner-xylem** (or wood) is composed of cells and fibers, which is reinforced by a mixture of cellulose and lignin. The **primary heart wood** is inert. The **secondary sapwood** conducts water and nutrients. The**raywood** comprising bands of living parenchyma cells store carbohydrates.

(ii) The **outer phloem layer** (or bast) has most of the **living cells**. They store and transport complex organic products.

(iii) The **cambium layer** is composed of **growth cells.** They initiate the production of the secondary sapwood. This helps to increase the trunk's girth.

The width and cell size of the annual growth rings show the seasonal variation in growth. Finally, the outer layer of epidermal and cortical cells form a protective bark the thickness of which may vary.

Although the maximum potential growth height is genetically controlled, the actual height attained depends on site conditions.

The tallest species are found in humid temperate areas, such as the eucalyptus of Australia and the conifers of north-west America. In humid temperate and tropical regions, the average maximum height of the dominant trees range between 40 m and 60 m.

Root Systems

Trees have **extensive root systems.** They are needed (i) to **anchor the large above-ground biomass,** and (ii) **to provide an adequate supply of water and nutrients for growth.**

In the beginning all saplings produce anchoring taproot. This may or may not be there as the tree matures. With the passage of time, it produces a broad mat of ramifying feeding roots, most of which are found within 18-20 m under soil surface. Actual root-depth depends upon soil-depth and soil consistency.

Life-span of Trees

The life-span of most of the tree species is more than that of most living organisms. Till date, no absolute tree-age limit has been established. In spite of that, there is an age after which the rate of growth declines. Eventually, growth becomes negligible. The tree then falls easy prey to disease and wind-throw. However, regrowth may continue even after the wood begins to decay. This growth is continued by suckers produced by adventitious buds on the fallen trunk and branches.

Tree Life-forms

There are 3 principal categories of tree life-forms :

(i) the evergreen narrow-leaved conifers;

(ii) the broad-leaved deciduous;

(iii) the broad-leaved sclerophyllous.

(i) There are **650 conifers in all,** belonging to 8 families and 50 genera. The conifers evolved earlier than all others. They mostly **occur in colder areas of the northern hemisphere** and the **high altitude mountainous regions of the tropics. Their growth and rate of wood accumulation is greater** than the other forms. These trees **retain their needles up to 7 years. Leaf fall is not seasonal,** hence coniferous trees can **start on photosynthesis**

as soon as environmental conditions become congenial. Thus, unlike deciduous species, they do not need to use energy to produce new leaves.

Conifers are the **world's largest plant-forms.** They attain tremendous girths and heights between 80-120 m.

The world's tallest trees are the Californian redwoods, often achieving heights of about 150 meters (450-500 feet), i.e. a 50 storeyed building ! Among the redwoods is the world's oldest tree — 'Eternal God' — 12,000 years old !! (Source : GUINNESS BOOK OF RECORDS —1999)

(ii) The deciduous broad-leaved trees are commonly **found in the forest ecosystem in humid, temperate lowlands**. Here, seasons vary from cool spring to warm/hot summer and form mild autumn to cold winter. Under suitable light and temperature conditions, their **mesophyllous (thin) leaves are capable of rapid photosynthesis.** This is due to freer and stronger sap flow than in conifers. The deciduous species undergo**annual leaf loss,** because **mesophyllous leaves cannot tolerate cold or drought.** However, the annual loss of leaves is compensated by regular and rapid recycling of their nutrients.

The growth in height attained by deciduous trees may be similar to that of conifers, but the **girth attained is much less.** In this regard, only poplars can be compared with conifers.

(iii) Although evolutionarily younger, the broad-leaved sclerophyllous evergreen and deciduous trees became dominant over coniferous species in the hot humid Tertiary era. Since they are frost sensitive, they are now found in **humid, warm tropical to mild temperate regions.**

Factors Responsible for Limiting Tree-growth

1. Insufficient moisture and heat for the production, germination and establishment of seedlings.

2. A very short growing season which does not allow the production of new wood before the onset of unfavourable conditions.

3. Growing deficiency of soil-water availability and/or accessible ground water, because of which trees adapted to periodic drought and low precipitation show slow growth.

4. Insufficient rooting depth inhibits plant growth.

5. Water-logged soil prevents normal plant growth.

6. High wind-force is inimical to growth — when trees have to withstand high wind-force, they become stunted, along with flattened or distinctly asymmetrical, wind-sheared crowns.

7. The most ubiquitous agent that is limiting tree-growth is direct or indirect human activities. Grazing of domestic livestock and protected wild herbivores, promotion of fire, deforestation etc. are such instances that inhibit regeneration.

The causes of industrial overpopulation are —

(a) the decline of a single or an entire group of industries, such as the textile industry disaster of Britain, where the fall of a single industry affected the population.

(b) technical progress resulting in increase of production and uselessness of labour,

(c) temporary declines in the trade cycles, such as the world crisis (Great Depression) of 1929-1934, which cause temporary overpopulation.

Even underpopulated countries sometimes show 'islands' of overpopulation where resources are abundant, people flock to such regions in order to improve their lives. Ultimately, a time comes when there is a population-resource imbalance. For instance, these discrepancies are found in Indonesia, where Java and some parts of Sumatra and Celebes are overpopulated while Borneo, the Moluccas, the Lesser Sunda island and West Iran, New Guinea are underpopulated.

Desert Ecosystem

Deserts are those areas where biological processes are controlled by severe climatic aridity and crop-based agriculture is impossible without irrigation. Aridity, is however, a relative condition. It depends upon temperature, precipitation, slope and aspect of the terrain and soil texture.

Climate

Desert climate is characterised by a low mean annual precipitation. It can vary from almost none to over 600 mm. The amount as well as the spatial and temporal occurrence of rainfall is very irregular. The reliable sources of water in deserts include dew, coastal fog and ground-water at such a depth that can be tapped by organisms. The amount of effective rainfall, i.e., the rainwater that becomes available for plant growth, is determined by the rate of evapotranspiration, ambient temperature, wind speed, relative atmospheric humidity and the infiltration rate of the soil.

In Tropical deserts the diurnal ranges of temperature are very high (50°-60°C). They have high maximum temperatures (45°-70°C).

In Temperate deserts, the winter temperatures often fall below 0°C. The annual range of temperature is also very wide.

There is not enough water to maintain permanent river flow. Surface run-off is also intermittent, ending in local depressions or intermontane basins. But rivers who have their sources beyond the desert can maintain their flow across arid areas.

The fine and medium textured desert soil are highly saline. There is an accumulation of saline salts (sodium chloride, sulphates, carbonates) below the surface, the depth depending on the percolation of water and/or the level of ground water table from which salts can be translocated by the capillary fringe near or to or on the ground surface.

When the salts are translocated near the ground surface, leaching is incomplete. Soluble salts are washed out of the upper soil and deposited at 10-100 cm below the surface.

When the saline ground water is brought near the surface, due to fluctuation of the water table and precipitation, salts are deposited below or near the soil surface.

Desert Vegetation

Desert vegetation is extremely simple. Its structure shows poor development. As aridity increases, its cover becomes more and more open and discontinuous.

Hills (1960) classified arid vegetation into 4 categories, in association with decreasing availability of water :

1. FRUTESCENT PERENNIAL SCRUBS, under which are the cactus communities of south-western USA and low woody scrub.

2. SUFFRUTESCENT PERENNIAL VEGETATION, comprising a few species of dwarf, succulent, low shrubs and perennial grasses.

3. EPHEMERAL OR SEASONAL HERBACEOUS VEGETATION composed of both perennials and annuals. They are mostly dominated by grass.

4. ACCIDENTAL VEGETATION which are found as occasional carpets of ephemeral annuals. They are common in areas of low and intermittent rainfall, where the soil can retain enough moisture.

Under the most regionously arid conditions, the land can be devoid of vegetation because of intense evaporation and/or extreme soil mobility or salinity.

The best adaptor are Halophytes and, more particularly, SUCCULENT EPIPHYTES. They absorb moisture directly from the atmosphere.

Energy Flow in Desert Ecosystems

Deserts are water controlled ecosystems. Here, total peak bio-mass and NPP are lowest among all ecosystems. Water input controls the energy flow in the desert ecosystem. This water input comes in short, discontinuous pulses. There may be only 10-50 rain days in a year, that occur in 3-15 rainy periods. Out of this, only 5-6 may be of biological significance. The Biotic response to a sequence of Rain PULSES is determined by the time interval between the pulses.

In some deserts, nutrient deficiency may reach a critical point. This can be either because (1) the organic litter is unevenly distributed over the ground, or (2) the mineral component is nutrient-poor. Also, (3) the rapid growth of annuals following a rain can cause fast depletion of the store nutrients, while their return to the soil after decomposition is slow.

The animal populations in deserts also show annual fluctuations.

(a) Arthropods have high fertility rates and short life cycles. They are, therefore, subject to alternating high population growth, as well as rapid decline.

(b) Mammals, birds and reptile show less fluctuation.

In most cases, these variations in animal population directly depend on rainfall. Other factors — such as the quality and quantity of food available, competition, predation and inherent demographic characteristics — exercise great control.

The herbivores play an important role in the desert ecosystem, like all others. 2-10% of the primary production is directly consumed by them. GRAMINIVORES such as rodents and ants may eat up as much as 90% of the seed production. Nevertheless, it is said that, prey-predator relationships are very weakly developed in the more arid deserts.

An important feature of the desert ecosystem is that, because of a variable and unpredictable environment, along with low primary production, both plants and animals show an opportunistic and flexible behaviour. This enables them to take advantage of resources when they become available. That is why most desert animals are GENERALIST FEEDERS.

Organic Adaptations to Desert Conditions

Organisms which inhabit the hot, dry deserts of the world have to be well-equipped in order to cope with the excessive heat and drought. This will ensure that neither internal temperatures nor tissue dehydration will reach dangerous levels. Desert animals and plants have, therefore, developed some morphological, physiological and behavioural strategies.

The tolerant organisms can survive extreme environmental conditions because of the fact that they possess the means of controlling their water loss and their temperatures.

The two principal strategies to survive under extreme desert conditions are avoidance and tolerance of heat and water stress :

(a) Most of the desert flora are EVADERS.

They can survive periods of stress in an inactive mature or premature stage. They can also live temporarily or permanently in cooler and/or moisture microhabitats, such as in the cracks of rocks, below stones on shrubs or below ground.

(b) 75% of desert animals are GEOZONTS, or sub-terranean, with wet surface activity.

In dry air, herbaceous plants can tolerate temperatures up to 50°-55°C. It is lower in the case of animals, ranging between 40°C and 50°C. Arthropods, such as scorpions and beetles, can tolerate 50°C, or more than that.

Both animals and plants have developed certain strategies to combat the desert environment :

(i) **Change in the orientation of a specific organ or of the entire body**; this minimises the areas and/or the time to which they remain exposed to maximum heat input.

(ii) **Light coloration and surface texture**; this maximises reflection of light and minimises absorption.

(iii) **Surface growth, such as spines, hairs etc.** :

(a) they absorb and/or reflect a significant portion of the incident radiation, and hence keep the underlying surface cooler, and

(b) they create a layer of air around them, thereby insulating the underlying surface.

(iv) **Body-size,** which is of particular importance because it controls the rate of heat flux between the organism and its environment.

Under such arid conditions, desert animals and plants become conservative users of the available water and reduce loss of water by one means or the other. Water loss from plants can be controlled by the following means —

(a) diurnal stomatal movements, and

(b) xeromorphic adaptations, such as surface hairs, thick cuticles and sunken stomata.

The most drought resistant higher plants are the succulents, such as cacti. They are XEROPHYTES. They possess well-developed storage tissues, low circular transpiration, small surface-to-volume ratios and rapid stomatal closure.

In heat-resistant cacti, the stomata remain closed during the day. They open at night to take carbon dioxide for photosynthesis. Many desert plants can exert a grater suction pressure than others. This way, they can extract more water from fine, water-retentive soils.

Also, some plants are capable of producing roots very fast with the onset of rain. Many cacti have shallow, lateral roots, so as to make use of brief rain spells efficiently.

Many animals have surface which reduce the rate of moisture-loss from perspiration. In addition to this, their excreta tends to be dry, and they also produce little and extremely concentrated urine.

Grassland Ecosystem

Grasslands occupy almost 19% of the earth's surface. The most commonly employed criteria to differentiate types of grasslands may be listed as follows :

(a) the presence or absence of trees and/or shrubs,

(b) the luxuriance and growth form of the dominant grass species, and

(c) the nature of the physical habitat.

Types of Grasslands in the World

A basic distinction can be made between the different grasslands of the world depending upon soil, climate, topography and nature of the grass.

The principal grasslands of the world are —

(i) **Prairies of North America**

(ii) **Pampas of South America**

(iii) **Savanna of Africa**

(iv) **Downs of Australia**

(v) **Veldts of South America**

(vi) **Steppes of Russia.**

TEMPERATE GRASSLANDS

Location : They are the Prairies of North America, Pampas of South America, Steppes of Eurasia, Veldts of South Africa and Downs of Australia.

Abiotic Components :

These includes the nutrients present in soil and the aerial environment.

Climate : The Northern Hemisphere Grasslands experience a continental climate while the Southern Hemisphere Grasslands have a moderate climate.

Temperature : Temperature varies between 20°C in summer to –15°C in winter in the Northern Hemisphere. In the Southern Hemisphere it ranges between 20°C and 10°C.

Rainfall : Mean average rainfall varies between 250 mm and 750 mm. Low annual precipitation is accompanied by high rate of evapotranspiration.

Soil : In the semi-arid grasslands, as we have already said, low annual precipitation is accompanied by a high rate of evapotranspiration. Therefore, available soil water is limited. Leaching is also limited. Only the most soluble cations, of which calcium is the most common, are leached easily. They are leached from the upper part of the soil profile and then precipitated at a depth. This depends on the balance between precipitation and evapotranspiration.

The process of leaching calcium results in the **Calcic** (calcium-enriched) horizon of soil. It is accompanied by a humus-rich upper horizon. A large part of this organic matter is derived from the deep, dense root system.

The most common soils found here are the dark **Chernozem** (Black Earth) and **Chestnut** soils of the North American grassland biome. Besides organic matter, the soil is rich in carbon, hydrogen, oxygen, nitrogen, phosphorus, sulphur etc.

Biotic Components

Producer

As the name suggests, producers here are mainly grasses.

The Prairie grasslands cover a wide range of precipitation and temperature. This east-west humidity gradient reflects itself in the transition from the tall-grass to short grass communities :

(a) Where rainfall exceeds 20″, tall nutritious prairie grass is found.

(b) Where rainfall is less than 20″, short, steppe grass is found.

The tall grass prairie is dominated by the genera **Andropogon, Agropyron** and **Stipa.**

The short-grass Prairie has **gamma grasses, bruchloe dactyloides** in the north and **boutelina gracilis** in the south.

Although, the grasses have extensive root systems, the leaf-surface area is minimum. This reduces transpiration to a minimum.

The **ecotone** between the tall and short grass prairies is the **Mixed-Grass Prairie.** It is composed of components from both the long and short grass communities.

Consumers

(a) **Primary Consumers** are the herbivores feeding on grasses. They are **grazing animals**, such as cows, buffaloes, deer, sheep, **burrowing animals** such as rabbits, mice etc. Termites and millipedes also feed on leaves and grasses.

Bisons, Pronghorns and Prairie-dogs are commonly founds in Prairies.

Kangaroos (Mansupials) are found in the Australian Downs.

(b) **Secondary Consumers** are the carnivores feeding on herbivores. These include animals like fox, jackal, snakes, frogs, lizards, birds etc.

Reptiles are **ovoviviparous**, i.e. whose eggs hatch within themselves.

(c) **Tertiary Consumers** are often Hawks.

Decomposers

They are the microbes active in the dead and decaying organic matter.

Tropical Grassland or Savannah

Location : latitudinally, the Savannah Ecosystem is found to extend between 10°–20° North and South.

In the Northern Hemisphere, they include West African Sudan, parts of East Africa and Llanos of the Orinoco Basin in Venezuela.

In the Southern Hemisphere, they cover Pampas of the Brazilian and Argentinian Highlands and Australian Savannah.

Abiotic Components

Climate is characterised by distinct wet and dry seasons, abundant insolation and high average temperature.

Temperature does not fall below 20°C.

Rainfall ranges between 250 mm and 500 mm.

Soil is mainly ferralosolic, accompanied by an impermissible, near-surface lateritic crust.

Biotic Components

The Savannah flora can be traced back to the tertiary era. In comparison to the temperate grasslands, Tropical Savanna shows a much greater diversity of composition, form and habitat.

The principal — sometimes the only — components are the more or less xerophytic, perennial grasses and sedges. They form the dominant herbaceous stratum.

In addition to this, there may be varying proportions of drought-resistant woody plants. They range from low shrubs to quite tall trees.

The Savannah vegetation can be arranged in **3 distinct layers** —

(i) **The Ground Stratum**, which is composed of grasses and herbaceous plants, such as African Elephant Grass.

(ii) **The Middle Stratum** consists of shrubs and very stunted woody plants.

(iii) **The Top or Canopy Stratum** is formed by trees, whose characteristics depend on the availability of water.

So far, 5 major kinds of savannah vegetation have been identified. They are **open woodland, parkland, grassland, low tree shrub** and **scrub.**

Huntley (1982) has distinguished between moist and arid savannah biomes :

(i) The **moist savannah biome** or **sour veldt** is marked by nutrient-deficient herbage with high bulk but low nutritive value. It supplies a low density of ungulates.

(ii) The **arid savannah biome** or **sweet veldt** is rich in nutrients. Here, large herbivores (elephants, buffalo) and many ungulates attain higher densities.

It is noted that the loss of grazing value during the dry season is greater in the sour than the sweet veldt.

Consumers

A large portion of the savannah has been subjected to grazing, burning and shifting agriculture, over a long period of time. The evolution of savannah flora, that can be traced back at least to the Tertiary era, has been accompanied by that of a multi-species fauna of large herbivores. It attained its maximum richness in the later Tertiary and Pleistocene eras.

Primary Consumers are the **herbivores.** The African savannah accounts for the largest number of **grazing vertebrate mammals**. They are giraffe, zebra, elephant, antelope, hippopotamus etc.

The Australian savannah is dominated by **Marsupials** such as kangaroo.

There are many **camouflaged species** who are well-occupied for self-defence. Most of the African herbivores — other than the elephant and ostrich — are ungulates with flocking and migratory habits.

Secondary Consumers are the carnivores feeding on the herbivores, such as lion, tiger, jaguar, jackal, puma. They have powerful jaw and teeth.

Along rivers and marshes are reptiles and mammals, such as crocodiles, alligators, giant lizards and snakes

Decomposers are the microbic life in the soil.

Forest Productivity

Forest ecosystems are highly productive. This is related to their structural development which allows the use of a large resource volume, which we shall discuss :

(1) The photosynthetic tissue are concentrated in the canopy. The weight of leaves can vary between 1 and 10 tonnes ha^{-1} dry weight. The LAI, or Leaf Area Index, at maximum crown development, can reach a value of 8+. The seasonal duration of active leaves is longer than in many herbaceous plants.

(2) The vertical above-ground development of the forest ecosystem is completed by the extent and volume of root system, which taps the necessary volume of water and nutrients required to maintain the high level of productivity.

A high proportion of the energy trapped and nutrients absorbed in primary production is stored in that part of the eco-system that is non-assimilating. In all forest eco-systems, a large percentage of the nutrient capital in the woody tissue remains immobile for a long time. The percentage of the NPP that is stored in the wood annually varies with age. During rapid growth in youth, it is a maximum of 30-50%. In old age it is reduced to 10-15%. In a mature forest, the cumulative effect is such that 70-90% of the nutrient content of the plant biomass may be locked up in the woody tissues. It is because of this that when forest resources are depleted at a rate greater than their renewal, the consequences are dangerous.

Firstly, there will be nutrient depletion due to the high cumulative uptake and the high plant : soil nutrient ratio, this can ruin the soil to a great extent.

Secondly, it modifies the microclimatic and associated habitat conditions, which might retard or inhibit regeneration.

Classification of Forests

At a global scale, forests can be classified and spatially delimited, taking into account one or a combination of three attributes —

(1) Environmental condition, particularly climate, basing on which tropical, temperate and cold forest zones have been delimited;

(2) The form of the Dominant Trees, which is determined by the shape, size, duration and durability of leaves, whether broad, narrow or needle; large or small, divided or undivided; hardness of cuticle (sclerophylly or mesophylly); evergreen, deciduous or mixed.

(3) The Composition, basing on the dominance or co-dominance of plant taxonomic groups; flowing (angiosperm) or coniferous (gymnosperm), family and/or genus and species.

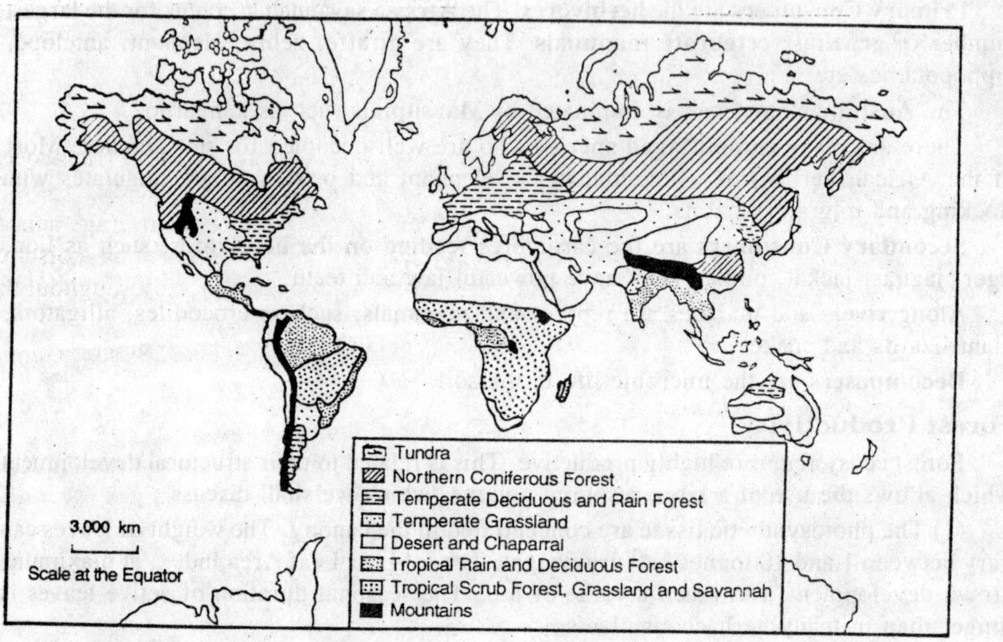

Fig. 12. Distribution of Forests

Forest Resources of India

According to environmentalists, at least 33% of any country should be under forest cover. This is essential in order to maintain the ecological balance and for proper functioning of the ecosystem that is required to help us lead healthy lives.

However, satellite images have revealed that only 19% of India's total geographical area is under forest cover. Studies have shown that the total area under forest cover is steadily declining. The pressure of an ever-increasing population demands more and more space for agricultural and industrial pursuits. Added to that, the demand of wood for fuel and other purposes is leading to felling of trees at an alarming pace. If deforestation is not controlled now, India will gradually become a desert.

The forests in India are not uniformly distributed. 70 to 75% of the forest cover is found in the Deccan region, and 15 to 20% is found in the mountainous Himalayan region. The extensive alluvial plains are almost devoid of forest cover.

Madhya Pradesh is the state which boasts of having 25% of the country's forested area. This accounts for the highest percentage of forest cover. West Bengal has 1.6% of the same.

Classification of Indian Forests

The natural vegetation of India is diverse. This is because of the climatic variations in the country — from mountains to desert, India is truly a land of diversity.

Based on the type and characteristics of the natural vegetation, the forests of India have been divided into seven categories :

(1) Evergreen Forests
(2) Dry Deciduous Forests
(3) Humid Deciduous Forests
(4) Scrub and Thorn Forests
(5) Desert Vegetation
(6) Himalayan Vegetation
(7) Tidal or Mangrove Forests.

(1) Evergreen Forests

(a) **Location :** Evergreen forests are found in the Terai region of eastern Himalayas, the western slope of the Western Ghats and the Andaman and Nicobar Islands.

(b) **Characteristics :** Evergreen forest are found in areas where the average annual rainfall exceeds 200 cms. Due to abundant rainfall, the soil is never deficient in moisture. Therefore the trees never lose their leaves. The leaves also remain green throughout the year.

(c) **Species :** The common trees are Rosewood, Toon, Poan, Rubber, Sissoo, Goran, Mahogany, Bamboo etc.

(2) Dry Deciduous Forests

(a) **Location :** Dry deciduous forests are found in western Bihar, eastern Uttar Pardesh, eastern Rajasthan, Maharashtra, Tamil Nadu, Karnataka, Madhya Pradesh and other arid regions in the Deccan plateau.

(b) **Characteristics :** These forests are prevalent in warm, arid regions, where the annual average rainfall ranges between 50 and 100 cms. The temperature also remains high throughout the year, and evaporation of water from the soil and vegetation is rapid.

(c) **Species :** The important trees found are Teak, Sal, Tendu, Palas, Rosewood, Satinwood, Amaltas, Bel, Lendi etc.

(3) Humid Deciduous Forests

(a) **Location :** These forests are also known as Monsoon Forests, since the vegetation is largely influenced by the Monsoon climate of the subcontinent. Humid Deciduous Forests are found in the eastern slope of the Western Ghats, the plains, plateau and coast of West Bengal, the plateau and Gangetic plains of Bihar, and the plains of Assam.

(b) **Characteristics :** These forests are common in regions where the annual average temperature varies between 100 and 200 cms. The climate here is characterised by hot, humid summers and dry winters. The trees shed their leaves during the cold season. The trees are well-adapted to combat the dry winter season. They are conservative water users and hence shed their leaves in time to reduce transpiration loss. Hence they are known as deciduous trees.

(c) **Species :** The commonly found trees are Mango, Neem, Shimul, Mahuya, Shirish, Sal, Teak, Arjun, Jarul, Amla, Tamun, Kusum, Kanju, Palas etc.

(4) Scrub and Thorn Forests

(a) **Location :** Scrub and thorn vegetation cover the extremely arid regions of western Rajasthan, Kutch and Kathiawar areas of Gujarat and the rain-shadow areas of the southern plateau.

(b) **Characteristics :** This type of vegetation is found in regions marked by very scanty rainfall, ranging between 25 and 50 cms annually. This acute scarcity of water inhibits the growth of trees.

(c) **Species :** The commonly found ones are date Palm, Cactus, Babul, Neem, Piluri etc.

(5) Desert Vegetation

Desert vegetation is restricted to the Thar Desert of western Rajasthan. The region suffers from extreme aridity, hence vegetation is essentially 'xerophytic' in nature. Cacti are the most common species. They have thick fleshy stems that store water and throns as modified leaves, so as to check transpiration loss. The roots of desert plants reach far deep into the soil since the ground water level is extremely low.

(6) Himalayan Vegetation

The natural vegetation here is so diverse that it is almost amazing. Due to the great height of the mountain range, climatic characteristics vary from the foothills to the peak. As one goes higher and higher, the temperature declines at a steady rate, and the amount of rainfall received is also affected. Moreover, temperature and rainfall characteristics vary between the Eastern and Western Himalayas.

The Himalayan vegetation is dominated by altitude. This gives rise to three distinct zones :

(a) **The Tropical Zone**, found at an elevation of 500 to 1,600 meters. It stretches along the 'Terai', or the sub-mountain belt of the Himalaya. The forests here are dense evergreen in the east and deciduous in the west. Sal forests are found in this zone. Other species include, Mango, Sal, Sissoo, Bamboos, and various types of grasses and fern climbers are found in plenty, as are bamboo and wild bananas.

(b) **The Temperate Zone,** extends between 1,600 and 3,500 meters. This is the coniferous forest belt. Oak, beach, maple, birch, pine, deodar, alder, poplar, elm, willow, etc. are found here, along with a variety of herbs and shrubs. At higher altitudes, blue pine, fir, deodar, silver fir, cypress, juniper etc. are found.

(c) The **Alpine Zone** extends from 3,500 to 4,500 meters. Vegetation is sparse in this zone.

Rhododendrons, Chrysanthemum, Primula etc. adorn these regions.

At an elevation above 4,500 meters, eternal snow prevails.

(7) Tidal or Mangrove Forests

(a) **Location :** The Mangrove Forests are found in the deltaic regions and in and around the tidal creeks. They can be found in the deltas of the Ganga, Brahmaputra, Mahanadi, Godavari, Krishna and Cauvery. The densest and most continuous mangrove forests are found in the Sunderbans in the Ganga delta.

(b) **Characteristics :** The forests are composed mainly of evergreen species. The trees have to survive in saline soil amidst constant rise and fall of tides and deep accumulation of mud. The trunks are supported by "stilt-roots". These act as respiratory roots under submerged conditions. One of the main feature of such forests is profuse growth with tangle of climbers.

(c) **Species :** The most common tree in the Sundarbans is Sundari, which gives the forest its name. Other important mangrove trees are Garan, Gewa, Hetal, Keya, Keora, Bogla etc.

QUESTIONS FOR EXAMINATION

A. Essay-Type Questions

1. Explain the nature and properties of Ecosystem.
   Ans. Pp. 41-43
2. Describe the different types of ecosystem.
   Ans. Pp. 43-45
3. Analyse and describe the characteristics of ecosystem in the world.
   Ans. Pp. 43-46
4. Describe the environmental interaction with plants and animals.
   Ans. Pp. 45-48
5. Describe the different forest products in the world.
   Ans. Pp. 49-50
6. Explain the Ecological importance of forests.
   Ans. Pp. 50-51
7. What are the different processes of forest conservation in the world ?
   Ans. Pp. 51-52
8. Explain the forest ecosystem in the world.
   Ans. Pp. 45-48
9. Discuss the different factors that are responsible for the growth of trees.
   Ans. Pp. 51-54
10. Explain the desert ecosystem.
    Ans. Pp. 53-56
11. Explain the grassland ecosystem.
    Ans. Pp. 56-59
12. Analyse the different types of forests in India.
    Ans. Pp. 60-62

B. Short Answer-Type Questions

1. What is Ecology ?
   Ans. Page 42
2. Define Ecology.
   Ans. Page 42
3. What is Autecology ?
   Ans. Page 42
4. What is community ecology ?
   Ans. Page 42
5. What is Human ecology ?
   Ans. Page 42
6. What is applied ecology ?
   Ans. Page 43
7. What is systems ecology ?
   Ans. Page 43

8. What is habitat ecology ?
   Ans. Page 42
9. What is ecosystem ?
   Ans. Page 43
10. Define ecosystem.
    Ans. Page 43
11. How many types of ecosystem are there ?
    Ans. Page 44
12. What is Nano-ecosystem ?
    Ans. Page 44
13. What is Natural ecosystem ?
    Ans. Page 44
14. What is Artificial Ecosystem ?
    Ans. Page 44
15. Give a few names of the principal ecosystems in the world.
    Ans. Page 44
16. What is plant biomes ?
    Ans. Page 45
17. What is animal biomes ?
    Ans. Page 45
18. What is forest ecology ?
    Ans. Page 48
19. Define the forest ecology.
    Ans. Page 48
20. What is the economic importance of forests ?
    Ans. Page 49
21. Give examples of minor forest products.
    Ans. Page 49
22. What is afforestation ?
    Ans. Page 51
23. Name the major grasslands of the world.
    Ans. Page 56
24. Give a few name of the grasslands in the world.
    Ans. Page 56
25. What is forest productivity ?
    Ans. Page 59
26. How many types of forest are there in India ?
    Ans. Page 61
27. Where do you find mangrove forests in West Bengal ?
    Ans. Page 62

Chapter 4

POPULATION AND ENVIRONMENT

INTRODUCTION

When we have to discuss the various factors that have led to the uneven distribution of population over the globe, we cannot subscribe to the purely deterministic point of view, because it believes that the natural elements are the sole controlling factors of population distribution. However, this is not true. Whether it is India or Canada, England or Argentina, physical factors alone will not explain the pattern of population distribution. Their influence may be greater in some places in comparison to others. Numerous social, economic, political, demographic and historical factors must be taken into account. No one factor can be responsible, but interrelated influences result in a specific pattern of population distribution. But everywhere man exercises some control over his habitat. The diversity of population distribution must be explained in terms of all these influences, as an important part of a dynamic process. Population distribution changes with respect to time and space.

Human Population Distribution

The factors which determine the pattern of population distribution are complex and diverse. The factors may be grouped in the following manner :

1. **Physical or Natural Factors**

(a) Geographical Location

(b) Topography

(c) Climate

(d) Soil

(e) Natural Vegetation

(f) Rivers, lakes and other water-bodies

(g) Mineral Resources.

2. **Non-physical or Socio-economic and Cultural Factors**

(a) Economic development and level of technology

(b) Birth and death rates

(c) Migration

(d) Political factors.

CAUSES OF UNEVEN DISTRIBUTION OF POPULATION

It has already been mentioned that population distribution in India is extremely uneven. The following factors account for the uneven distribution —

I. **Physical Factors**

(i) **Relief** — (a) The high elevation and rugged topography of the northern Himalayan region, the north-eastern hills, and the hilly regions of the peninsula have made them sparsely populated since economic activities cannot be carried out easily.

(b) On the other hand, the plains of the North and along the coasts are densely populated due to excellent agricultural prospects, communication facilities, location of industries, employment opportunities etc.

(ii) **Climate** — (a) The adverse climatic conditions of the Rajasthan desert region or the Kutch region of Gujarat has led to sparse population here.

(b) The plains of the Ganga or the coastal regions are densely populated due to a congenial climate that encourages human habitation.

(iii) **Presence of Rivers and Water Bodies**

In the north, the valleys of the Ganga and the Brahmaputra, and in the south the valleys of Mahanadi, Godavari, Krishna and Cauvery are densely populated. These rivers help in irrigation, navigation, electricity generation, fishery development and drinking water supply.

(iv) **Soil** — (a) The river valleys and delta regions are densely populated due to the rich alluvial soil that supports agriculture.

(b) The black soil of the Deccan is extremely fertile and is most well-known for cotton cultivation. Here population is dense due to agricultural facilities.

(c) The stony, infertile soils of the mountains as well as the regions having lateritic or sandy soils do not attract population.

(v) **Natural Vegetation** — The dense forests at the foothills of the eastern Himalayas and the western slopes of the Western Ghats do not encourage human habitation.

(vi) **Mineral Resources** — In spite of infertile soils, the Deccan plateau and Chota Nagpur plateau are rich in mineral deposits. Mining activities and allied industries have given rise to pockets of population concentration in these areas.

II. **Non-Physical Factors**

(i) **Transport and Communication** — The plains of North India are very well-connected by road, rail and air and, therefore, the region is densely populated. In comparison, states like Madhya Pradesh and Orissa do not have such communication facilities. The sparsely populated north eastern states are linked to the rest of the country by air, which makes communication very expensive for the common people.

(ii) **Industry** — The location of industries give rise to settlements since here people find employment opportunities in plenty. The Calcutta conurbation, Durgapur-Asansol region are examples.

III. **Cultural Factors**

Education, knowledge, capacity to work, ability to exploit the available resources and proper planning can also overcome the constraints set by hostile nature. Today, the Indira Gandhi Canal has worked wonders to improve the agricultural scenario of the 'Thar Desert' in Rajasthan.

Thus, all these factors, in isolation or in combination, have influenced the distribution of population in India.

World Population Trend and Present Position

Man first appeared on earth almost 1,000,000 or 2,000,000 years ago, although there is no concrete evidence supporting this view. Not only in those days, even today, there are quite a few regions and countries where the exact size of the population cannot be determined. The population data of the world prior to the 1800s was definitely far from accurate.

From the end of the 18th century, the global population has been increasing at a rapid rate. Till the middle of the 18th century (1750), it occurred slowly, due to natural calamities, war, diseases like malaria, cholera, plague etc. The birthrate was high, but the death rate was even higher. Consequently, the growth of population was extremely slow.

By the end of the 18th century, the Industrial Revolution in Europe changed the entire scenario. Transport and communication improved, agricultural and industrial production reached new heights and medical facilities took a new turn. Overall, there was an upliftment of the living standards of the people. All these factors resulted in the decline of death rates. Therefore, in the next 150 years (1800-1950), the world population more than doubled itself.

Based on the various population data available, population scientists have given us an idea regarding the world population trend over the years —

(1) **10,000 B.C.** — the global population was almost **5,000,000**.

(2) **6000 B.C.** — the population number increased to **86,500,000**, since agricultural techniques came into vogue between 10,000 B.C. and 6,000 B.C.

(3) **1 A.D.** — the world population was **250,000,000.**

(4) **1650 A.D.** — the rate of growth of population was extremely slow and reached **540,500,000.**

(5) **1750 A.D.** — in 100 years the population increased by only 183,400,000. Hence, at that time, the population was only **728,400,000.**

(6) **1800 A.D.** — After 1750 A.D., as it has already been discussed, the Industrial Revolution brought in dramatic changes. In 50 years population increased by 180,000,000 and became **905,600,000.**

(7) **1850 A.D. — the world population rose to 1,171,000,000, increasing by 265,400,000.**

(8) **1900 A.D.** — the world population was steadily increasing and reached 1,608,000,000.

(9) **1950 A.D.** — The trend of population growth remained unchecked and reached 2,486,000,000.

(10) **1995 A.D.** — The global population reached almost 5,700,000,000. Therefore, during the last 45 years, the world population has increased by 3,190,000,000.

The Present Population Trends

On 12 Oct. 1999, world population touched 6 billion and in 2000 it was 6.069 billion; by 2025 A.D. it will be 8.25 billion ! This alarming growth of population may be termed as **"Population Explosion"**.

Although the population numbers are increasing at an alarming rate and creating a pressure on the limited resources available, the scenario is not the same everywhere.

(1) Countries that are rich in technology, or the so-called **developed countries,** have **very low birth and death rates.** Therefore the annual population growth rate in these countries vary between 0.1% and 1%. Due to this, in the coming decades, the population in these countries will remain **stationary.**

Countries under this category are USA, Japan, France, Italy, Austria, Germany, Hungary, Bulgaria and UK.

(2) The **less developed and developing countries** of Africa, Asia and Latin America have **very high birth rates** and a frightening **annual growth rate of 2% to 3%.**

The principal factors responsible for this situation are —

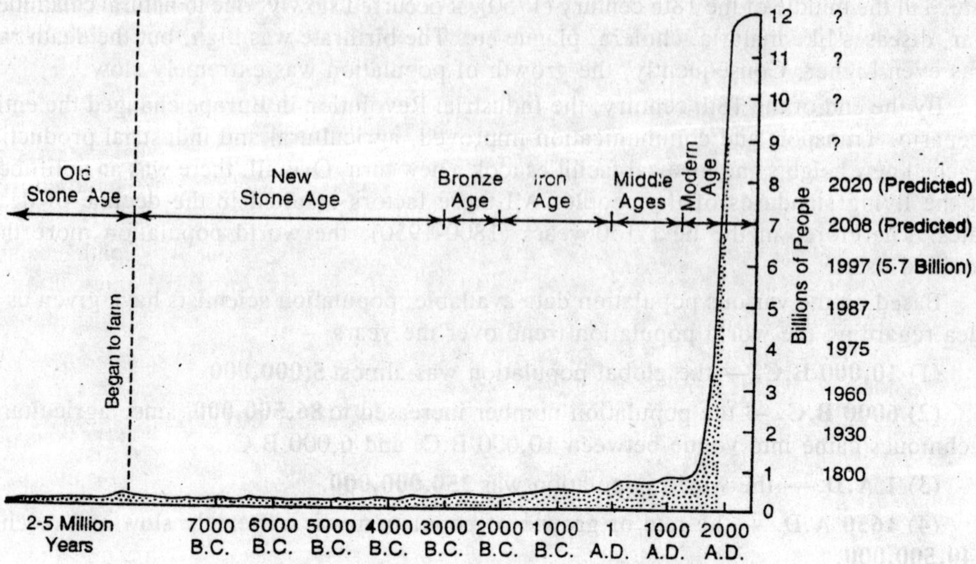

Fig. 13. World Population Growth

(a) widespread illiteracy
(b) low per capita income
(c) low standard of living
(d) religious beliefs and superstition
(e) child-marriage
(f) medical facilities controlling epidemics and decling mortality.

The growth rate in countries like Ethiopia, Iran, Yemen and Pakistan vary between 3% and 4%. However, increasing urbanisation, industrialisation, spread of education and medical facilities, government assistance and social awareness have lowered the population growth-rate in some countries, such as China, India, Brazil, Argentina etc.

Latitudinal Distribution of Population

The distribution of population by latitudes is also not uniform.

The southern hemisphere, which is mostly occupied by oceans, is inhabited by even less than 10% of the world's population. Just over 10% inhabit the region between the Equator and 20°N, almost 50% between 20°N and 40°N and 30% between 40°N and 60°N, and less than one-half percent lives in the permanently frozen region north of 60°N.

Vertical Distribution of Population

Let us look at the following facts —

(1) Roughly, 56.2% of the world's population live between 0 and 200 m of sea-level, which accounts for only 27.8% of the total land area.

(2) Only over four-fifths of the world's populace live under 500 mts. This covers 57.3% of land area.

Analysing the vertical distribution of population all over the world, Staszewski concluded that the population numbers and densities are inversely proportional to altitude, i.e. population densities decrease with increasing altitude.

Continentality and Insularity

(1) Population tends to concentrate along the margins of continents. The interiors of continents are sparsely populated. Three-quarters of the world's population have chosen to live within 1,000 km of the sea, and two-thirds within 500 km of the sea.

This fact proves that human beings are attached by coasts and discouraged by continentality. Here, the principal factors involved are climatic congeniality and commercial opportunities.

(2) The disposition, shape and size of the continents also determine population distribution, especially in high latitudes.

The northern high latitudes, because of countries with wide longitudinal extent, have limited maritime influence. This factor has made these continents repellent to population concentrations.

On the other hand, southern continents taper to the south. This characteristic has led to the reverse condition in southern high latitudes.

Where the equator passes through South America and Africa, and the tropic of Cancer passes through Africa, the longitudinal extents of the continents are very wide. This has directly influenced the scarcity of population in these regions, as these latitudes are directly related to the size of tropical rain forests and deserts.

The densely populated islands of the world prove that insularity attracts human concentration. We can take the instances of Sri Lanka, Indonesia, Philippines, Taiwan, West Indies, Japan, British Isles and many more. However, no simple and direct relationship exists between insularity and population concentration. The geographic and economic potentialities are very important, along with size, situation and historical background.

Coasts, all over the world, show diversities. No wonder coastal populations are not always evenly distributed. Population concentrates in pockets at ports or other favourable sites.

The respective influences of continentality and insularity do not hold good in isolation. Several other factors are associated and thus give rise to exceptions.

Population Growth and Natural Resources

We already know that distribution of population is not even all over the world. Man has the tendency to settle down in areas where he receives the maximum benefits. In doing so, the numbers are either too great or too low for the full utilization of the available resources in a certain area. When we have to confront this problem, we are made to consider the concepts of minimum, optimum and maximum population.

What is Resource ?

According to the Dictionary of Human Geography, resource is **"a concept employed to denote sources of human satisfaction, wealth or strength. Labour, entrepreneurial skills, investment funds, fixed capital assets, technology and cultural and physical attributes may all be referred to as resources of a nation (or region, company or household)."**

Natural resources can be broadly classified into —

(i) Stock or Non-renewable Resources (minerals and land), which are available in a fixed amount and have taken millions of years to form.

(ii) Flow or Renewable Resources, which can provide new supply units by natural regeneration, within a human time-span. For instance, solar energy is a Flow Resource.

Resources evaluation is essential while considering the distribution or growth of population numbers vis-a-vis resources.

Resources evaluation will determine the value of a resource, in physical, economic or perceptual terms, as well as the long-term effects and adequacy of resource-management strategies.

Resource Management

Resource Management is a broad, multi-disciplinary area. Its study deals with the management of all available natural resources (renewable and non-renewable), regardless of whether managed by public-sector agencies or by private-enterprise.

The aims of a resource-management programme, according to the Dictionary of Human Geography, will be :

(a) explanation of the physical, socio-economic and political processes that lead to resource exploitation, supply and consumption;

(b) analysis of the resource products and services allocated over space and time;

(c) evaluation of management systems, practices and policies regarding resource exploitation;

(d) development of alternative management strategies and evaluatory tools, for the Earth to sustain further increase in population and the consequent economic activities.

The quantitative measurement of resources is virtually impossible. Moreover, different populations differ in their cultures, ideals, customs and, therefore, needs. It has already been mentioned that resources are substances or properties which satiate human needs, and, therefore, availability of resources rise with the aims, efforts, skills, economic and cultural attainment of the population and their capacity to exploit resources.

Population and Resource Evaluation and Indices

From the previous discussion, it is evident that population/resources ratios are often highly subjective. Political and socio-cultural beliefs play an important role here.

No simple indices can be formulated for optimum population, over-population or under-population.

The U.N. volume "The Determinants and Consequence of Population Trends" examines eight indices, to which we may add the dependency ratio [the number of children (aged 0-14) and elderly people (aged 65 or over) in a particular population as a ratio of the number of adults (aged 15-64)] :

1. Per capita income
2. Level of employment
3. Existence of diminishing returns
4. Volume and direction of migration
5. Changes of consumption patterns
6. Life expectancy
7. Changes in terms of international trade
8. Measures of population density.

The concepts of over-population, under-population and optimum population vary with time and space.

Optimum population in one region may be considered over-population or under-population in a similar region, but with a population exhibiting socio-economic and cultural characteristics.

The movement (natural and external) of population — as well as technological advancement — are mostly responsible for this. The rate of technical progress has not been equal in all parts of the world. Therefore, there have been different results in different regions.

Under-population

If, in a region, the resources could support a larger population — without resulting in lower living standards or without increasing unemployment — or the population is so small that it cannot fully utilize the resources, then the region is said to be under-populated.

Absolute under-population can rarely be found, other than in the case of isolated populations, where the numbers are so low that they are incapable of normal demographic replacement, as well as of sufficient economic production. In some places, such as in the southern continents, we find **relative under-population**, where the available resources have not undergone sufficient development.

Under-population occurs in regions where (a) the living standards of the people are very high, and,

(b) extensive farming is practiced, such as in the Prairies and parts of Australia and New Zealand,

(c) the technical levels are very low, such as among the pastoral nomads who wander in the arid regions of the world.

Over-population

If, in a region, the existing population is excess over the utilized or potential resources, the region is said to be over-populated.

The principal factors leading to over-population may be listed as —

(a) an increase in population

(b) a fall in the demand for labour

(c) a decline in available resources

(d) a low rate of technical progress

(e) a combination of all the factors.

Thus, over-population takes place where the place of resource development does not match the population growth, and where the growth of tertiary services lags far behind technical progress.

Relative over-population is more commonly found than absolute over-population.

Absolute over-population occurs when —

(a) living standards are low, and

(b) absolute limit of production has been attained, in spite of the low living standards of the people.

Relative over-population occurs when the existing production is insufficient for the population, although greater production can be made possible.

Over-population can be found at different levels —

(a) regional

(b) national

(c) rural

(d) industrial.

Rural over-population is mostly found in under-developed, highly populated countries.

The best example can be South-East Asia. It is marked by high fertility, declining mortality, intensive agricultural practices, minimum mechanization, and fragmentation of land. In these regions, history shows evidence of natural checks to population.

There are some other factors also that have influenced rural overpopulation :

(a) decline in the demand for agricultural labours, due to increased mechanization,

(b) uneven distribution of land among farmers,

(c) rapid rate of growth among the rural population, and

(d) again, a decline in the demand for labour due to a change from cultivation to livestock farming.

Many of the old European countries show these features that lead to overpopulation.

The Optimum Theory of Population

The optimum theory of population was put forward as a reaction to the Malthusian theory of population. Malthus (1766-1834), in his famous book 'Essay on the Principle of Population' (1798), stated that : Population increases faster (in geometric progression) than means of subsistence (in arithmetical progresion).

However, the Malthusian Theory deals with the relationship between population growth and food supply, while the Theory of Optimum Population studies the relationship between population size and the production of wealth.

Optimum population refers to a state where the size of the population is neither greater nor lower than the socially desirable level.

Definition of Optimum Population

The concept of Optimum Population arose from the fundamental relationship between population and resources.

Edwin Cannan (1861-1935), who was a British economist, has been credited for having introduced the term and framing the theory. He published the "Wealth" in 1924. His idea was discussed and made popular by Carr Saunders, Dalton and Robbins.

If the different views are studied, we would find that they emphasized on various aspects of the optimum size of population, such as requirements of the population, productive activity of the economy, requirement for equitable distribution etc.

Assumption of the Theory of Optimum Population

(1) With the growth of population, the ratio between total population and working population remains unchanged.

(2) The hours of work and production per head of working population will remain constant.

(3) A time may come when a country's population will increase with that of the available natural resources. Under such a condition, technical know-how and capital will not change. So, after some time, the law of diminishing returns begins to operate. When the combination of factors is not suited for production, it will be impossible to maximise production.

According to the exponents of the theory, from the national point of view, population should be treated as a labour force. Every increase in the labour force creates an opportunity to utilize the material resources available in the country.

Interpretation of the Optimum Population

In order to understand the concept of optimum population, the following points are to be studied carefully :

(1) Population is the manpower needed to exploit the natural resources and thereby promote economic growth.

(2) As long as the optimum point is not reached, the nation shall remain unable to exploit the natural resources to the maximum possible extent, i.e., properly and fully.

(3) If the population crosses the optimum point, then the nation shall not get the maximum return. This is because the large population will create pressure on other resources, The burden on those resources will become disproportionate.

(4) If the population is at the optimum point, the resources are properly and fully utilized. It gives the ideal combination of factors of production. Moreover, it helps in suitable division of labour, resulting in very high national gross production and per capita income. At the optimum point, external economies are fully utilized.

As an empirical theory, the optimum theory is very scientific. Given a criterion, the theory establishes that the function y(P) increases over a range of low value of P, reaches a maximum point and then decreases as the value of P increases :

$$Y = y(P),$$

where y = per capita real income

P = Population.

From Fig.13A, we can understand the theory. Here, the optimum population function is represented as a simple curve which is concave to the X-axis. The curve has a single hump.

The point P shows the optimum point. Here, the per capita income is highest. Till the poin 'P' is reached, the growth in population is accompanied by a corresponding increase in per capita income. When we go beyond the point OM, any further increase in population results in a fall in per capita income.

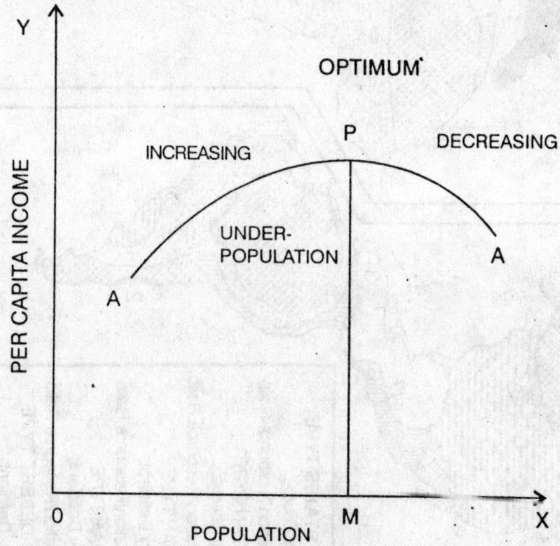

Fig.13A. The Concept of Optimum Population

Here, we can refer to the laws of production.

According to the law of increasing returns, as the population increases, marginal and average productivity also increases. When the point of optimum population is reached, the law of constant returns operates. Now, with further increase in population, the law of diminishing returns tends to overtake the economy.

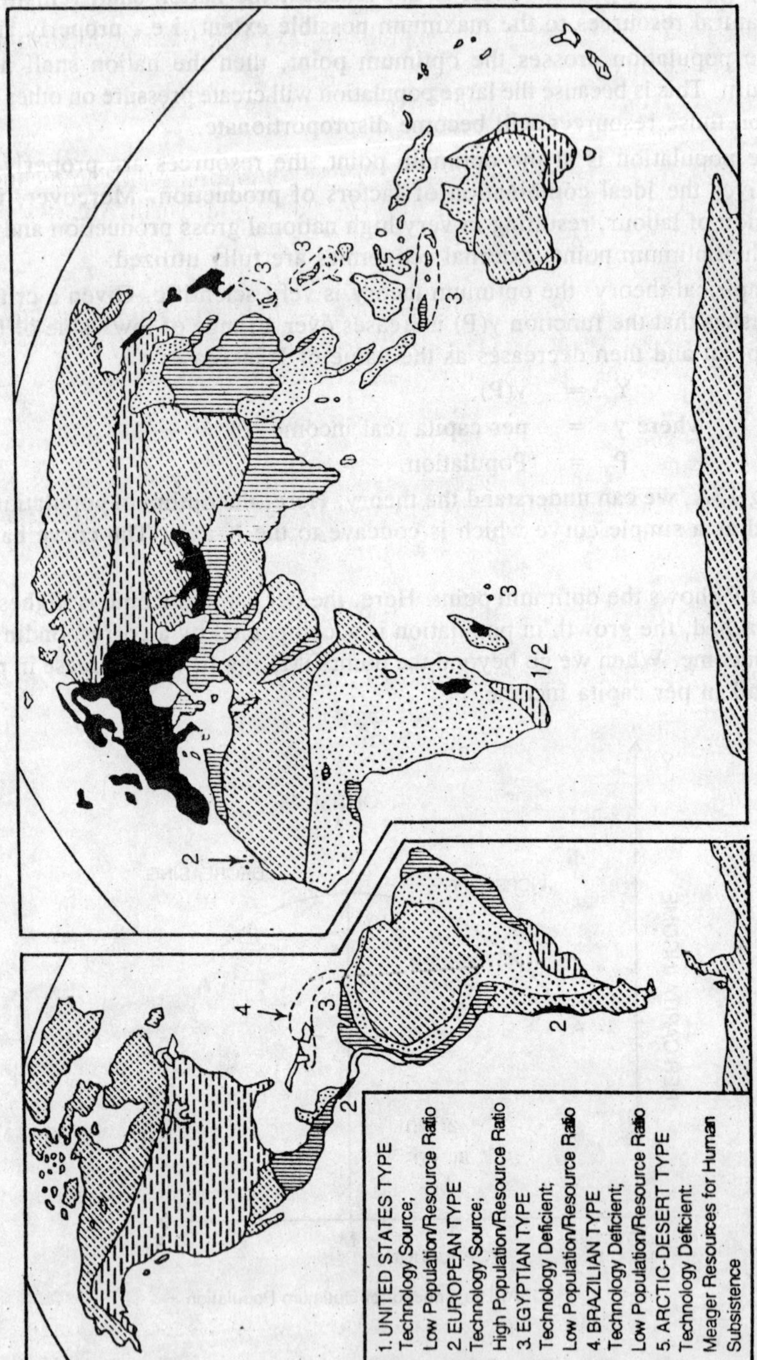

Fig.14. Population/Resource Regions of the World

Population-Resource Regions

Ackerman has classified the population of the world on the basis of population-resource ratios and the availability of technology.

The five population-resource regions are :

(1) **United States Type**

About (1 billion=) one-sixth of the total world population reside in technology-rich areas where population : resource ratio are low, such as in North America, Australia, New Zealand and erstwhile U.S.S.R.

(2) **European Type**

About (1 billion=) one-sixth live in such areas where technology has advanced and population : resource ratios are high. Industrialization and technology have resulted in an expansion of resources through international trade, such as in Japan and a vast part of Europe.

(3) **Egyptian Type**

Approximately, one-half (3 billion) lives in these technology-deficient areas. Population resource ratios are high, such as in India, Pakistan and China. Severe population problems are experienced here.

(4) **Brazilian Type**

One-sixth (1 billion) live in areas that are deficient in technology. Population : resources ratios are low, often resources remain unused due to problems to overcome hostile environmental difficulties. Most of Latin America, Africa and South-east Asia fall under this category.

(5) **Arctic Desert Type**

Regions that are under ice-caps, Tundras and deserts are mostly poor in technology and have very little food-producing potential.

Carrying Capacity

Just as the use of terms 'metabolism' and 'energetics' have been controversial, the recent re-introduction of the term **'carrying capacity'** into the environmental debate is sure to make waves.

However, this does not hold any surprise. When ecologists first used the term 'carrying capacity', they referred to the size of the optimum population of any particular species, which, in a given habitat, could be supported indefinitely. When the term is applied to the study of humans, critics immediately point out the human ability to innovate for survival and increase in numbers, very often at the expense of less innovative species. Here, humans are unlike other species such as cows and dogs. It is assumed that human beings will continue to exercise their ability to innovate, thereby constantly expanding the ability of the earth to carry them.

This assumption faces challenge from two observations :

(i) Only some of the human population about 1 billion is truly prospering due to this innovative process. The rest — the majority of the population (about 5 billion) — is fighting a difficult situation.

(ii) The assimilative capacity of the important environmental sinks has now been reached. By this, it is meant that society needs a change of direction. If there is any further belt-tightening, it will have some tough implication for the first observation, i.e. the inequality between people.

It is true that the twentieth century has seen the rapid growth of innovation, and at the same time the rapid growth of disparities between people living in different parts of the world.

Therefore, when we talk about the carrying capacity of the earth, we should do so including the whole of humanity. We have to make realistic and pragmatic adjustments that will ensure a planetary human habitat not only for us, but for the generations to come.

But how did this illusion about an endless stream of innovations and an ever-expanding carrying capacity continue for such a long time ? The answer is colonisation and empire-building by the Europeans. From the birth of the European empires of the sixteenth century to the multinationals (MNCs) of the present, the wealthier people of the more prosperous countries have taken possession of global hinterlands to meet the requirements of their increasing urban citizens.

From the self-glorification of the initial empire-builders to the 'global-sources' of today, this has been acknowledged by all. And all has been covered under the flawless credentials of so-called free-trade and international competition for markets. Eventually, no matter what the stock-exchanges tell us, at the base of everything is an energy basis for all life, including human life. That is what the concepts of metabolism and carrying capacity try to capture.

Definition of Carrying Capacity

Originally, the term was used to delimit the optimum population density for a certain species (plants, animals, insects as well as humans) in a particular "Ecological Niche" (ecological niche — The functional position of an organism in its environment, comprising the habitat in which the organism lives, the periods of time during which it occurs and is active there, and the resources it obtains there). It has been applied to the human population in relation to the earth, but this application is controversial because carrying capacity will vary greatly according to the efficiency with which humans use the resources around them.

SUSTAINABLE DEVELOPMENT

The most important objective of development is the satisfaction of human needs and aspirations. The basic needs of the people — food, clothing and shelter — go unnoticed in the developing countries. Beyond these basic needs, the people still yearn for an improved quality of life. A world where poverty and inequality have become a way of life will always be susceptible to ecological and other crises. This is where sustainable development is required, for meeting the basic needs of all and giving them the opportunity to satisfy their aspirations for a better life.

Definition of Sustainable Development

The most significant problem today is that human beings sometimes make use of resources without keeping in mind the limits or constraints on their use.

There are 3 important policy issues concerning the use of resources :

1. **Depletion** of resources, especially to meet the demand for energy.
2. **Destruction** of resources through pollution.
3. **Maximum utilisation** of resources for the worlds food supply.

(i) In 1987, the United Nations World Commission on Environment and Development, chaired by Gro Harlem Brundtland, published its title **"Our Common Future"**. It is popularly known as the **Brundtland Report.**

According to the Brundtland Report : "sustainable development is development that meets the needs of the present without compromising the ability of future generations to meet their own needs."

There are two key concepts here —

(a) The concept of needs refers to requirements of the world's poor, to which the most priority should be given.

(b) The concept of limitations, imposed by the state of technology and social organisations, or the capacity of the environment to meet present and future needs.

(ii) According to R. K. Turner (1988 — Sustainable Environmental Management, Belhaven, London), sustainable development "would seek to maintain an 'acceptable' rate of growth in per-capita real incomes without depleting the national capital asset stock or the natural environmental asset stock."

(iii) According to G. R. Conway (1987 — 'The Properties of Agroecosystems', Agricultural Systems), sustainable development is 'The net productivity of bio-mass (positive mass balance per unit area per unit time) maintained over decades to centuries."

It can be concluded by saying that sustainable development aims at maintaining development over time.

Three Basic Principles for Sustainable Development

As population numbers grow, the changing technologies have also simultaneously increased. This is not only affecting the present, but will have long-term consequences in the future states of the environment.

There are three major principles underlying the process of sustainable development :

I. Principle of Inter-Generational Equity or Principle of Futurity.

This principle is to ensure that, in considering any human activity, one has to consider the effects it might have on future generations to meet their needs.

II. Principle of Social Justice

This is concerned with the present generation, where poverty is found to be the principal cause of degradation. Sustainable development calls for an evenly exercised control over the distribution of resources, keeping in mind the basic needs of common aspiration.

III. Principle of Trans-Frontier Reponsibility

Wherever possible, the impacts of any human activity should not involve any geographical displacement of environmental hazards that will remain uncompensated, i.e., transfrontier pollution must be identified and controlled.

In this regard, wealthy nations should not overexploit the resources of other nations, that might lead to an imbalance in regional economies and ecosystems. Similarly, the detrimental effects of urban activities should not go beyond the metropolitan boundaries.

Strategic Imperatives

1. **Reviving Growth**

Since proverty increases the pressure on environment, sustainable development must stress on the issue of proverty, to stimulate growth in the developing countries.

2. **Changing the quality of growth**

"Growth" must be made less materialistic, less energy intensive and its impact more equitable. Economic and social development must be "mutually reinforcing".

3. **Meeting essential human needs**

More food is needed, not merely to feed people, but also to attack undernourishment. Housing, fresh water supply, medical facilities and energy should be supplied. Energy consumption patterns should change, so that the need for energy all over the world can be satisfied.

4. **Ensuring a sustainable level of population**

The highest rates of population growth, especially in developing countries, is to be tackled. This will ensure improved quality of life and higher per capita income. The distribution of population between urban and rural areas must be equitable.

5. **Conserving and enhancing the resources base**

There is a rising demand for efficient, low-waste technologies for preserving agricultural resources (land, soil, water), forestry, fisheries and energy.

6. **Reorienting technology and managing risk**

The implications of 1-5 are for the reorientation of technology in the two following ways —

(a) the capacity for innovation must be greatly increased in developing countries, and

(b) technological development, in general, must lay special emphasis on environmental factors. This is especially linked to the issue of "risk management", by which we can minimise environmental impact.

7. **Merging environment and economics in decision-making**

Economics and ecology are two interlocking subjects that go hand in hand in sustainable development.

In order to achieve 1-7, the Brundtland Report sees the following essential requirements—

A **political system** that secures effective citizen participation in decision-making.

An **economic system** that is able to generate surpluses and technical knowledge on a self-reliant and sustained basis.

A **social system** that provides for solutions for the tensions arising from disharmonious development.

A **production system** that respects the obligation to preserve the ecological base for development.

A **technological system** that can search continuously for new solutions.

An **international system** that fosters sustainable patterns of trade and finance.

An **administrative system** that is flexible and has the capacity for self-correction.

Sustainable Development in Practice : Sustainable Energy Project, Haryana State, India

In 1984, the Tata Energy Research Institute, New Delhi, instituted the sustainable energy project, on an experimental basis. They focussed on only one village, Dhanawas. Their aim was to demonstrate the practical achievements of work in the field, by using the local renewable sources of energy. Their objective in the long run was to spread the idea to the other villages of the state.

The project involves the participation of the villagers. The village council's cooperation and the funding from TERI, the FAO and the Government of India have made the project possible.

The principal features of the project are —

(a) A **seven hectare plantation** has been established on very poor saline soils, that had once supported only scrub vegetation. This initiative was taken for long term improvement of soil quality, by using tough, nitrogen-fixing species, such as acacia and mesquat. These can also be used as fuelwood on a sustainable basis. All the trees here are held as a common property resource.

(b) **Biogas makers** have been set up. They use a mixture of dung and water. The capacity of each unit is 2 cubic meters a day. This is sufficient to support 5 hours of cooking on modern stoves or 10 hours of lighting. Enough number of these biogas makers are to be introduced, so that the village becomes self-sufficient in renewable fuel sources. This will eventually reduce the consumption of fuelwood in conventional cook-stoves.

(c) A **gasifier** has been developed. This uses pellets made of a mixture of shredded mustered stalks, dungs and water. This equipment is capable of generating an equivalent of 5 kilowatts of electricity with an 80%/20% gas/diesel mix.

(d) The villagers have been taught the use of **solar-powered water heaters.**

Haryana is the one among the agriculturally most productive states of India. Therefore, it was easier to convince the villagers of Dhanawas village to participate since their village is "richer" than the others. Poorer villages mostly concentrate on other priorities, such as access to safe drinking water, increased income, higher standard of living.

By the efficient use of renewables, the villagers can cut down on the cost of conventional fuel consumption. With the spread of awareness, education and development will go hand in hand.

Density of Population in India

The crude density of population is the man/land ratio, or, the number of people per unit area. Therefore

$$\text{Population Density} = \frac{\text{Total population of the country}}{\text{Total area of the country}}$$

The salient features of population density of India, as per the 1991 census are :

(1) Population density of **India** is 267/km^2.

(2) The state with **highest population density** is **West Bengal** (766/km^2).

(3) The state with **second highest population density** is **Kerala** (747/km^2).

(4) Although **Uttar Pradesh** is the most populated state of India, it is the **fourth most densely populated state** (471/km^2).

(5) The state with **third highest population density** is **Bihar** (497/km^2).

(6) The **most densely populated Union Territory** is **Chandigarh** (5,620/km^2).

(7) The density of population of **Delhi** is the highest (6,319/km^2).

(8) The **Union Territory** that is **least densely populated** are the **Andaman and Nicobar Islands** (34/km^2).

(9) The **state** that is **least densely populated** is **Arunachal Pradesh** (10/km^2).

Population Density Zones of India (census 1991)

Basing on the census data of 1991, India can be broadly divided into 3 population density zones :

(1) **Thickly populated regions** where the population density is **greater than 501/km^2.**

States and Union Territories under this category are West Bengal, Kerala, Delhi, Chandigarh, Lakshadweep, Pondicherry, Daman and Diu.

(2) **Moderately populated regions** where the population density is **between 201/km^2 and 500/km^2.**

States and Union Territories under this category are Uttar Pradesh, Tamil Nadu, Punjab, Haryana, Goa, Assam, Tripura, Maharashtra, Andhra Pradesh, Karnataka, Gujarat, Orissa, Dadra and Nagar Haveli.

(3) **Poorly populated regions** where the density of population is **less than 200/km^2.**

The states and Union Territories falling under this category are Madhya Pradesh, Rajasthan, Himachal Pradesh, Manipur, Meghalaya, Jammu and Kashmir, Nagaland, Sikkim, Mizoram, Arunachal Pradesh and Andaman and Nicobar Islands.

Population Distribution in India

For any country, population is undoubtedly a very important factor. Due to low population numbers, countries like Australia and Canada are suffering since the available resources cannot be adequately exploited. At the same time, most of the countries of South-East Asia are growing under the pressure of overpopulation. However, economists and social scientists are of opinion that no matter how overpopulated a country is, systematic planning can give fruitful results. Keeping this in mind, it is necessary to maintain accurate records of population numbers, distribution and density. This is the reason why India conducts a census every ten years. The first Census was conducted in India in 1872, but since 1881, it is done regularly at an interval of ten years. The census of 2001 has been completed and the results are awaited.

India is one of the most populated countries of the world. After China, India is the second most populated country of the world. [The population of China was 1,265 million in 2000, while the population of India was 1,002 million]. India accounts for more than 16% of the total global population, i.e., among every 6 persons in the world, 1 is Indian, although India accounts for only 2.42% of the total land area of the world.

India's Population Growth

At present, the rate of population growth in India is 2.1% and the country's population was 1,002 million in 2000.

The table below gives an idea of the rapid rate of population growth in India :

Year	Population
1901	240,000,000
1951	360,000,000
1981	683,329,097
1991	846,332,688
2000	1,000,000,000

We see from the table that both from 1981 to 1991 and 1991 to 2000, i.e. recently, every 10 years the population has increased by almost 16 crores. Therefore, every year the numbers increased by roughly 16,000,000.

Causes of Rapid Growth of Population in India

During the past few decades, the population of India has shown a rapid rate of increase. Although India ranks as the seventh largest country in the world, she is the second most populated country.

A few factors are responsible for the rapid growth of population in this country —

(1) **High Birth Rate** in comparison to the developed and developing countries of the world. This is due to wide-spread illiteracy, acute poverty, superstition, religious beliefs, child-marriage and various other reasons.

(2) **Low Death Rate** accompanied by a high birth rate has aggravated the problem. During the past few decades, especially after independence, medical facilities have improved, which along with improved communication facilities, have made it easy to aid the victims of floods, droughts, famine and any natural calamity. No wonder advancement in the field of medicine and communication has increased average life expectancy.

(3) **High Rate of Immigration** from the neighbouring countries during the post-partition

period worsened the population problem. The constant flow of refugees had put enormous pressure on the government. Illegal infiltration is still continuing.

(4) **Scientific and Technological Developments and Rise in Economic Standards.** After independence, the country has been blessed with technological advancement, in both agriculture and industry. The Green Revolution resulted in an increase in food production and states like Punjab and Haryana, especially, were blessed. Industrialization also provided employment to many. As a result, the average living standards of the people improved.

Science and technology have enabled the common man to foresee nature's whims. The satellite images warn us before a catastrophe and the government takes adequate measures to fight the calamity. This saves life and property and indirectly results in a rapid growth of population.

Distribution of Population In India (according to 1991 Census)

During the census of 1991, it was noticed that although India is a highly populated country, the distribution of population is not even.

While the Northern Gangetic Plain and the Malabar Coast are densely populated, the Rajasthan Desert and the Himalayan region remain sparsely inhabited. In central India, the population is somewhat dispersed, and the North-Eastern mountainous region has almost very low population.

Let us study the salient features of population distribution in India :

(1) The **most populated state** is **Uttar Pradesh** (139,100,000 approximately)

(2) The **second most populated state** is **Bihar** (86,300,000 approximately)

(3) The **third most populated state** is **Maharashtra** (78,900,000 approximately)

(4) The **fourth most populated state** is **West Bengal** (68,100,000 approximately)

(5) The **least populated state** is **Sikkim** (406,000 approximately)

(6) The **most populated Union Territory** is **Pondicherry** (807,000 approximately)

(7) The **least populated Union Territory** is **Lakshadweep** (52,000 approximately).

(8) The population of Delhi is 9,400,000 approximately.

(9) Although Madhya Pradesh is the largest state, it ranks sixth in population (66,200,000 approximately).

Population Education

Education is probably the only effective short and long-term instrument that can bring about numerous desired changes in the world. Human activities have produced irreversible changes in the global environment for the last 300 years. Humankind has shown progress over the years, and material advances became synonymous with the extract of resources, accompanied by the gradual transformation of the landscape to support growing numbers. When we consider the rising population numbers across the globe, the world no longer seems to be vast and inexhaustible.

India is already over-populated. It should be remembered that the future course of population growth in India will depend mainly on the reproductive behaviour of the people. In order to make the people aware of the ecological as well as socio-economic imports that large population exert on the world around them, population education has become a must, especially in developing countries.

Population Education Through Community Contact Programme

The implementation of Population Education in the formal education system will make every school an integral part of the community. The most effective method to impart population education in developing countries must be through community contact programmes by schools, planned and co-ordinated at the developmental block level.

The modus operandi of the population education programme may be :

(i) a conference of the local leaders, community health volunteer, officers and personnel from the block health centre, educationists and school teachers from a cluster of 10 to 15 villages, in order to explore the possibility of participation and cooperation of the people in the proposed programme;

(ii) orientation of the school teachers before implementing the programme, and organising discussion meetings after two to three months;

(iii) a contact programme between pupil and teachers, and occasional door-to-door contact with the parents of the pupil, so as to involve the community as a whole;

(iv) regular supervision by educational supervisors;

(v) regular and systematic assessment of the programme by block-level health, education and development officers.

If the proposed programme is implemented suitably, it can be utilized to introduce important messages and educate the masses about national objectives, and further get them translated into action.

National Population Education Project (India)

National Population Education Project (School Education) was launched in India in April 1980. It aims to institutionalise population education in the school education system.

This project is —

(a) executed by the Ministry of Human Resource Development,

(b) monitored by the Ministry of Health and Family Welfare, and

(c) implemented by the National Council of Educational Research and Training (NCERT).

This project has been implemented in 29 states and Union Territories and also in the Higher and Adult Education section. Three cycles of the project has been completed so far. They have emphasized on —

(i) integrating population education in the syllabi and text-books;

(ii) development of prototype curricular, instructional and training materials for all stages of school education;

(iii) conducting teachers' training programmes in population education throughout the country, and

(iv) incorporating sustainable development, ageing and other related concerns in the population education elements in all NCERT text-books.

Impact of Economic Development on Environment in India

The post-independence period in India was marked by a sudden upsurge in both agricultural and industrial sectors. This was simultaneously accompanied by large scale population of the natural environment. This was probably the nightmare that was dreaded the most, since environmental pollution is the obvious consequence that follows industrialization and urbanization.

The growing population is the most important source of pollution in India. The states which offer the population maximum prospects for a better livelihood and good standard of living are the most populated. Thus, particular states and a number of cities attract population, resulting in large scale consumption of resources and creation of wastes. The problem of environmental pollution in our country is further complicated by widespread poverty of the masses. A large proportion of the country's population lives below poverty line. The slum dwellers have to be contented even though they are constantly exposed to various health hazards due to complete lack of civic amenities.

Development of the Industrial Sector in the Planning Era

Immediately after independence, the necessity to take solid steps for the betterment of the industrial scene was badly felt. It was realised that only industrialization could breathe life into the shattered economy of the country and lead her on the path of progress and prosperity. The most remarkable progress in the field of industry took place during the first two Plan Periods.

The First Five Year Plan (1951-56) emphasized on increasing the capacity of already existing industries, rather than starting new ones. Thus, sugar, vanaspati, cement, paper, cotton textile, chemical and engineering industries prospered. The new industries that emerged during this Plan were transport equipment, newsprint, paints and varnish, power looms and medicines.

The Second Five Year Plan (1956-61) emphasized on the development of basic and heavy industries. Iron and steel, heavy engineering, lignite projects and fertilizer industries showed marked imporvement. The existing steel plants at Jamshedpur, Kulti-Burnpur and Bhadravati were expanded. Three new state-owned plants at Rourkela, Bhilai and Durgapur were either initiated or completed. The Hindusthan Machine Tools (HMT) Limited plant at Bangalore, Chittaranjan Locomotive Factory, the Hindusthan Sphipbuiding Yard at Vishakhapatnam and The Sindri Fertilizer Factory were expanded. At Nangal and Rourkela, two new fertilizer plants were set up.

Thereafter, a steady rate of industrialisation followed. However, industrial development has been localized in certain areas. Various pockets of the country have remained unexplored and neglected, such as the tribal areas of Madhya Pradesh and hilly terrain of the north-east.

The Tourism industry has, however, flourished in otherwise underdeveloped areas. The popular resorts in the Himalayas, the desert and historical ambience of Rajasthan and various such places depend solely on the inflow of tourists for their economy. During peak seasons, a sudden rise in population often disturbs the usual or natural life of the original inhabitants of such places. For instance, water crisis in Darjeeling takes almost the shape of a drought during the summer months. However, illegal construction of hotels and guest houses on unstable slopes often result in disaster.

In southern India, Bangalore and Hyderabad have become popular destinations for the educated, skilled labour force since the software industry has prospered here.

Soil or Land Pollution in Rural India — an Impact of the Green Revolution

With the commencement of the Green Revolution in 1966-67, the use of chemical fertilizers and biocides in agriculture gained momentum.

High yielding varieties (HYV) of seeds were combined with chemical fertilizers and pesticides, such as DDT, BHC, aldrin, endrin, dieldrin organophosphorus compounds etc. When excessive quantities of these chemicals are used, the soil particles absorb the remnants, which eventually contaminate the crops. The herbivores consume these crops and the harmful chemicals are transferred through carnivores to the human bodies in course of food chains.

The overall per hectare consumption of fertilizers was only 0.55 kg in 1950-51. This rose to 67 kg in 1992-93. No wonder Punjab, Haryana and western Uttar Pradesh are facing serious threats of soil pollution, since the Green Revolution had truely had an impact on the agriculture in these states.

Problem of Water Pollution in India

Water resources can be broadly categorised into —

(1) **Surface Water**, that include river, canals, lakes, ponds and even the seas, and

(2) **Ground Water**, that we can get from wells, tubewells, hand pumps, springs and so on.

At present, water pollution in India has reached an alarming situation.

Causes of Water Pollution in India

(1) There are about three hundred class 1 cities in India. The sewage from most of these cities (when each city generates almost 10,000 million liters of sewage everyday) is dumped into adjacent water courses, without any treatment.

The Ganga is the most sacred and the most worshipped river of the Hindus. Yet, it happens to be the most polluted river of India !

The Ganga carries with it agricultural, industrial, urban and human filth. Along its courses, the river collects surface run-off, domestic garbage, industrial effluents, municipal sewage and pesticides from agricultural run-off.

(2) Numerous industrial towns are situated on the banks of rivers. Toxic chemicals are constantly being added to the rivers from industrial waste water and effluents.

The following table shows important rivers and the source of their pollutants :

RIVER	PRINCIPAL SOURCES OF POLLUTANTS
1. Yamuna	Industrial and urban wastes mainly from Delhi, Mathura, Agra and Allahabad.
2. Kali	(a) Industrial units of western UP, (b) domestic affluents and waste water from printing and dyeing industry of Farrukhabad
3. Gomti	Industrial effluents from — (a) sugar mills at Sitapur (b) distilleries of Lucknow
4. Damodar	Wastes from the various industries in the mineral rich Chota Nagpur region

(3) Since 1960, the Green Revolution brought about widespread changes in the agricultural practices in India. It introduced the use of huge quantities of fertilizers, pesticides, herbicides, insecticides etc. Some of these toxic chemicals are drained by rain water and poured into the rivers. This causes large scale pollution of river water.

(4) The sea water near the coasts is being polluted due to unrestrained disposal of urban and industrial waste. For instance, the fuel leakages in Mumbai High in 1982 and 1987 polluted the Arabian Sea.

Oil slicks also affect marine life.

Air Pollution in India — an Aftermath of Industrialisation and Urbanisation

Air pollution in India has assumed alarming proportion. This has been an effect of the rapid pace of industrialisation and development during the post-Independence period.

The injection of gases, liquids and solid particles into the atmosphere, that are detrimental to human health, may be referred to as air pollution.

(a) **Delhi** is the fourth most polluted city in the world. It has been estimated that the following are the principal sources of air pollution in Delhi —

Automobile — 64%
Thermal Power Plants — 16%
Industry — 12%
Domestic Sector — 8%

The vehicles (over 3 million in number) release 1,063 tonnes of carbon monoxide, 400 tonnes of hydrocarbon, 323 tonnes of nitrogen dioxide, 179 tonnes of sulphur dioxide and large quantities of suspended particulate matter (SPM) daily.

The industries located at Lawrence Road, Wazirpur, Kirti Nagar, Najafgarh Road, DLF Industrial Area and Moti Nagar have made them the most polluted area.

(b) **Calcutta** is world's sixth most polluted city. A report submitted by National Environment Engineering Research Institute (NEERI), Nagpur, in 1981, said that total daily emission from all sources amounts to 1,305 tonnes in Calcutta Metropolitan District (CMD). Of this, 900 tonnes of pollutants are produced in the industrial belt of Calcutta, while the rest come from the Howrah Industrial Belt.

Besides industry and transport sectors air pollution is also caused by large amount of garbage, lack of sanitary facilities, sewer wastage and cigarettes, cigars and bidis.

(c) Air pollution in rural area is also caused by the large scale use of pesticides and insecticides in the agricultural field. This has risen especially during the past four decades. The life style of the Indian rural masses is also closely related to air pollution since they burn wood, cow dung callus, coal and kerosene oil in unventilated kitchens.

QUESTIONS FOR EXAMINATION

A. Essay-Type Questions

1. What are the causes of uneven distribution of population in the world ? Explain with examples.
   Ans. Pp. 65-69
2. Explain the world population trend and present position.
   Ans. Pp. 66-68
3. Discuss the distribution of population in the world.
   Ans. Pp. 67-69
4. Discuss the relation between population and resources.
   Ans. Pp. 69-71
5. Discuss the different theories of optimum population.
   Ans. Pp. 72-73
6. Analyse the population-resource regions in the world.
   Ans. Pp. 73-75
7. Explain the density of population in India.
   Ans. Pp. 79-81
8. How is population growth related to natural resources ? — Discuss.
   Ans. Pp. 73-75
9. What are the causes of rapid growth of population in India ? — Explain.
   Ans. Pp. 80-81
10. Explain the population education system.
    Ans. Pp. 81-82
11. Explain the impact of economic development on environment in India.
    Ans. Pp. 82-85
12. Discuss the nature and principles of sustainable development.
    Ans. Pp. 76-79

B. Short Answer-Type Questions

1. What is population density ?
   Ans. Page 79
2. What is resources ?
   Ans. Page 69
3. What is renewable resources ?
   Ans. Page 69
4. What is resource management ?
   Ans. Page 70
5. What is over-population ?
   Ans. Page 71
6. What is under-population ?
   Ans. Page 71
7. What is optimum population ?
   Ans. Page 72

8. Define optimum population.

   Ans. Page 72

9. How many population resource regions are there in the world ?

   Ans. Page 75

10. How many population density zones are there in India ?

    Ans. Page 79

11. What is population education ?

    Ans. Page 81

12. What is economic development ?

    Ans. Page 82

13. What is National Population Education Project in India ?

    Ans. Page 82

14. What are the sources of land pollution ?

    Ans. Page 83

15. What are the principal sources of water pollution ?

    Ans. Page 83

16. What is carrying capacity ?

    Ans. Page 75

17. Define carrying capacity.

    Ans. Page 76

18. What is sustainable development ?

    Ans. Page 75

19. What are the principles of sustainable development ?

    Ans. Page 77

20. What are the strategic imperatives ?

    Ans. Page 77

21. What is 'Green Revolution' ?

    Ans. Page 83

22. What are the impacts of Green Revolution on environment ?

    Ans. Page 83

23. What in 'Ecological Niche' ?

    Ans. Page 76

Chapter 5

LAND AND WATER USE OF THE EARTH

INTRODUCTION

Land and Society : Land denotes both physical objects and social institutions. It comprises a bundle of earth materials and vegetation cover along with a bundle of legal rights to their use. As such, discussion of the human impact on the land is a discussion of how human land uses alter the biophysical land cover.

Today, much land is held or managed as common property. They can be used as cropland, pasture and range, woodland, hunting and fishing grounds.

Common lands are areas collectively controlled and managed. The resources are used by individuals belonging to the community, but under the community's rules. Control can be exercised on the use of resources but there is no guarantee that it will be. There is also no guarantee that control will be exercised for the benefit of the community or the environment. In some cases, the powerful members of the community may use the land in such a way that they will derive benefits while others suffer losses. However, the network of institutions makes the prevention of overuse possible by different means.

Changes in Land Cover

The most important land-use and land-cover classes are —

(i) cultivation
(ii) forest
(iii) grassland
(iv) wetland
(v) settlement.

The changes in land cover can occur in two forms :

(a) The process of **conversion** refers to the change of the cover from one class to another, such as, when forest is cleared for pasture, cropland is converted into urban settlement, wetland drainage for cultivation and so on,

(b) The process of **modification** is an alteration of the existing cover that does not convert it to a different cover type. All over the world, cultivation has replaced less productive land uses, such as forest, pasture, rangeland and "wastelands" of different kinds.

However, cultivation has also suffered the fate of conversion, where more lucrative land uses — in the form of sprawling urban areas — devour cropland.

Modification of land cover has occurred where forests have been thinned, the grass cover has been improved or nibbled down and urban infrastructure has undergone redevelopment.

The most dramatic and rapid land-use and land-cover change occur in zones of frontier expansion :

"Virtually all human societies have experienced that dynamic form of changing land use referred to as frontier. The frontier is that period and area in which a peripheral region is created or extended. We are all familiar with the transient frontier epoch during which time forests, grasslands, and even deserts are transformed into agricultural, pastoral, and urban landscapes of settlement and sedentary agriculture. Populations of diverse human 'tribal' societies — hunter-gatherers, pastoralists, shifting cultivators — succumb to the urgent claims of pioneer settlers backed by the modernizing state. Populations of wild animals are displaced by domesticated draft and grazing animals or are eradicated altogether." (Richards 1990 : The Earth as Transformed by Human Action, 165-66)

The lowland rain-forests on either side of the Amazon river has attracted settlers not only from Brazil, but also from the mountainous regions of Amazonia (Bolivia, Peru, Ecuador and Colombia). A similar phenomenon of rapid population influx accompanied with a classic transformation can be noted in the lowland Terai zone of Nepal.

Cultivation

The principal processes of land-cover changes associated with cultivation include —

(i) conversion — of forest, grassland or wetland to cropland, and

(ii) modification — the intensification of agricultural use.

When rise in population is followed by an automatic rise in consumption, it prompts the increase of agricultural output by either of the two means. The options will be —

(i) cultivation of more land at the expense of some other land cover, or

(ii) more intensive use of already formed lands, and addition of more inputs to reap larger crops.

Let us note the following facts —

(a) In the past three centuries, the world's cultivated land has expanded by more than 450%.

(b) In 1700, the world had 2.65 million square km of land under cultivation, but today it has grown to 15 million square km.

(c) From 1700 to the present century, the average net conversion of land to cropping was more than forty thousand square km per year. However, between 1950 and 1980, the average net conversion was well over a hundred thousand square km annually. The most rapid expansion following World War II (1939-45) took place in the developing countries. Retirement and abandonment of croplands have been comparatively more common in the developed countries. Much of land that remains under agriculture does so only because of state subsidy.

The definition of most of the world's land as unfit for agriculture is not simply a physical one, but also a techno-economic one. Crops can be grown anywhere, as Isaiah Bowman, the American geographer, wrote that we could, if we wished to do so and were willing to meet the costs, raise pineapples in greenhouses at the South Pole.

When technologies have been employed, irrigation has helped to expand the area that can be profitably farmed — since the end of the seventeenth century, the world's irrigation land has increased 50 times.

In spite of the progress in the agricultural sector, a number of unwanted threats have been observed which should not be allowed to aggravate any further. The environmental degradation that have been caused by advanced agricultural technology in association with unscientific agricultural practices are :

(1) The Effects of Intensive Use of Land

In order to achieve maximum production from the same land, the land starts losing its fertility. As a result of such intensive use, there is a decrease in the productivity of soil due to extreme soil erosion through ploughed furrows, or loss of fertility due to destruction of organic soil, and the burning of vegetation.

(2) The Effects of Over-Utilisation of Irrigation Water

Constant use of irrigation water dwindles the level of underground water, which again affects capillary action and the soil structure. It also results in water logging which increases salinity.

(3) The Effects of Overdoses of Chemical Fertilizers

Overdoses of chemical fertilisers may temporarily increase the productivity of the land, but, in the long run, the physical and chemical properties of the soil are so affected that the once rich soil may turn sterile. Moreover, the food value of crops grown on artificially enriched soils decreases.

The Impact of Pesticides and Undesirable Pollution of the Surroundings

In the West, pesticide contamination amounts to 1.79 gm per hectare, the figure is 300 gm per hectare in India.

The direct consequences of stubborn persistence of pesticides on land or soil are :

(i) The green foliage of plant tissues that are enriched with nitrogen are attractive to insects. During the months of winter, when the intensity of solar energy is low, blight and similar crop diseases are common.

(ii) Pesticides hamper the organic matter synthesis in the soil by hindering the microbial activities. This makes humus formation almost impossible and the soil becomes nutrient-deficient.

(iii) During the hours of daylight, pesticide residuals on soil/plant tissue or leaves undergo photo-chemical reaction. This causes photo-toxicity which retards healthy photosynthesis.

(iv) When animals consume the crops, vegetables, grasses, straw and fodders crops grown on contaminated soil, the toxic substances are accumulated in their body, fat and milk. Human beings consuming such contaminated crops, milk and meat are seriously affected, and suffer from asthma, gastroenteritis, short-sightedness, throat irritation etc.

Forest

We all know how important a component of the ecosystem the forest is. It provides a habitat to different types of plants, animals and microorganisms. Forests give us nutrient-rich soil having high organic matter content. Forests play a vital role in increasing precipitation, preventing soil erosion, reducing surface run off, as well as the frequency and dimension of floods, encouraging percolation of rain water, increasing recharge of ground water potentials, providing domestic fuelwood to numerous people, providing raw materials to various forest-based industries, and also offering food and shelter to innumerable animals. The task of assessing the direct and indirect importance of forest land use in a comprehensive manner is indeed an extremely difficult one. However, it is obvious that as a sole component of environmental system, the forest plays a crucial role in the stability of environment and ecosystem, as well as in the restoration of ecological balance.

At present, an increasing population and ever-increasing human needs and desires have resulted in massive deforestation. When forested land is converted into other land uses, particularly urban and industrial, it leaves a serious impact on the environment that proves harmful to human society.

The most common causes of deforestation are —

(i) conversion of forest covered land into agricultural land
(ii) practice of shifting cultivation in hilly terrains
(iii) conversion of forest land into pastures
(iv) overgrazing by animals
(v) lumbering for domestic and commercial interests
(vi) natural and man-induced forest fires
(vii) development of large scale multipurpose river valley project and also others
(viii) unscrupulous destruction by ambitious timber traders
(ix) illiteracy and lack of consciousness among the rural masses, etc.

Shifting cultivation has affected the forest cover in many states of India, especially in the North-East.

The following table shows the loss of forest cover in India (due to shifting cultivation) as also in West Bengal, where forest lands are diverted or likely to be diverted for non-foresty purposes.

Table : Annual Loss of Forest Cover by Shifting Cultivation in India

Province	Area affected due to shifting cultivation (sq km/year)	Population dependent on shifting cultivation ('000)
1. Orissa	5,298	706
2. Meghalaya	760	350
3. Nagaland	730	400
4. Arunachal Pradesh	703	270
5. Assam	700	403
6. Mizoram	600	260
7. Manipur	500	300
8. Andhra Pradesh	173	116
9. Tripura	170	100
10. Bihar	162	61
11. Madhya Pradesh	81	116
12. Kerala	19	16

Table : Extent of Forest Area Under Encroachment in West Bengal

District	Forest Area Encroached (ha)
1. Darjeeling	1,482.12
2. Jalpaiguri	1,059.23
3. Cooch Bihar	1,759.90
4. Malda	174.40
5. West Dinajpur	13.68

District	Forest Area Encroached (ha)
6. Nadia	20.27
7. Bankura	3,628.00
8. Midnapore	3,604.39
9. Burdwan	348.64
10. Hooghly	2.15
11. Purulia	5,657.50
12. Birbhum	157.56
13. 24-Parganas	0.08
Total	**17,907.56**

For the dangerous rate at which deforestation is carried out in various parts of our country, as well as globally, we should be prepared for drastic consequences. Deforestation causes severe environmental problems, such as :

(i) accelerated rate of soil erosion

(ii) increase in the sediment load of rivers

(iii) sialation of reservoirs and river beds

(iv) rise in the frequency and dimension of both floods and broughts

(v) changes in the pattern of distribution of precipitation

(vi) intensification of green house effect and rise in temperature

(vii) intensification of the devastating force of atmospheric storms.

Deforestation also causes economic losses, since

(i) floods and droughts damage agricultural crops

(ii) erosion of the fertile top soil hampers agricultural production

(iii) unscrupulous and random felling of trees decreases supply of raw materials to the industries and building materials to the urban and rural areas

(iv) loss of forest cover will cause a significant decrease in fodder to animals, and

(v) the various causes will cumulatively bring in poverty and there will be a rise in crimes and other social problems.

Grassland

Grassland used as rangeland or pasture form the largest share of the world's land area that is directly used for productive activities.

Grassland is a kind of land cover, while rangeland and pasture are kinds of land use. Both land-use practices primarily involve livestock grazing on the grass cover, that is sparse and unimproved in rangeland, while in pasture the grass cover is cultivated and often integrated with ordinary farming.

The following are the important grasslands of the world

(i) The Prairies of North America

(ii) The Pampas of South America

(iii) The Steppes of Russia

(iv) The Savanna of Africa

(v) The Veldts of South Africa

(vi) Downs of Australia.

Most rangelands are found in arid zone unsuited to farming, but some grassland lies in regions receiving high and medium rainfall.

In today's world, almost 68 million square km of the land surface is grassland. This also includes many lands that are too barren for any sort of grazing.

Livestock raising on rangelands follows one of the two patterns :

(a) **ranching**, which is **market-oriented** and practiced in a **fixed place**, and

(b) **pastoralism,** which is **subsistence-based** and **migratory** in nature.

In the nineteenth century, ranching spread across many of the world's grasslands — from North and South America to the interior of New Zealand, Australia and South Africa.

In comparison, pastoralism is still the dominant form of production over the largest class of the earth's directly exploited lands. Yet, it supports considerably less than 1% of the world's population. The practice of cropland expansion has cut down the area of range available for grazing, and, at the same time, the expansion of livestock herds has increased pressure on the vegetation cover of the area that remains.

The most severe forms of grassland degradation have been termed as **desertification,** which describes the loss of vegetation or agricultural productivity and the damage caused to soil, water and land cover in grasslands or in arid or semi-arid zones.

Even if desertification is not the case, overgrazing of rangeland and the cultivation of semi-arid regions can create, extend or further degrade non-productive landscapes because of the following circumstances :

(i) When the grass cover has been overgrazed or impoverished,

(ii) When the soil has been salinized by irrigation or loosened by ploughing,

(iii) When the land is degraded and societies dependent on the land are devastated due to a rise in subsistence needs of high human and livestock population and the addition of pressures for production of a commercial economy.

Wetlands

The term "Wetlands" refers to land that is covered throughout or part of the year with water, but not so deeply or permanently as to be classed as water surface.

Wetlands include a variety of sub-types, such as swamps, marshes, bogs and peatlands, river margins and so on. They overlap with many common land-cover classes, such as cropland, grassland and forests. For instance, a paddy field can be said to be a cultivated wetland. Wetlands are found in both salt and fresh-water environments.

The conversion of wetland to dryland through drainage or filling is the most drastic form of wetland alteration. Almost 200,000 square km have been altered by drainage in Europe and Russia, and up to half a million sq. km in the USA. Australia has lost all of the original 20,000 square km of wetland.

At present, 8.5 million square km of the present world area is under wetlands. The area lost to drainage — mainly for agriculture — is almost 1.5 million square km.

Settlement

According to some eminent Russian soil scientists, non-agricultural land uses occupy about 6% of the world's total land area. They include settlement, industry, transportation and communication routes, reservoirs etc, among which human settlement is the most significant. While agricultural frontiers are gradually fading in importance, urban land-use practices are growing everywhere. Every urban-rural fringe zone is a miniature example of drastic land use/cover change, where cropland that once displaced forest, wetland or grazing is now displaced by settlement.

In the Third World, rapid urbanization coupled with rural-to-urban migration have created huge and exploding cities, often overtaxing the built infrastructure and the resource base. In this context, let us take the example of Mexico City, which happens to be today's epitome of uncontrolled Third World megacity growth. From 1950 to the late 1980s, the metropolitan area of Mexico City grew almost by six times. In the early twentieth century, the city's population density reached its peak, at around 20,000 people per square km. Today, in spite of a population that is twenty times higher and settled area vastly greater, Mexico City's overall density has come down to less than 15,000 people per square km.

Urban land cover has some distinctive features that bring about both local and regional alterations in the environment, thus affecting the climate, water flows, plant and animal diversity and creating new human hazards of health and safety.

The degree to which the land cover has been transformed varies from one city to another, and also between various areas within a city. Built-up area and paved land represents a relatively small part of most cities land area.

The environmental problems of a city may be exported to its hinterland also. It occurs physically through pollution of air and water and resource extraction. The most obvious impact is the consumption of land. In the outskirts of cities in developing countries, transformation of land to urban cover is proceeding most rapidly and with the severest consequences. The impacts of urbanization spread in exurban waves far beyond the area actually converted to settlement. Fuel, water, timber are extracted from zones surrounding cities to fulfil their needs, and urban wastes — air pollutants, landfills, waste water — are sent out in return.

However, urbanization may also have positive environmental impacts, since rural-to-urban migration can relieve pressure or rural land-cover.

Conclusion

From the dawn of civilization till the present day, land surface has been greatly altered by humankind. Much modern change in the most densely populated lands occurs not from a largely natural state to a human-shaped one, but from one human-shaped state to another. Today, much urban construction is actually redevelopment, especially in the developed world. For example, forest that is removed now is not being cut for the first time. The intensification of land use has taken the shape of a world-wide drive for an increase in production, keeping pace with the exploding population, growing markets and competition from several producers. Land alteration is an objective fact, while land degradation exists in the eyes of the beholder.

From where do we get water ?

There are only a limited number of ways to get significant amounts of offstream fresh water. They can be listed as —

(a) direct capture of precipitation

(b) desalination of saline water, mostly sea water

(c) recycling of used water (this includes a water that is put back into the water system but does not include treated waste water that is returned into streams and the ground)

(d) diversion of water in lakes, streams and rivers, called offstream surface water

(e) extraction of ground water, commonly obtained by drilling of wells and pumping, and also by diversion of ground-water fed springs.

We shall discuss the first three methods :

(i) Desalination and direct capture of precipitation can be said to be insignificant for somewhat different reasons.

Desalination is a very expensive process. It is used only where there are no other options.

Capturing precipitation is cheap. However, it is only done on a small scale and hardly provides a sufficiently steady supply of water. Hence people cannot depend on it as their sole source of water.

(ii) In most developed nations, reclaimed water is the fastest growing source of water. In the United States, between 1980 and 1990, offstream and ground water use declined, while use of reclaimed water increased by 50%. Yet, reclaimed water still only accounts for 0.02% of water use. If its current growth rate continues, the use of reclaimed water would not account for even 1% of total U.S. water consumption for almost 100 years.

(iii) Large-scale extraction of groundwater generally involve the use of more money, energy and technology than what people have. Therefore, people are more dependent on surface water even though it is a very imperfectly distributed source.

Demand for Water

We all know that water is extremely essential to all of us — from cooking our meals to various industrial uses, water is something without which life becomes impossible. The different uses/demand of water can be classified in the following categories :

(i) domestic demand
(ii) industrial demand
(iii) institutional demand
(iv) fire fighting demand
(v) unaccounted use of water.

We will analyse each demand in order to get an accurate picture of requirement of water.

(i) **Domestic Water Need —**

Under this category is included the various domestic needs, such as cooking, washing, drinking, cleaning, flushing toilets etc. The consumption of water in any city depends on its population.

The minimum rate of domestic consumption of water should be 70 to 100 liter per capita per day (lpcd). How this water can be used per head for a town-resident is shown below, but this is totally based on assumption :

(a) drinking	2 liters
(b) cooking, washing, cleaning	10 to 12 liters
(c) bathing, washing cloths	40 to 60 liters
(d) flushing toilets	25 liters
(e) other requirements	10 liters
Total	70 to 100 liters (approx.)

The rate of domestic water demand in a city is closely associated with the size, economic condition as well as non-domestic needs of the city. In rural communities houses do not have water connections, and supply is through hand pumps, wells, tanks etc. Here the water demand should be around 40 lpcd. But in the few houses with connections, the rate shall be 70 lpcd, to make the scheme self paying.

(ii) **Industrial Water Need —**

The industrial demand for water in a town depends on the number, nature and size of industries. The table below gives the rates of water demand in various industries.

TABLE : DEMAND FOR WATER IN INDUSTRIES

Type of Industry	Units of Production	Need for Water (liters/day)
Automobiles	Vehicle	40.000
Fertilizer	Tonne	80,000-2,000,000
Paper	kg	200-400
Leather	kg (tanned)	40
Steel	Tonne	200,000-250,000
Petroleum Refinery	Tonne (crude)	1,500-2,000
Textile	kg	80-140
Sugar	Tonne	1,000-2,000
Thermal Power	Mega Watt	150,000-160,000
Coke	Tonne	14,000
Wood Pulp	Tonne	240,000
Ice	Tonne	1,850

(iii) **Institutional Water Need —**

Under this category comes the quantity of water needed by various public buildings and institutions. Therefore, since the water is used for public utility purposes, it is sometime known as public demand. The following table shows the different water utility rates :

Table : Institutional Demand for Water

Institution	Need for Water (lpcd)
Hospital with laundry	
(a) less than 100 beds	340
(b) more than 100 beds	455
Hostels and Boarding Houses	135
Restaurant	70 (per seat)
Hotel	180 (per bed)
Stations (railway junctions)	70
Day school/college	45
Factories	45
Offices	45
Cinema/Theatres	15

Watering of parks and gardens, cleaning streets, roadside fountains and other beautification measures, maintaining public swimming pools and other entertainment centers etc. come under this kind of demand.

(iv) **Fire-Fighting Need —**

Water is stored for fighting sudden fire-outbreaks. The tanks are filled from nearby water bodies by water tankers wherever possible and then used when needed.

High-rise buildings (above 25 m height) must be provided with their own water storage, other than the water used for domestic purposes.

(v) **Unaccounted Use of Water —**

A huge quantity of water is lost due to thefts, negligence, ignorance etc. Some loss also occurs due to technical problems, such as leakages at the joints and valves. Proper vigilance, inspection and timely maintenance can reduce unaccounted loss of water to a large extent.

Agriculture, Land Use and Water

Agriculture represents a long-standing and probably the world's most important source of impact on water resources.

Where rainfall and soil-moisture are inadequate, water is withdrawn from surface or aquifer for the purpose of irrigating crops. The water flowing back from cultivated fields may be polluted with sediments, fertilizers, salt, pesticides. Changes in land cover by deforestation and ploughing also affect the rate and volume of surface flows.

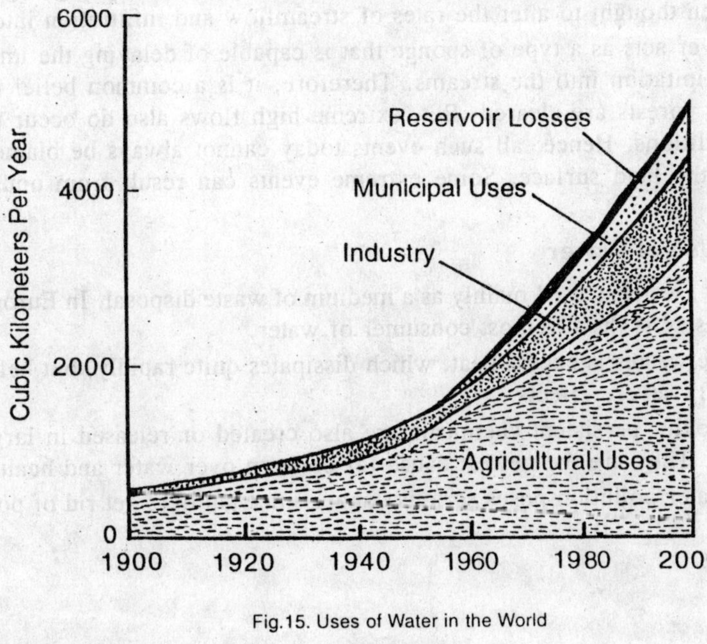

Fig.15. Uses of Water in the World

Impact of Irrigation

Every year, most of the water tapped from the global hydrological cycle (almost three-fourth) is used for irrigation. In the late seventeenth century, the figure was almost 100 cubic km. It has risen 25-fold in three centuries, and today it is nearing 2,700 cubic km. This rise has occurred during the period when the global population has grown only about seven-fold, and artificially watered farmland over the world has increased 50-fold, from about 50,000 square km to almost 2.5 million square km.

Compared to other uses of water, irrigation is truly extremely consumptive. Since large volumes are lost to evapotranspiration and seepage, little water after use returns to the system of flow. Currently, 85% of the water withdrawn for irrigation is actually consumed. This figure, however, depends on the natural setting of the basin and the crops and technologies involved.

The importance of irrigation in the water budget is spatially quite uneven. Asia represents almost 90% of the total water demand. Irrigation is not as important in other continents. In North America and Europe, industry and power generation withdraw most of the water.

The world land area under irrigation grew at a steady but slow pace during the 18th and 19th centuries. The rate of growth never exceeded 2% per year. The foremost agents in nineteenth century expansion of irrigation were the British colonial engineers in the Nile Valley and in India. Irrigation in Egypt facilitated the large-scale growing of cotton for the world market.

In India, work began with the restoration of decayed irrigation works from the Mughal period (1526-1857) and proceeded to new construction. By 1947, independent India had 60 million acres under irrigation. Despite rising problems of salinization, expansion and intensification have continued.

Land Use and Stream Flow

Running water shapes the landscape, and at the same time water is affected by the character of the land surface over which it flows. Deforestation and ploughing of grasslands have often been thought to alter the rates of streamflow and infiltration into the soil.

Forest cover acts as a type of sponge that is capable of delaying the immediate run-off of all precipitation into the streams. Therefore, it is a common belief that flooding increases after forests are cleared. But, extreme high flows also do occur under purely "natural" conditions. Hence, all such events today cannot always be blamed on human disruption of the land surface. Some extreme events can result from unusual weather conditions.

Industrial Use of Water

In industry, water is used mainly as a medium of waste disposal. In Europe and North America, industry is the foremost consumer of water.

Among the wastes is excess heat, which dissipates quite rapidly, but before doing so can have locally severe effects.

Possibly toxic, persistent chemicals are also created or released in large quantities into the water. They are the newest cause for concern over water and health.

Ground water pollution poses serious danger since aquifers get rid of pollutants very slowly.

QUESTIONS FOR EXAMINATION

A. Essay-Type Questions

1. Discuss the different types of land cover in the world.
   Ans. Pp. 88-89
2. Describe the agricultural land use in the world.
   Ans. Pp. 89-92
3. Give an account of the principal grasslands in the world.
   Ans. Pp. 92-93
4. Explain the human habitation or settlement and land use pattern in the world.
   Ans. Pp. 93-94
5. Describe the different sources of water and its uses.
   Ans. Pp. 94-96
6. How many types of water uses are there in the human society ?
   Ans. Pp. 95-97
7. What are the importance of water in agriculture ?
   Ans. Pp. 97-98

B. Short Answer-Type Questions

1. How many types of land use are there ?
   Ans. Page 88
2. What is wetland ?
   Ans. Page 93
3. Where do we get water ?
   Ans. Page 94
4. What are the principal sources of water ?
   Ans. Page 94
5. What are the principal demands of water ?
   Ans. Page 95
6. How much domestic water is needed in an urban area ?
   Ans. Page 95
7. How much domestic water is needed in a rural area ?
   Ans. Page 95
8. How many types of water uses are there in agriculture ?
   Ans. Page 97
9. How many categories of water uses are there in industries ?
   Ans. Page 98
10. What is land use and stream flow ?
    Ans. Page 98

Chapter 6

AIR POLLUTION

INTRODUCTION

Breathing is indispensable for the survival of all living beings. A normal human being breaths, on an average, 15 times per minute, 22,000 times a day. In doing so, he takes in 16 kilograms of air which he gets from the atmosphere rich in oxygen. Terrestrial animals, too, depend on air for survival. Not only terrestrial animals, fish and other organisms living under water breathe in oxygen dissolved in water. Thus air rich in oxygen is essential for human and animal life on earth.

On the other hand, plants depend on CO_2 which is obtained from the air, for photosynthesis. We all know that green plants having chlorophyll make use of sunlight, water and CO_2 in order to manufacture food for themselves. Through this process, O_2 is released, which, in turn, is used by humans and animals. From here it is evident how important air is for all types of life in the biosphere.

Air is a chemical mixture of a number of gases, mainly, Nitrogen (78.09%), Oxygen (20.95%), Carbon dioxide (0.03%), other trace gases, such as hydrogen, helium, neon, krypton, xenon and ozone, are also present.

The presence of these gases in the atmosphere in correct proportions is what is needed for the functioning of life in the biosphere. Therefore, air is the most important resource.

Composition of Air

The principal constituents of the atmosphere are Oxygen (O_2) and Nitrogen (N_2). Besides these two constituents, certain other gases are also present in traces in the atmosphere.

The regions of the atmosphere above the seas and mountains are purer, and the air here may contain 21.99% of O_2. On the other hand, the oxygen content in air in an overcrowded hall may be as low as 20.65%.

Carbon dioxide (CO_2) is obtained by various method, such as combustion, fermentation, putrefaction and respiratory processes of animals. A rise in CO_2 content by 1.5% will produce nausea, headache and depression. If the figure becomes 2.5%, it will extinguish the candle, and when it becomes 5% by volume, it will result in fatal accidents.

Definition of Atmospheric Pollution

Scientists all over the world differ in their views regarding the various sources of atmospheric pollution. According to some, pollution means the increase (or even decrease), of any atmospheric constituent, from the value that whould have existed had there not been any human activity.

The constitution of the earth's atmosphere has undergone profound changes throughout its lifetime. Forest fires, volcanic eruptions and sand storms result in striking local and regional variations in atmospheric constituent values.

Weber (1982) has defined atmospheric pollution as : "The presence of substances in the ambient atmosphere, resulting from the activity of man or from natural processes, causing adverse effects to man and the environment."

Therefore, air pollution may be defined as : "the presence of substances or energy in the atmosphere, in such quantities and of such duration that they may harm human, plant or animal life, or damage man-made structures and materials, or changes in the weather and climate, or interfere with the normal enjoyment of life or property or other human activities."

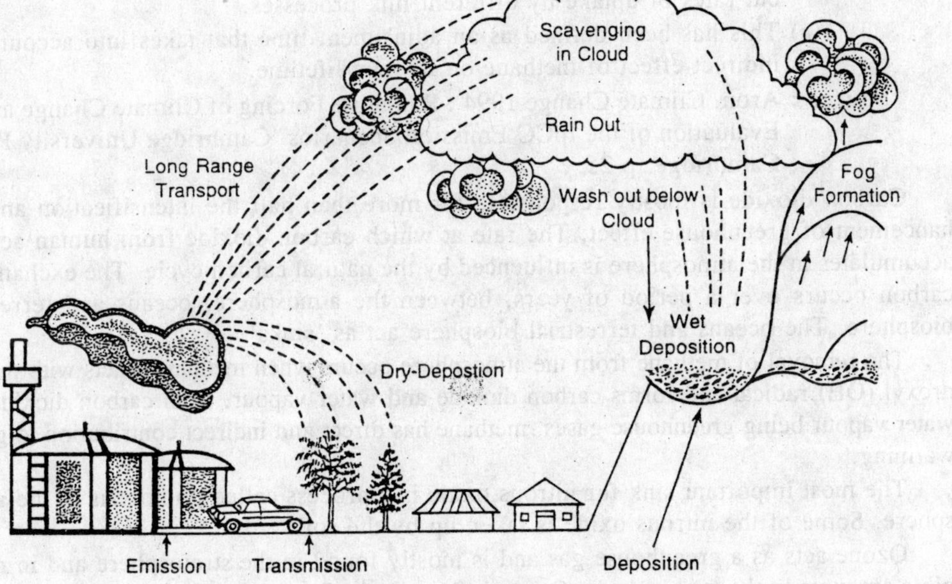

Fig.16. Air Pollution

Greenhouse Gases — Gases which cause Global Warming

At present, the gases that are known to cause the greenhouse effect are carbon dioxide (CO_2), methane (CH_4), nitrous oxide (N_2O), chlorofluorocarbons (CFCs), and two CFC substitutes — hydro-chlorofluorocarbon (HCFC-22), and perfluoromathane (CF_4).

Table : Summary of Key Greenhouse Gases Affected by Human Activities

	CO_2	CH_4	N_2O	CFC-12	HCFC-22	CF_4
Pre-industrial concentration	280 ppmv[(a)]	700 ppbv[(b)]	275 ppbv	zero	zero	zero
Concentration in 1992	355 ppmv	1,714 ppbv	311 ppbv	503 pptv[(c)]	105 pptv	70 pptv
Recent rate of Cocentration	1.5 ppmv/yr	13 ppbv/yr	0.75 ppbv/yr	18-20 pptv/yr	7-8 pptv/yr	1.1-1.3 pptv/yr
Change per year (during 1980s)	0.4%/yr	0.8%/yr	0.25%/yr	4%/yr	7%/yr	2%/yr

	CO_2	CH_4	N_2O	CFC-12	HCFC-22	CF_4
Atmospheric lifetime (in years)	50-200[d]	12-17[e]	120	102	13.3	50,000

Note : (a) parts per million by volume
(b) parts per billion by volume
(c) parts per trillion by volume
(d) No single lifetime for carbon dioxide can be defined because of the different rates of uptake by different link processes.
(e) This has been defined as an adjustment time that takes into account the indirect effect of methane on its own lifetime.

Source : Aron, Climate Change 1994 : Radiative Forcing of Climate Change and an Evaluation of the IpCC Emission Scenarios, Cambridge University Press, Cambridge, p 25.

Carbon dioxide is mostly responsible for more than half the intensification and enhancement of greenhouse effect. The rate at which carbon dioxide from human activity accumulates in the atmosphere is influenced by the natural carbon cycle. The exchange of carbon occurs over a period of years, between the atmosphere, oceans and terrestrial biosphere. The oceans and terrestrial biosphere act as 'sinks'.

The removal of methane from the atmosphere occurs when methane reacts with the hydroxyl (OH) radical and forms carbon dioxide and water vapour. Both carbon dioxide and water vapour being greenhouse gases, methane has direct and indirect contribution to global warming.

The most important sink for nitrous oxide is a process called photolysis in the atmosphere. Some of the nitrous oxide is taken up by the soil.

Ozone acts as a greenhouse gas and is mostly found in the stratosphere and in negligible amounts in the troposphere. Ozone influences both solar and infrared radiation. The contribution of ozone to greenhouse effect cannot be easily assessed since its concentration varies regionally and vertically, and it also has a short life span in the atmosphere.

Greenhouse Gases and their Main Anthropogenic Sources

Carbon dioxide (CO_2)	Fossil-fuel burning Wood fuel Deforestation and land-use change Cement manufacture
Methane (CH_4)	Releases from gas, oil or coal production or transmission Enteric fermentation from ruminants (eg. cattle, sheep, goats) Wetland rice cultivation Landfill waste sites Burning and decay of biomass
Chlorofluorocarbons (CFCs)	Used for solvents, refrigerants, aerosol spray propellants, foam packaging etc.
Nitrous oxide (N_2O)	Fertilizers Fossil-fuel burning Tropical deforestation and wildfires Land conversion for agriculture

ALSO, GASES INVOLVED IN GENERATION OF LOW-LEVEL OZONE	
Nitrogen oxides	Fossil-fuel burning Bio-mass burning
Carbon monoxide	Fossil-fuel burning Bio-mass burning
Non-methane hydrocarbons	Evaporation of solvents and liquid fuels

Greenhouse Effect

Currently, the Greenhouse Effect is probably one of the most popular global environmental issues. In 1896, the Swedish scientist Svante Arrhenius first said that industrial activities associated with carbon dioxide emission might lead to a rise in average global temperature. However, it was as late as 1979 when government representatives and scientists discussed the perilous aftermath of such a climatic change, at the First World Climate Conference.

What is Greenhouse ?

Let us first discuss how a greenhouse works. A greenhouse is actually made of glass and is meant for plants. In cold countries, the total insulation received, especially during winter, is not enough to encourage plant growth. The glasses of the greenhouse work in such a way that visible sunlight can come in, but long-wave infrared rays cannot go out. Thus the resulting heat is trapped inside.

The glass in the greenhouse allows the temperature to be maintained, because it prevents the warm air inside from mixing with the cold air outside.

Therefore, a greenhouse allows the incoming shortwave solar radiation to come in but the outgoing long-wave terrestrial infrared radiation is not allowed to escape.

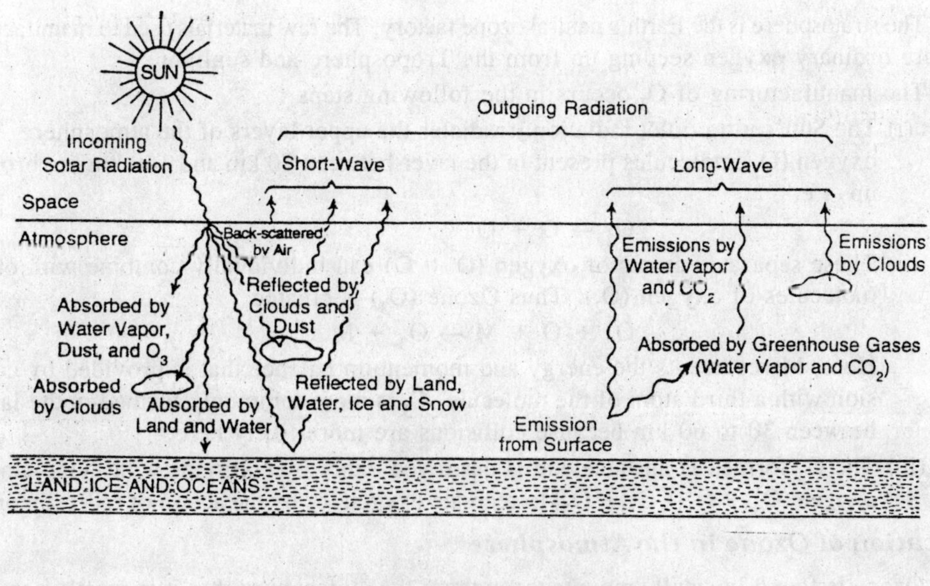

Fig.17. The Greenhouse Effect in the Earth's Atmosphere

What is the Greenhouse Effect ?

According to the Oxford Dictionary, the Greenhouse Effect means "progressive warming up of the earth's surface due to the blanketing effect of man-made carbon dioxide in the atmosphere".

The atmosphere surrounding the earth can be selective in its response to different kinds of radiation.

The short-wave solar radiation from the ultraviolet end of the energy spectrum passes through the atmosphere, unaltered, and heats the earth's surface.

The energy that the earth has absorbed is reradiated into the atmosphere. However, this time the terrestrial radiation is long-wave infrared. Instead of being transmitted, this is absorbed. As a result, the temperature of the atmosphere rises. A part of the energy absorbed by the atmosphere is given back to the earth's surface, resulting in a rise in its temperature.

Without the greenhouse effect, global temperatures would be much lower than what they are at present. The existing average of +15°C would be as low as –17°C.

The behaviour of the atmosphere as a Greenhouse is made possible by a group of gases, which make up even less than 1% of the total volume of the atmosphere.

There are almost 20 of these Greenhouse gases. Carbon dioxide is the most common and abundant greenhouse gas. Besides, methane, nitrous oxide and the chlorofluorocarbons are also important; water vapour also shows greenhouse characteristics.

Any change in the volume of these greenhouse gases will alter the flow of energy in the earth-atmosphere system. The effect will be felt in the changing global temperature pattern.

What is Ozone ?

Ozone is an unstable, allotropic triatomic form of oxygen. It is pale blue in colour and has a pungent odour. It is a powerful oxidising agent, formed by silent electrical discharge in oxygen or naturally by action of ultraviolet light. The chemical symbol of Ozone is O_3.

The Formation of Ozone (O_3) in the Atmosphere

The stratosphere is the Earth's natural ozone factory. The raw materials used to manufacture O_3 are ordinary oxygen seeping up from the Troposphere and sunlight.

The manufacturing of O_3 occurs in the following steps :

(i) The Sun's ultraviolet radiation irradiates the upper layers of the atmosphere. The oxygen (O_2) molecules present in the layer between 80 km and 100 km are broken up, i.e.

$$O_2 \rightarrow O + O.$$

(ii) These separated atoms of oxygen (O + O) can individually combine with other molecules of oxygen (O_2). Thus Ozone (O_3) is created

$$O_2 + O + M \rightarrow O_3 + M.$$

Here, M represents the energy and momentum balance that is provided by collision with a third atom of the molecule. O_3 is most commonly formed in the layer between 30 to 60 km because collisions are more likely here.

(iii) The O_3 formed is unstable and is destroyed either by collisions with mono-atomic oxygen ($O_3 + O \rightarrow O_2 + O_2$) to recreate oxygen, or by the action of radiation on it.

Location of Ozone in the Atmosphere

Ozone is found in small amounts throughout the atmosphere, but it is mostly concen-

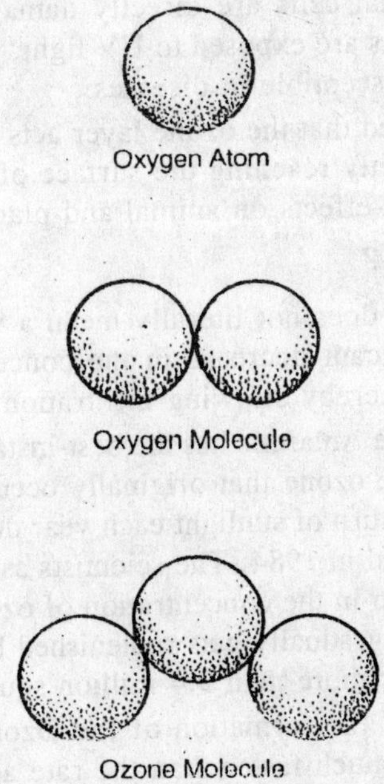

Fig.18. Atom in a Molecule

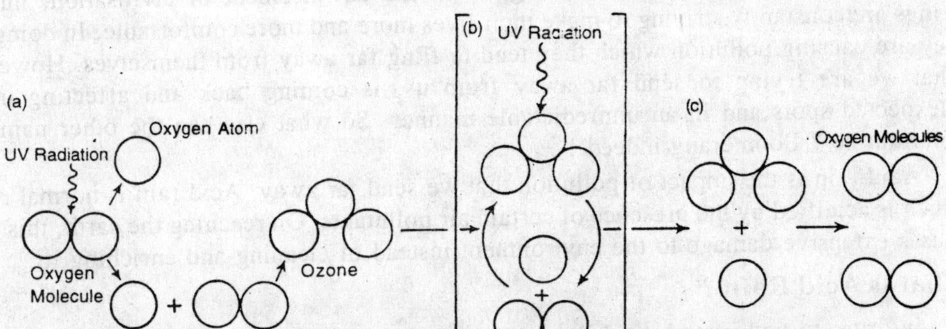

Fig.19. (a) Ozone is created when UV radiation breaks-up an oxygen molecule with other oxygen molecules. (b) The ozone so formed is repeatedly broken-up and reformed, until (c) it is destroyed by collision with an oxygen atom

trated in the Troposphere and Stratosphere, between 15-35 km 90% of the total ozone is found in the Stratosphere, due to which this is called the Ozone Layer.

Although ozone is formed at higher levels in the atmosphere, upper air atmospheric circulations transport it to heights as low as 12 km.

Importance of the Ozone Layer

Most of the harmful ultraviolet rays of the sun are absorbed by the ozone present in the atmosphere. The ozone layer thus prevents the ultraviolet rays from reaching the earth's surface.

The depletion of the ozone layer has detrimental effects on human beings. The UV rays affect eyes and skin, causing sun-burns, skin-cancer, cataract and so on. The DNA or genetic material of animal cells are directly damaged by the UV rays. It has been observed that when mammals are exposed to UV light, the rays act on the immune system and make the body more susceptible to diseases.

Thus, it can be concluded that the ozone layer acts as a "sunscreen" that prevents the harmful UV rays from directly reaching the surface of the earth. This helps in reducing the risks of mutation and ill-effects on animal and plant life.

What is the Ozone Hole ?

The term 'Ozone Hole' does not literally mean a void in the earth's atmosphere. It actually refers to the significant decrease in the concentration of ozone in a particular region of the atmosphere, thereby allowing infiltration of the harmful ultraviolet rays.

The ozonosphere over the Antarctic has the best-instance of an Ozone Hole. At present, it has only about 50% of the ozone that originally occurred there. The Ozone Hole over Antarctica occurs with the return of sunlight each year during spring in the southern Hemisphere. This was first detected in 1984. The scientists associated with the British Antarctic Survey observed that the drop in the concentration of ozone in the stratosphere above Antarctica begins in August and gradually gets replenished by the end of November. In 1993, the ozone hole extended over more than 9.4 million square miles (24 million sq. kms).

The main reason behind the formation of the Ozone Hole is that the rate at which ozone is being destroyed is much faster than the rate at which it is formed.

ACID RAIN

Pollution is just like a boomerang. With the advancement of civilisation, human beings are constantly striving to make their lives more and more comfortable. In doing so, they are causing pollution which they tend to fling far away from themselves. However, what we are trying to send far away from us, is coming back and affecting us at unexpected spots and in an unpredictable manner. So what else can the other name of pollution be ? Boomerang indeed !

Acid rain is the impact of pollution that we send far away. Acid rain is normal rain, which is acidified by the presence of certain air pollutants. On reaching the earth, this rain causes extensive damage to the environment instead of cleaning and enriching it.

What is Acid Rain ?

In order to understand Acid Rain, we have to understand how the acidic strength of any medium is judged. This is done by pH of the medium, pH being the negative logarithm of the hydrogen ion activity of the medium.

(a) When the pH > 7 the medium is alkaline (basic).

(b) When pH < 7, the medium is acidic.

(c) When the pH $= 7$, the medium is neutral.

The lower the pH, the stronger is the acidity. Therefore, a medium, where pH $= 1$, is strongly acidic, while if the pH $= 6$, the medium is mildly acidic.

The formation of rain is an integral part of the hydrological cycle. When the water vapour in the clouds condenses, rain droplets are formed. As the droplets travel to earth through the air, they dissolve floating chemicals and other particles that are suspended in air. When the air is clean and unpolluted, the rain can dissolve only natural substances such as pollen, dust and some CO_2, as well as some chemicals produced by lightning and volcanic eruptions. These substances make the rain slightly acidic, where the pH is of about 6. This level of acidity is not detrimental. When the pH of rain is less than 5.6, it is said to be Acid Rain.

Chemistry of Acid Rain

Six basic steps are involved in the formation of acid rain :

(1) The atmosphere receives oxides of sulphur and nitrogen from natural and man-made sources.

(2) Some of these oxides fall back directly to the ground as **dry deposition**, either close to the place of origin or some distance away.

(3) Sunlight stimulates the formation of photo-oxidants (such as ozone) in the atmosphere.

(4) These photo-oxidants interact with the oxides of sulphur and nitrogen to produce H_2SO_4 and HNO_3 by oxidation.

(5) The oxides of sulphur and nitrogen, photo-oxidants, and other gases (like NH_3)

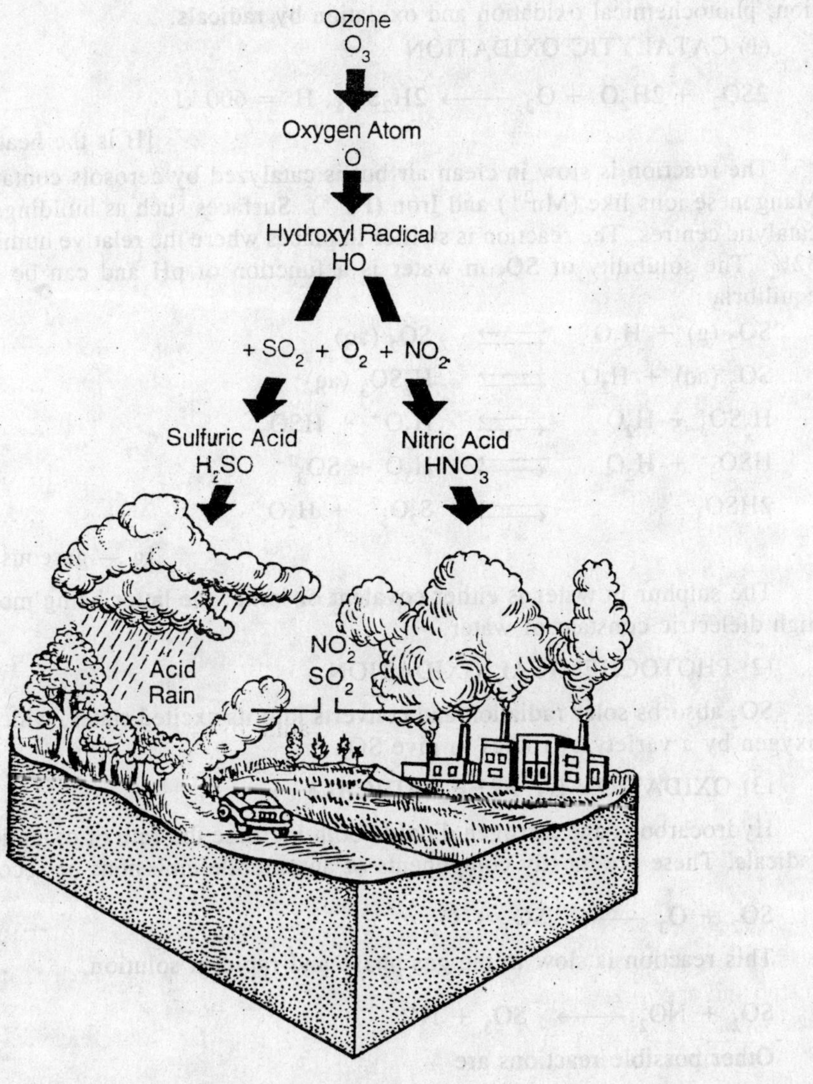

Fig. 20. Acid Rain

dissolves in the droplets of clouds and rain to produce acidic cations (hydrogen ions, H^+ and ammonium ions, NH_4^+), sulphates (SO_4^{2-}) and nitrates (NO_3^-).

(6) Acid rain containing ions of sulphate, nitrate, ammonium and hydrogen falls as **wet deposition.**

Chemical Reactions involved in Acid Rain

Oxidation of Sulphur Dioxide

In the atmosphere, sulphur dioxide gets oxidized to sulphur trioxide which reacts with water or alkalies to give sulphuric acid or sulphates. The acid or sulphates, in particular ammonium sulphate and bisulphate, occur as aerosol.

The process is illustrated by the following equation :

$$SO_2 \xrightarrow{(O)} SO_3 \xrightarrow{H_2O \quad NH_4OH} H_2SO_4/(NH_4)_2SO_4 \quad NH_4HSO_4 \quad \ldots\ldots\ldots \quad (1)$$

The oxidation step proceeds in one or more of three ways, namely, catalytic oxidation, photochemical oxidation and oxidation by radicals.

(1) CATALYTIC OXIDATION

$$2SO_2 + 2H_2O + O_2 \longrightarrow 2H_2SO_4, H = 600 \text{ kJ} \quad \ldots\ldots\ldots \quad (2)$$

[H is the heat of the reaction]

The reaction is slow in clean air but is catalyzed by aerosols containing metal — of Manganese ions like (Mn^{2+}) and Iron (Fe^{3+}). Surfaces such as buildings may also act as catalytic centres. The reaction is swifter in places where the relative humidity is more than 32%. The solubility of SO_2 in water is a function of pH and can be described by the equilibria :

$$SO_2\,(g) + H_2O \rightleftharpoons SO_2\,(aq) \quad \ldots\ldots\ldots\ldots\ldots \quad (3)$$

$$SO_2\,(aq) + H_2O \rightleftharpoons H_2SO_3\,(aq) \quad \ldots\ldots\ldots\ldots\ldots \quad (4)$$

$$H_2SO_3 + H_2O \rightleftharpoons H_3O^+ + HSO_3^- \quad \ldots\ldots\ldots\ldots\ldots \quad (5)$$

$$HSO_3^- + H_2O \rightleftharpoons H_3O + SO_3^{2-} \quad \ldots\ldots\ldots\ldots\ldots \quad (6)$$

$$2HSO_3^- \rightleftharpoons S_2O_5^{2-} + H_2O \quad \ldots\ldots\ldots\ldots\ldots \quad (7)$$

[g — gaseous, aq — aqueous]

The sulphur in water is either covalent or ionic, the latter being more soluble due to high dielectric constant of water.

(2) PHOTOCHEMICAL OXIDATION

SO_2 absorbs solar radiation and converts into its excited states, which then react with oxygen by a variety of routes to give SO_3.

(3) OXIDATION BY FREE RADICALS

Hydrocarbons and nitrogen dioxide both increase the rate of oxidation of SO_2 to free radicals. These are mostly components of automobile emissions or secondary products :

$$SO_2 + O_3 \longrightarrow SO_3 + O_2 \quad \ldots\ldots\ldots\ldots\ldots \quad (8)$$

This reaction is slow in the gas phase and rapid in solution.

$$SO_2 + NO_2 \longrightarrow SO_3 + NO \quad \ldots\ldots\ldots\ldots\ldots \quad (9)$$

Other possible reactions are

$$SO_2 + HO_2 \longrightarrow SO_3 + HO \quad \ldots\ldots\ldots\ldots\ldots \quad (10)$$

$$SO_2 + RO_2 \longrightarrow SO_3 + RO \text{ [R indicates } CH_3C = 0] \quad \ldots\ldots\ldots\ldots\ (11)$$

$$HO + SO_2 \longrightarrow HOSO_2 \quad \ldots\ldots\ldots\ldots\ (12)$$

$$HOSO_2 + O_2 \longrightarrow HOSO_2O_2 \quad \ldots\ldots\ldots\ldots\ (13)$$

$$HOSO_2O_2 + NO \longrightarrow HOSO_3 + NO_2 \quad \ldots\ldots\ldots\ldots\ (14)$$

$$\downarrow\uparrow$$

$$H_2SO_4$$

The dissolution of SO_3 in water gives sulphuric acid which can reduce the pH of the rain to as low as 2 !

Rise of Sea Level

The global warming expected by the middle of this century may cause the polar ice-caps to melt substantially, and increase the water-level in the oceans.

There are two main reasons for rising oceans :

(i) the thermal expansion of water as the world warms.

(ii) the melting of the ice above sea level in mountain glaciers and at the poles.

A 1990 estimate is that over the last 100 years the global sea level has risen by about 1 mm. to 2.5 mm. a year, i.e. 10 cm. to 25 cm. in total. The possible or prediction of the sea level rise is given in the diagram (Since 1990 to 2100).

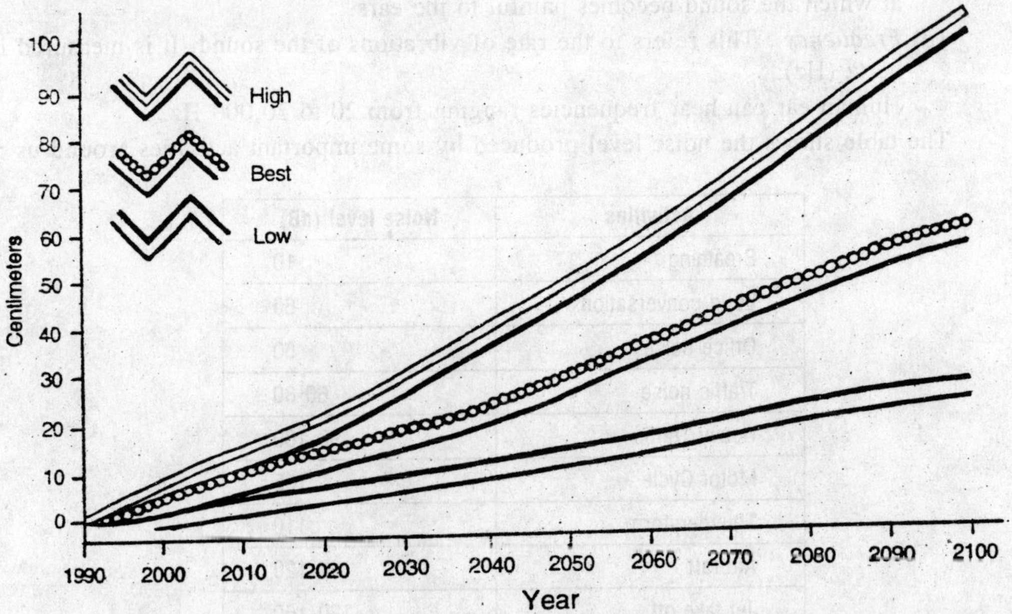

Fig. 21. The Rise of Sea Level (prediction if no action is taken)

Noise Pollution

A musical programme on the radio at full volume may give pleasure to the listener, but it can be extremely annoying to an ailing person in the neighbourhood. Similarly, the screeching of a car at the dead of night can disturb the sleep of many people in the locality.

Noise pollution is a common phenomenon in cities, offices, institutions and even houses. It is proportionately related to the developmental activities that are indispensable for industrialization, urbanization, transport and communication.

Definition of Noise Pollution

J. Tiffen, an industrial psychologist, has defined it as —

"Noise is a sound which is disagreeable for the individual and which disturbs the normal way of an individual."

According to the Encyclopedia Americana : "Noise by definition is unwanted sound. What is pleasant to some ears may be extremely unpleasant to others depending on a number of psychological factor. The sweetest music, if it disturb a person, who is trying to concentrate or to sleep, is a noise to him, just as the sound of a pneumatic riveting hammer is noise to nearly everyone. In other words any sound may be noise if circumstances cause it to be disturbing."

We can conclude by saying that any sound which is disagreeable to the individual and which hampers the normal way of the individual is noise.

Properties of Noise

There are two properties of noise —

(i) *Intensity of Noise :* This depends upon the amplitude of vibrations which initiate the noise. The unit of measuring the intensity of sound is "decibel", abbreviated as dB. 60 dB is considered as a normal conversation intensity. 140 dB is the level at which the sound becomes painful to the ears.

(ii) *Frequency :* This refers to the rate of vibrations of the sound. It is measured in hertz (Hz).

Human ear can hear frequencies ranging from 20 to 20,000 Hz.

The table shows the noise level produced by some important activities around us :

Activities	Noise level (dB)
Breathing	10
Loud conversation	60
Office noise	60
Traffic noise	60-80
Heavy Traffic	90-100
Motor Cycle	105
Thunderstorm	110
Aircraft	90-120
Jet take off	120-160
Classroom	30-40
Ordinary Conversation	30-60

The *National Pollution Control Board* has permitted the following as maximum permissible noise level in Indian cities :

CATEGORY	LEVEL OF NOISE (dB)	
	DAY	NIGHT
Residential Area	55	45
Commercial Area	65	55
Industrial Area	75	70
Silent Zone	50	40

Sources of Noise Pollution

There are numerous sources of noise pollution. The two broad categories of the sources are — (A) Industrial sources of Pollution, and (B) Non-Industrial sources of Pollution.

The various sources of noise pollution that fall under these broad categories have been discussed below :

(i) *Industries :* Noise is caused due to manufacturing processes in industries. The most offending noises come from industries such as grinding mills, looms, printing presses, compressors, furnaces, generators, looms etc.

(ii) *Loudspeakers :* In India, loudspeakers are used in public meetings, social occasions as well as in religious ceremonies.

(iii) *Construction :* To keep pace with development, many construction activities are being taken up for building houses, roads, dams etc. Maximum noise is produced during demolition of old buildings, in using grenade for repairing roads etc.

(iv) *Road Transport :* In recent years, road transport vehicles have increased manifold. The main reason behind vehicular sound pollution is blowing of horns and use of defective silencer pipes.

(v) *Rail Transport :* Where railway tracks pass through residential areas, sound pollution is the maximum. Steam engines produce a lot of noise also.

(vi) *Air Transport :* The higher the speed of an aircraft, the greater is the noise pollution. The supersonic jet planes can break window panes and shake buildings by their 'sonic boom'. The problem of noise pollution is the most acute in localities near airports.

(vii) *Satellite Communication :* This is a relatively new source of sound pollution. High explosive rockets that are used to launch satellites in space produce deafening noise when the satellites are launched. The atomic explosions (experimental) also create heavy noise pollution.

(viii) *Household Gadgets :* The modern urban households need some gadgets that have become a part of life today. Mixer-cum-grinder, washing machine, coolers, air-conditioners etc. produce noise while they function and may also prove dangerous to health.

(ix) *Radio and Television :* The entertainment media have entered almost every household. The playing of televisions, radio, stereos interfere normal conversation, cause headache and restlessness and affect students during examinations.

(x) *Agricultural Methods and Machines :* The machinery used in modern agricultural practices have become a major source of noise pollution.

Effects of Noise Pollution

To all of us living in today's scientific and industrialized society, the effects of noise pollution can have far reaching consequences. The major effects of noise pollution have been discussed under the following heads :

(i) *Health Hazards*

(a) Sudden loud noise can damage the eardrum and the tiny hair cells in the internal ear.

(b) Prolonged noise causes temporary loss of hearing or even permanent damage.

(c) If the sensory and nervous system is affected, several related physical ailments will follow.

(d) Noise beyond 25 to 45 dBs disturbs health, comfort and peace of mind.

(e) Noise at the level of 45 to 80 dBs disturbs the digestive system.

(ii) *Physiological Effects*

Noise pollution causes physiological changes, such as —

(a) rise in blood pressure, respiratory rate, heartbeat rate,

(b) giddiness and nausea

(c) fatigue

(d) insomnia

(e) sharp muscular contractions

(f) abortions and other congenital defects in urban children.

(iii) *Behavioural Effects*

Exposure to high level noise often results in behavioral changes in human beings and animals.

(a) Sudden noise creates nervousness in people.

(b) Undesired noise often causes annoyance.

(c) Noise causes irritation and hampers learning abilities, especially among children studying in school situated in busy areas.

(iv) *Personality Effects*

Prolonged exposure to noise causes —

(a) deficiencies in children, like lack of confidence and poor perception about his or her ownself,

(b) decrease in performance in individuals,

(c) reduction in a worker's efficiency.

(v) *Effects on Non-living things*

Extreme noise can shatter glass panes, shake buildings and thus reduce the value of property.

Table : Sources and Effects of Noise on Human Beings

Source	Sound Pressure (dynes/cm^2)	Decibels (db)	Power at Ear (watt/cm^2)	Effects
Shotgun Blast (1 m)	—	150	10^{-1}	Instantaneous damage
Stereo Headphones (full vol.)	2,000	140	—	Hearing damage in 30 sec.
50 hp siren (at 100 m)	—	130	10^{-3}	Pain threshold
Jet take-off (at 100 m)	200	120	—	Hearing damage in 7.5 min.
Heavy metal rock band	—	110	10^{-5}	Hearing damage in 30 min.
Motorcycle	20	100	—	Damage in 2 hr.
Heavy City traffic	—	90	10^{-7}	Damage in 3 hr.
Loud Classical Music	2	80	—	Occupational safety and Health Agency (OSHA) * 8 hr. standard

Source	Sound Pressure (dynes/cm²)	Decibels (db)	Power at Ear (watt/cm²)	Effects
Vacuum Cleaner		70	10^{-9}	Concentration disrupted
Normal conversation	0.2	60	—	Speech disrupted
Background Music	—	50	10^{-11}	—
Bedroom	0.02	40		Quiet
Library	—	30	10^{-13}	—
Soft Whisper	0.002	20	—	Very Quiet
Leaves rusutling in the wind	—	10	10^{-15}	Barely audible

Source : WHO

Table : Effects of High Intensity Noise on Human Health

Noise (dB)	Effects Observed
0	Threshold of hearing
110	Stimulation of receptors in skin
120	Pain threshold
130	Nausea, vomiting, dizziness, interference with all activities
140	Pain in ear, extreme limit of noise tolerance
150	Significant change in pulse rate, prolonged exposure causing damage to skin, extreme emotional disturbances
160	Minor permanent damage to hearing on prolonged exposure
190	Major permanent damage to hearing in a short time.

Source : WHO

Measures to Control Noise Pollution

Noise pollution has taken the shape of a major problem in both developed and developing countries. It poses a serious threat to existing eco-systems and quality of environment. At this stage, it is virtually impossible tu control noise pollution completely. Yet, if we adhere to certain rules and take strict measures, we will certainly be able to reduce the noise pollution to its minimum.

The following measures, if adopted, can control present noise pollution :

(i) *General Awareness*

The public media must be used to educate the masses on the ill-effects of noise pollution. The users of loudspeakers and other sources of entertainment must not be sources of irritation to their neighbours.

(ii) *Noise Reduction at Source*

This can be done through proper planning and layout of plant and mechinaries in factories. Well-maintained, regularly repaired machines produce less noise. Noisy processes should be replaced with noise-free equipments.

(iii) *Screening the Noise Source*

This can be done by screening the noise source with thick walls and other absorbing materials, such as rubberized material and antivibration pads. Machinery in factories should be operated in covered sheds and not in the open.

(iv) *Screening the Noise Receiver*

The workers in industries that produce noise should be provided with ear-muffs and protectors. Their working hours must be so adjusted as to restrict them to acceptable limits.

(v) *Reduction in Traffic Pollution*

The noise created by the numerous vehicles can be effectively reduced by banning honking, ensuring good body and silencer designs and streamlining traffic flow. Heavy vehicles should be restricted to ply only on certain routes during peak hours.

(vi) *Removal of Noise Sources*

Sources of noise must be removed to areas where the noise created will not affect the surrounding. For instance, a factory should not be located near a locality.

(vii) *Coordinators between Planners and Environmental Authorities*

The authorities responsible for the development of towns and cities must essentially consult the Pollution Control Board Authorities before the planning and execution of certain schemes. Clearance from the Pollution Control Board must be made mandatory. Modern devices to control the noise pollution created by traffic and construction work must be developed and introduced.

(viii) *Noise-Free Zones*

Noise-free zones should be created around schools, hospitals, residential areas etc. Movements of vehicles, construction works, use of loud-speakers must not be allowed here.

(ix) *Plantations*

Green belts must be developed around metropolitan cities and industrial towns since plants are efficient absorbers of noise.

Odour Pollution

Smell causes distress and discomfort, while odour, under different conditions, can be pleasing.

The osmogenic molecules (smell) enter the nasal cavity through the nostrils. They excite the osmoceptors. The specific impulse travels along the myelinated nerve fibers to the receptor centres in the brain in the form of specific electric discharges. The message is processed and delivered to the evaluation centres in the brain. Here olfactory information is compared with stored experience (the memory), and finally the interpretation of message is relayed back along other nerve paths.

Sources of Odour Pollution

Stale air is characteristic of areas that are populated or overpopulated — whether residential, commercial or industrial. Stale air is deprived of its full oxygen value. Instead, it carries a considerable surplus of carbon dioxide :

(i) *Perspiration* is probably the most common metabolic sources of odours. A worker in a hot and humid environment is likely to lose up to 900 g sweat per hour. Normal sweat from a healthy person does not have any particular odour. It becomes repulsive when the urea content (normally about 0.03%) or butyric acid (normally about 0.001%) increase slightly. Sometimes sweat also contains valeric acid, which, in combination with butyric acid, forms the characteristic body odour.

(ii) *Various diseases* may also create odour and pollute the air, such as cancer in advanced stages, tinea versicolor, osteomyelitis, ozaena etc.

(iii) *Certain pathological conditions,* such as bromidrosis produced by decomposing keratin of the feet, are characterized by offensively smelling sweat.

(iv) *Stale or fermented urine* smells of ammonia as well as cyclohexen-3-one.

(v) The *odours of the alimentary tract* are dependent upon the type of digestion taking place. Stools give off highly offensive smells when they are alkaline, indicating protein putrefaction.

(vi) Objectionable *cooking odour* originates from the production of sulphur compounds together with steam — while cooking vegetable or animal matter.

(vii) *Industries* give off various kinds of smells, according to the type of solvent used for the numerous natural and synthetic materials employed in the finishing trade.

Solvent vapours are extremely volatile and give rise to photochemical smog.

Effect of Odour Pollution

People have differing reaction to odour — the reponse to an odour may be affected by the subject's age, sex, profession, attitudes etc.

Odour may affect the well-being of people by eliciting unpleasant sensations, by triggering possible harmful reflexes and evoke psychological and physiological reactions.

Measures to Control Odour Pollution

(i) The concentration of odour in houses, schools, office, factories etc. must be checked once in a month and controlled when necessary.

(ii) The sudden outbreaks of steam smoke and other odour-producing fumes must be controlled.

(iii) A mobile laboratory fitted with a radio telephone transmitter and receiver for communication is needed to check the odoriferous dusts and fumes.

(iv) In localities around industrial areas, the concentration of oxides of carbon, nitrogen, sulphur and other pollutants must be evaluated every half an hour.

QUESTIONS FOR EXAMINATION

A. Essay-Type Questions

1. Describe the principal Greenhouse Gases in the atmosphere.
   Ans. Pp. 101-103
2. Explain the formation of Ozone (O_3) in the atmosphere.
   Ans. Pp. 104-106
3. Describe the functions of Acid Rain and their effect on the Biosphere.
   Ans. Pp. 106-108
4. Analyse the different sources of noise pollution.
   Ans. Pp. 111-112
5. Analyse the effects of noise pollution on human health.
   Ans. Pp. 111-113
6. How to take measures to control noise pollution ?
   Ans. Pp. 113-114
7. Describe the different sources of odour pollution.
   Ans. Pp. 114-115

B. Short Answer-Type Questions

1. What are the principal gases in the atmosphere ?
   Ans. Page 100
2. Define atmospheric pollution.
   Ans. Page 100
3. What are the principal Greenhouse gases ?
   Ans. Page 101
4. What is the Greenhouse ?
   Ans. Page 103
5. What is Greenhouse Effect ?
   Ans. Page 103
6. What is the basic formation of Ozone ?
   Ans. Page 104
7. What is O_3 ?
   Ans. Page 104
8. What is Ozone ?
   Ans. Page 104
9. Where is ozone layer situated in the atmosphere ?
   Ans. Pp. 104-105
10. What is the importance of ozone layer ?
    Ans. Pp. 105-106
11. What is the Ozone Hole ?
    Ans. Page 106
12. What is Acid Rain ?
    Ans. Page 106

13. What is sea level rise ?

    Ans. Page 109

14. What is noise pollution ?

    Ans. Page 109

15. Define noise pollution.

    Ans. Page 110

16. How many sources of noise pollution are there ?

    Ans. Page 111

17. What is odour pollution ?

    Ans. Page 114

18. What are the principal effects of odour pollution ?

    Ans. Page 115

19. How do you measure odour pollution ?

    Ans. Page 115

20. How do you control odour pollution ?

    Ans. Page 115

Chapter 7

ENERGY SOURCE

INTRODUCTION

In the earliest days of civilisation, human beings used their own strength in moving and carrying loads, trapping animals and in hunting them for food. The revolutionary discovery of fire by accident, was the first attempt of man to use energy from a source outside his body. The rapid advance of human progress that occurred during the Neolithic Era was characterised by the use of solar energy which through biological system produced grains and animals for human survival.

Later, humans used animal power and stones as tools to harness the soil for agriculture — man used his energy together with the sun's energy. Thus, first signs of stable human communities began to develop.

In the early days, the only significant energy sources were natural ones — the power of falling water and the use of wind for ships. In industry, the central energy source was fire, from the burning of wood. The first fossil fuels to be exploited were surface deposit of asphalt, peat and coal, oil from surface seepage and gas coming out from underground reservoir.

Petroleum came into prominence in the 17th century, when an oil well drilled in Modena, Italy, in 1640, provided fuel for street lighting. Wind was used for ship propulsion. Later, windmills were widely used for flour grinding, water flow and other purposes. Petroleum is widely used in cars, aeroplanes and industry.

Today, we all have some basic knowledge about the uses and application of energy by using petrol or diesel, to get energy to run scooters, cars, trucks etc. We also need kerosene, oil, gas and coal for domestic use. So, we live in a world with energy around us.

We need to know the different terms associated with energy. 'Work' means 'moving something against resistance'. When we do work, we use energy. Work and energy are both measured according to the distance an object is moved and the force that must be overcome to move it. Work done is, therefore, proportional to both the applied force and the distance through which the force acts.

When an object is moved against a force, work is done and energy is expended in the process by the agency responsible for the movement. Energy can be kinetic and potential.

Power is the rate at which something uses up or produces energy or work. As work is measured in joule and time is measured in second, the unit of power is the joules/second.

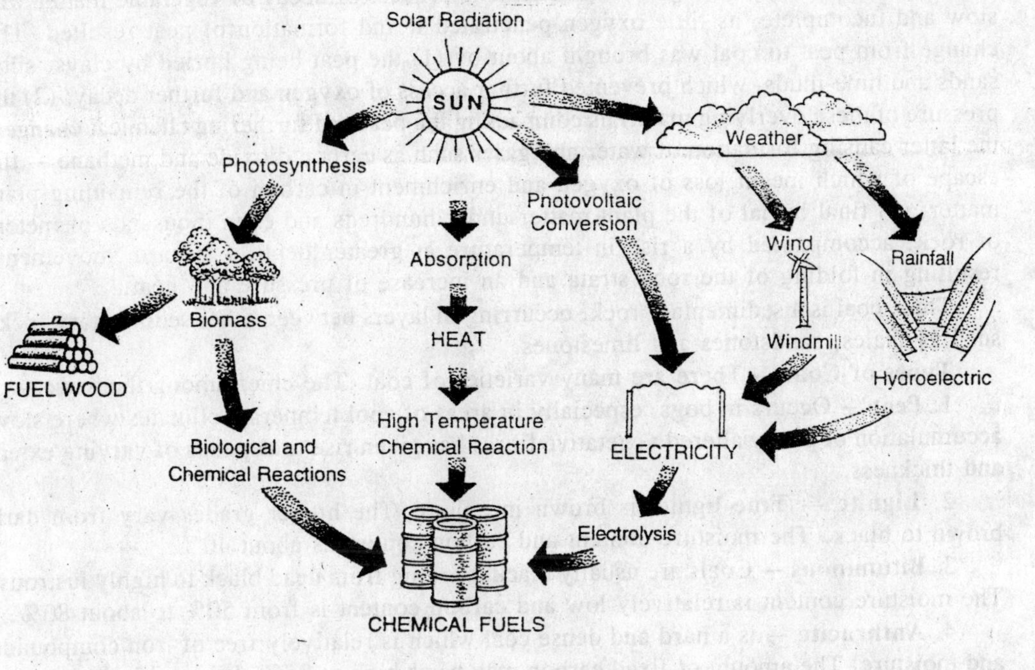

Fig. 22. Sources of Energy

Classification of Energy

Energy is converted from one form to another. Similar conversion can take place in respect of several different forms of energy. These are classified as :

(1) **Mechanical Energy** —Kinetic and potential.

(2) **Chemical Energy** — tied up in molecules of food or in fossil fuels such as coals and oil.

(3) **Radiant Energy** — including light, radio, X-rays, infrared and ultraviolet — which flood through the universe.

(4) **Heat Energy** — can cause gases to expand, drive engines and raise the temperature of water.

(5) **Nuclear Energy** — the forces that combine the atomic nucleus together.

(6) **Electro-Magnetic Energy** — derived from motion of electrons or protons orbiting the nuclei of atoms.

Conventional Energy

For untold thousands of years people kept warm around wood fires, which shed a cheerful heat but required constant care and replenishment. Only relatively late in history, probably in Greek and Roman times, did man discover a black rock, coal, which, though did not ignite as easily as wood, but once caught fire burned longer and evenly and yielded large amount of heat.

Formation — Two hundred and fifty million years ago, much of the world was warm, damp and green. In vast tropical like swamps was to be found a most luxuriant growth of vegetation and numerous species of animal and insect life. As the plant life breathed in carbon dioxide from the air and assimilated carbon, the first step in coal-making occurred. As the leaves, stalks, barks and wood fell into the water, acids were formed that arrested further decay of organic material. The process of decay of vegetable matter was slow and incomplete, as little oxygen penetrated it and formation of peat resulted. The change from peat to coal was brought about by (1) the peat being buried by clays, silts, sands and lime-muds, which prevented further access of oxygen and further decay; (2) the pressure of these overlying materials compacting the peat and furthering chemical changes, the latter causing formation of water and gases such as carbon dioxide and methane — the escape of which meant loss of oxygen and enrichment in carbon of the remaining plant matter; (3) final burial of the plant matter under hundreds and even thousands of meters of rock, accompanied by a rise in temperature at greater depth, (4) earth movements resulting in folding of the rock strata and an increase of pressure and heat.

Thus, coal is a sedimentary rock, occurring in layers between other sedimentary rocks such as shales, sandstones and limestones.

Types of Coal — There are many varieties of coal. The chief among them are —

1. **Peat** — Occurs in bogs, especially in areas of cool temperate climates where slow accumulation of partly altered vegetative fibres has given rise to deposits of varying extent and thickness.

2. **Lignite** — True lignite is brown in colour. The higher grades vary from dark brown to black. The moisture content and carbon content is about 40%.

3. **Bituminous** — Coals are usually black, varying from dead black to highly lustrous. The moisture content is relatively low and carbon content is from 50% to about 80%.

4. **Anthracite** — is a hard and dense coal which is relatively free of iron compounds and moisture. The amount of fixed carbon may be as high as 95%. It is jet black, lustrous and of excellent coherence.

Uses of coal — Coal is principally used as fuel for dometic fire and as power for factories, locomotives, steamships, for smelting ores of metals, for coke-ovens and for electric power houses and gas works. Peat is used for making thermal power. Lignite coal is used for manufacturing briquettes.

World Distribution of Coal — Coal is found in many countries of the world. The major producers are — USA, UK, CIS (former Soviet Union), China, India etc. In North America, the Appalachian coal-fields are the most important. The centres are Pittsburg, Cincinnati, New Orleans, Kentucky, Birmingham, Chicago, Oklahoma, Kansas etc. In United Kingdom, important coal centres are Northumberland and Durham, Lancashire, Warwickshire, Leicestershire, Shorpshire are other centres.

CIS (former Soviet Union) — Donetz basin is the largest coal field. Besides, Pechora, caucasus field supply coal. The Kuznetok basin and Kuzbas are most important. The other fields are Karaganda, Amur valley near Vladivostok, and island of Sakhalin.

In China, coal is found in the Loess Highland of Shanti, Shensi, Honan, Kansu.

The Raniganj, Jharia, Daltanganj, Wardha valley, Singarani are important centres of India.

Petroleum — is a mineral product found underground in the form of liquid, solid and gaseous form. It is an important source of power in modern world.

Uses — Petroleum is used for generating heat and power and for lighting and lubricating purpose. It is the best known lubricating oil in the world without which modern machinery would come to a halt. Besides, it has numerous by-products like kerosene, petrol or gasoline, asphals, paraffin, tar, petrol cake etc. Besides, a whole range of petro-chemical products like artificial rubber, chemical fertilizer, insectisides are obtained from petroleum.

World Distribution — Petroleum is found in many countries which can be categorised into three belts : (a) American belts (b) The middle eastern belts (c) The far-eastern region belts.

(a) **American belts** : The USA is the 2nd leading producer of petroleum in the world. The main regions are — The Appalachian region runs from south-western New York through western Pennsylvania, Eastern Ohio, west Virginia, Kentucky, Tennessee. The Lima-Indiana, Michigan, Illinois, Kansas, Oklahoma and Texas have many fields.

(b) **The middle eastern belts** : The countries of Saudi-Arabia, Iran, Iraq, Kuwait, Qatar are important. In Saudi Arabia, the important fields are Damman, Abquaiq, Qatif, Ghawar, Haifa are important centres. In Iraq, oil-fields are located at Baba Gagur, north of Kirkuk, Khanakin etc. In Iran, oil fields are at Musjid-i-Suleiman, Halt-kel, Goch Saran, Agha Jaria, Naft Safid, Lali etc. In Kuwait, the principal oil-field is located in Burgan hill district.

(c) **The far-eastern belt** : includes Myanmar (Burma), Indonesia, Sarawak, China, Sakhalin, Kamchatka, India. The principal regions of Indonesia are Balik, Papan and Pallenbang. In Myanmar, oil is found in Irrawaddy valley of upper Myanmar. In India, oil is found in Digboi, Lakhimpur, Nahar Katiya, Moran, Bappapung, Hansanpung, Masimpur, Badarpur and Patharia. Besides, Bomaby High region produces high quality petroleum oil.

Hydro-electricity

We use electric power in every aspect of modern civilised world. Electric power can be of two types — (a) Hydro-electricity and (b) thermal power.

Hydro-electricity is the most utilized source of power in the modern world. Water is a free gift of nature which, properly harnessed, can give unhindered source of electricity.

Distribution — Hydel power is found and utilized in countries like Africa, USA — Washington, Oregon, California, Switzerland, CIS (former USSR), Italy, Norway, France, Canada, Sweden, India and Japan.

Nuclear Power

In the modern world, nuclear power is the most important form of energy which has given power to some countries of the world. Scientists have acknowledged the fact that the source of energy lies in the atoms of various substances — or rather in the nuclear part of the atoms — and hence is called atomic or nuclear energy. In this type of energy, yield is closely related to metals like uranium, radium, thorium, lithium, plutonium etc.

Non-conventional Energy

Energy that is being utilised comes from conventional sources like coal, water, fuel, wood etc. However, alternate energy sources like solar, wind, tidal and geothermal should find wide application in future.

Solar energy : The sun provides us enormous amounts of energy in the form of solar radiation — energy that travels in small wave packets called photons, reaching the surface of the Earth from a distance of 150 million kms (93 million miles) in only 8 minutes. Solar energy can be used in production of heat, electricity, bio-energy etc. There are some simple devices using solar energy like solar cooker, solar water heater, solar desalinator, solar air heaters, solar space conditioner, solar refrigerator, solar steam generators, direct conversion to electricity, photovoltaic technology, solar cells and modules.

Bio-energy : includes those processes where biological forms of matter such as plants, vegetables, bacteria, enzymes etc. provide the basis for energy or its conversion from one form to another. The widest use of bio-energy is the traditional way where wood plants and agricultural matters are burnt to provide heat. Bio-mass includes both terrestrial as well as aquatic matter and can be grouped into new plant growth, residues and wastes.

The use of bio-mass as source of energy has tremendous potential. About 40% of total energy consumed in India even today comes from sources like wood-wastes and animal wastes etc. Most dry forms of bio-mass can be burnt directly to produce heat, steam or electricity.

Wind energy : is the kinetic energy associated with movement of large masses of air resulting from differential heating of the atmosphere by the sun. Wind energy is renewable and poses no major environmental threats. Small windmills with direct mechanical drive matched to a pump and tank storage are in extensive use in many parts of the world. Some new all-metal multi-bladed windmill designs have been developed; like the traditional multi-bladed windmills, they have a good starting torque, but lighter in weight, are simpler to fabricate and have slightly better efficiencies.

Animal energy : Draught Animal Power (DAP) is one of the important renewable energy sources which has served mankind from times immemorial. Animals have served humankind for work, food, skin. In urban areas also draught animals play a significant role in transportation.

Ocean energy : The sea — which is constantly receiving solar radiations and acts as the world's largest natural solar collector — has potential to provide a means of utilizing renewable energy. It acts not only as a collector but also has an enormous storage capacity. Energy from ocean is available in several forms such as — ocean thermal energy, wave, tidal, salinity gradient, ocean current, ocean wind and bio-mass.

Hydrogen energy : Hydrogen is a versatile fuel and can play an important role. Hydrogen has the highest energy content per unit of mass of any chemical fuel. It is a raw material for chemical industry. It can replace coke or coal as a metallurgical reductant. Liquid hydrogen can be used for automobiles, aircraft etc.

QUESTIONS FOR EXAMINATION

A. Essay-Type Questions

1. Describe the importance of energy resources.
   Ans. Pp. 118-119
2. Explain the different types of conventional energy resources.
   Ans. Pp. 119-121
3. Explain the different types of non-conventional energy resources.
   Ans. Pp. 121-122
4. Give an account of fuel energy resources in the world.
   Ans. Pp. 118-121
5. Give an account of the distribution and production of coal in the world.
   Ans. Pp. 120-121
6. Give an account of the distribution and production of petroleum in the world.
   Ans. Pp. 120-122
7. Describe the importance of hydro-power energy resources in the world.
   Ans. Pp. 121

B. Short Answer-Type Questions

1. What is energy ?
   Ans. Page 118
2. How many types of energy resources are there ?
   Ans. Page 119
3. What is conventional energy resources ?
   Ans. Page 119
4. What is non-conventional energy resource ?
   Ans. Page 121
5. What is the principal source of energy ?
   Ans. Page 119
6. What is the importance of energy ?
   Ans. Page 119
7. Why bio-gas is important for energy ?
   Ans. Page 121
8. How is the sun the ultimate source of energy ?
   Ans. Page 118
9. What is nuclear power ?
   Ans. Page 121
10. What is solar energy ?
    Ans. Page 121
11. What is wind energy ?
    Ans. Page 122
12. What is animal energy ?
    Ans. Page 122
13. What is the ocean energy ?
    Ans. Page 122
14. What is the hydrogen energy ?
    Ans. Page 122

Chapter 8

ENVIRONMENT AND PUBLIC HEALTH

INTRODUCTION

The terms Environment and Public Health are interdependent, because both are determined by the interplay and integration of two ecological universes — the internal environment of man himself and the external environment which surrounds him. On the other hand, public health plays a key role on the diseases which become epidemic in character and seem to be highly related to the ecological factors.

The Environment and Public Health of an individual, a community or a nation is determined by the three ecological factors (agent, host and environment) responsible for the disease. In the modern concept, disease is due to a disturbance in the delicate balance between man and his environment. Of the three ecological factors responsible for disease, the disease agent is usually identified with the help of the laboratory, the host is available for study; but the environment from which the patient comes is largely unknown.

What is Public Health : The meaning of the term **"Public Health"** may thus be summed up by saying : **the science of safeguarding health, the way of life, the quality of living that is exposed in the clean home, the clean farm, the clean business, the clean neighbourhood and the clean community.** Being a way of life it must come from within the people, it is nourished by knowledge and grows as an obligation and an ideal in human relation." In this regard the excerpts from the WHO, which defines Environmental sanitation as "the control of all those factors in man's physical environment which exercises or may exercise a deliterious effect on his physical development, health and survival". According to the World Health Organisation (WHO), health is defined as **"A state of complete physical, mental and social well-being and not merely the absence of disease and infirmity"**.

The effects of Environment and Public Health which centres round with the concept of controlling the environment with a view to prevent disease and promote health. As per view of the different environmentalists and public health experts, man has already controlled a number of factors in his environment, e.g. food, water, housing, clothing, sanitation. These controllable factors are those included in the standard of living. During the past century, in the developed countries, these controllable factors have been responsible for considerable improvement in the health of the people. However, man's mastery over his environment is not complete because old problems are in the way of getting solved but at the same time new problems are arising.

The demographic and fast urbanisation all over the world are bringing profound social and environmental changes in this regard. Air pollution is of growing concern in many urban cities. Apart from that, industrial growth has given rise to the problem of environmental pollution by industrial wastes. Advances in nuclear technology have produced the problem of radioactive pollution of the environment.

Therefore, the attainment of a healthy environment is becoming more and more complex. Proper environmental health now requires the services of the public health, qualified doctor, the epidemiologist, the public health engineer, the town planner, the sociologist, the economist, and the health inspector. It should be remembered that a purely medical or engineering approach by itself is no longer sufficient, a combined multi-disciplinary programme of the action is needed to achieve a healthy environment.

The conference of the United Nations held on **Human Environment in Stockholm in 1972 stressed the need to improve health by improving the environmental situation.**

The references of the underdeveloped and developing countries of Asia, Africa and Latin America with regard to Environment and Public Health can be summed up by saying that they are lagging behind considerably. The basic problems of sanitary disposal and safe drinking water supply are yet to be taken up. In this regard, the condition of India is far below satisfactory level because 80% of India's population lives in rural areas.

The first step in any health program is the elimination through environmental control of those factors which are harmful to health.

Sources of Diseases

As has been discussed earlier, ecological factors are responsible for the diseases which are mainly **Water borne, Food borne** and **Air borne** by nature. It is the environment factor which plays the key role for prevention and control of diseases. Unless the environmental factors which are basic and fundamental to individual and community health can be eradicated the basic concept of public health would be in jeopardy. Now the following diseases are discussed for any health programme in order to eliminate through environmental control.

Water Borne Diseases

The majority of these diseases are commonly spread by contaminated water, although the infractive agent is mainly excreted in the faces and subsequently contaminates the environment. They are intestinal infections such as typhoid, cholera, and other acute diarrheal diseases, while others are non-intestinal, such as hepatitis A and poliomyelitis.

Much of the ill health in the underdeveloped countries is largely due to lack of safe drinking water. There can be no state of positive community health and well-being without safe water supply. Since the beginning of the 20th century when international cooperation in public health began, safe water has been a major concern. A survey conducted by WHO in 1975 on Community Water Supplies revealed the fact that, in India, while 80 per cent of the population in water areas had access to community water supplies, only 18 per cent of the rural population has reasonable access to safe water.

The WHO attributed the slow pace of progress to shortage of funds and trained manpower, weakness in national programs, difficulties in system operation and maintenance and insufficient involvement of potential users.

Water intended for human consumption should not only be "safe" but also wholesome. A safe water is one that cannot harm the consumer, even when ingested over prolonged periods. Water may be safe, but if it has an unpleasant taste or appearance it may drive the consumer to other, less safe, sources. Therefore, **Drinking Water** should be not only completely safe but agreeable to use or wholesome, such a supply may be termed **"acceptable** or "**potable**". Therefore the definition of safe and wholesome water is **"free from pathogenic agents, free from harmful chemical substances, pleasant to the taste and usable for domestic purposes".** The causative agents of water and food borne diseases are numerous and include bacteria, viruses, protozoa, and helminths. The agent normally lives and multiplies in a person who either suffers from specific disease or is apparently healthy. It escapes from the reservoir of infection via the intestinal tract and is subsequently ingested by the susceptible host — either directly or indirectly.

Enteric Fevers (Typhoid and Paratyphoid)

Enteric fevers comprise typhoid and paratyphoid, and are caused by salmonella typhi and S. paratyphi A, B, and C, respectively. In developing countries, typhoid is more prevalent than paratyphoid. The predominant paratyphoid infection in S. E. Asia is paratyphoid A. Children and young adults are the susceptible population in endemic areas.

It is usually spread through iced drinks, shellfish, inadequately purified water, chlorinated or cross-contaminated between potable and polluted water or sewage.

Several types of whole-cell parenteral typhoid vaccines have been developed.

The remedy to be introduced for control of this disease is through epidemiological investigations. Food handlers who are found to be carriers should be kept under surveillance and prohibited from preparations and sale of food to the public as long as they are carriers.

Cholera and other acute Diarrheal Diseases

Cholera is an acute communicable disease of the gastrointestinal tract, caused by the bacteria Vibro-cholerae. The disease occurs in both epidemic and endemic forms.

The disease is spread by the feco-oral route, through ingestion of water or food contaminated by the bacteria from the stool of a cholera patient.

The control of cholera and other acute Diarrheal Diseases is through sanitation measures, immunization and educating the people via medias.

Dysenteries

Dysentery is an acute communicable disease characterized by gripping pain in the abdomen accompanied by the passage of frequent stools. It may be caused by bacteria or by a protozoan Entameba histolytica — and is called, respectively, bacillary dysentery and amebic dysentery.

It has a worldwide distribution and is endemic. However, epidemics frequently occur where there is poor sanitation. It is more common in children below 10 years.

The disease is spread by feco-oral route, through contaminated food and by direct personal contact. Persons transmitting the disease are generally those who observe poor personal hygiene.

Sanitation measures like improved methods of sanitation are of utmost importance in the prevention of dysenteries. In fact, that is how the occurrence of the disease has been considerably lowered in Western countries.

The following measures can be taken for the control and remedies of the disease :

(a) **Safe Water Supply :** This is very essential. In rural areas this can be achieved by chlorination of water, replacement of shallow wells by sanitary wells and boiling of drinking water.

(b) **Sanitation Barrier :** This implies the proper disposal of excreta so that infection does not reach water, soil, milk, food or flies. This is very crucial as the main source of infection is excreta. A sanitation barrier can be effectively achieved by the constructions and use of sanitary latrines.

(c) **Health Education :** It is essential to educate people for improvement in sanitation. Apart from that the people should be made specially conscious for improving their personal hygiene, i.e. the importance of washing the hands after defection and prior to handling food must be emphasized. Also, nails must be cut short and kept clean. People must be advised not to eat raw vegetables and fruits without washing them thoroughly in running water.

(d) **Food and Sanitation :** Boiling and pasteurization of milk help to control the spread of disease. Food should be protected from flies and dusts. Uncovered food, cut fruits and food from roadside vendors should not be eaten. Pre-placement and periodic examination of food handlers should be conducted.

(e) **Fly Control Measures :** These include proper disposal of garbage, to prevent fly-breeding, the use of insecticides and protection from flies by screening kitchen with wire gauze mesh for doors and windows.

(f) **Immunization :** It is recommended under the Expanded Programme on Immunization (EPI) that all children be immunized with vaccine at the time of entry to school, i.e, at the age of 5.

Infective Hepatitis

It is an endemic disease characterized by jaundice and caused by a virus. It is common in children and young adults.

The disease is spread by the feco-oral route. The virus is excreted in the stools of the patient and contamination of water and food may lead to explosive outbreaks. It is also spread by direct contact. Therefore, persons living is the same house are at great risk, particularly when standards of personal hygiene are low.

The improvement in sanitation is the only permanent method for reducing the occurrence of the disease.

The vaccine is now available, therefore immunization in adults and children are advised accordingly.

To sum up about water borne diseases, we must remember one thing — with the advancement of civilization, new diseases are also attacking human race which need special scientific and technology based attention from all advanced nations of the world.

The major water borne diseases prevalent in the underdeveloping countries are tabulated below.

The routes of transmission as well as the main preventive measures to control these diseases are also outlined.

Table : Types of Diseases

Disease	Major route of transmission	Major action for prevention
1. Cholera	Contaminated water	Safe disposal of human excreta
2. Dysentery	Contaminated food	Use Sanitary latrine
3. Common gastro-intestinal problems	Contaminated hands	Washing hands with soap or ash before handling food, after defecation
4. Diarrhea	Flies	Use of protected water sources

Air Borne Diseases

Air borne diseases include only those infectious diseases which are transmitted by air through the respiratory tract into the body. Apart from that, diseases which are not caused by an infectious agent but are caused by inhalation of polluted air, e.g. silicosis, asbestosis. Air borne diseases, grouped by their causative agents, include bacteria, viz. **pharyngitis, tonsillitis, bronchitis, pneumonia, mycobacterium tuberculosis,** which causes tuberculosis, viruses such as those causing measles, rubella, variola and influenza. Apart from these diseases, the most dangerous and notorious is plague which is caused by bacteria transmitted by rodents.

Plague

Plague is transmitted to man mainly through the rat flea which acts as a vector and transmits the disease from infected rodents. The infected rat flea transmits the disease mainly through bites. Pneumonic plague is transmitted from the diseased to a new host through droplet infection. The incubatory period of plague is usually 4-6 days which is followed by symptoms of fever, painful enlargement of lymph nodes, bodyache, headache and high fever, breathlessness.

The preventive and control measures of plague include destruction of rats, eradication of fleas, vaccination and chemoprophylaxis of human population. During the period of outbreaks, flea control is of primary importance. Spraying insecticides. eg. DDT, as also mass vaccination should be done during an outbreak. Rat burrows should also be insufflated with the insecticidal dust.

The other important measures to be taken are early diagnosis, Notification, **Isolation, Treatment, Disinfection of sputum, discharges from lymph nodes and articles used by the patient, Handling of dead bodies aseptically** and **Health Education.**

For prevention and control the same procedure of water borne diseases cannot be applied for airborne diseases. To whatever degree that air is contaminated, we cannot prevent human beings from breathing it. Specific protection is by immunization only. In general, only certain immunization programmes are carried out in such developing countries and these include diphtheria, pertussi, tuberculosis. Immunization against mumps, measles and rubella are carried out only in those countries which can afford these immunization programmes.

Food Borne Diseases

It is known that water borne and food borne diseases are very much interlinked. There is a large group of communicable diseases in which the infective agent is mainly excreted in the feces and subsequently contaminated the environment. The majority of these diseases are intestinal infections such as typhoid, cholera and other acute diarrheal diseases, while others are non-intestinal, such as hepatitis A and poliomyelitis. As these water borne and food borne diseases are closely related to environmental sanitation, they create major socio-economic and public health problems in many developing countries where basic sanitation and hygiene are inadequate. The most common food borne diseases in the developing countries are **Bacterial Food Poisoning, and poliomyelitis.**

Bacterial Food Poisoning

Food poisoning is a general term which refers to an acute attack of gastrointestinal illness with abdominal cramps, nausea, vomiting, diarrhea, with or without fever, acquired through ingestion of contaminated food or water. Bacterial food poisoning is usually mild and rarely fatal.

The other food borne diseases are mainly **Entameba gingivitis** which is generally found to be present in pus-pockets of teeth of pyorrhea infected persons and in the cysts of infected tonsils. It is usually transmitted by cooks who cough into the food at the time of dishing.

Then comes **Entameba histolytica** which is cosmopolitan in distribution ; it is commonly found in epidemic form in tropical and sub-tropical regions. The trophozoites of this parasite penetrates the wall of the intestine and feed upon its cells causing the formation of ulcers. These ulcers rupture and discharge blood and mucus into the intestine that pass out with the stool. The fecal contamination of drinking water and raw vegetables or contamination by infected and careless food handling are the mode of transmission of this parasite.

Under this category the other diseases which are most prevalent are **Entameba Coli, Balantidium Coli, Giardia lambila intestinalis, Schistosoma manooni** and **Ascaris lumbricoides**. The symptoms of all these other than Ascaris lumbricoides have many factors common with **Entameba histolytica.** But **Ascaris lumbricoides** — more commonly known as "Round Worm" — inhabits the small intestine of man and is more common in children, Round worms are cosmopolitan in distribution.

Poliomyelitis

The most dreadful disease of this group which calls the attention of all is paralytic poliomyelitis, an important childhood disease in developing countries. By the age of four years, more than 90 per cent of the children in some developing countries are already infected. The virus mostly enters by mouth and multiplies in the oropharynx and intestine before invasion of the nervous system. The infection is mainly spread by close contact with those with apparent infections, either by pharyngeal or intestinal route. The virus is readily, therefore, spread within the family. Indirect transmission by contaminated food, milk, water, and sewage is rare.

To sum up, the main causes of food borne diseases lie with the habits of personal hygiene of the people in general. With improvement in sanitation the chances of infection through food and water become less as the epidemiology and control of all these diseases are generally similar. A system of notification and epidemiological investigation of communicable diseases should be developed in areas where this is lacking.

Personal Hygiene Issue/Civic Sense

Introduction : The term personal hygiene is very much synonomous with urban population or urbanisation. As modern civilisation evolves around cities, towns and megacities, it is really unfortunate that modern decision-makers — who come from all branches of science and technology, social science and medical science — never take into account the conditions of the rural areas of the developing countries where, still, 80 per cent of the world population live without any accessible roads, modern housing, sanitations and safe drinking water ! Apart from these, education and proper food and health care are also suffering for these narrow parochial decision-makers.

Whenever the term '**personal hygeine**' is taken up the main issue is of slums which cover 50 per cent of the total area in any city or megacity. In most of these urban slums there is hardly any modern sanitary condition which aggravates the different kinds of communicable diseases. Even in the time of natural calamities people from these slum areas suffer from epidemics which are mainly either water, food and air borne by nature. Statistics are not wanting to show that disease rates are drastically cut down by an improvement in the quality of public water supply. Last but not the least is sewage system which controls the remedy of any communicable disease.

Health Consciousness in Urban Sphere

The improvement of the environmental hygiene of a community is of fundamental importance for ensuring health campaigns at various levels. Socio economic factors, social habits, customs and tradition may perpetuate the existence of a disease focus, despite the availability of methods for its prevention and control. Improvement in this respect is often difficult and seldom complete without intensive and continuing health education of the community at various levels.

It is well known that health consciousness in urban spheres can be taken up more easily in relation to improvements in the living conditions at slums because of the geographical, sociological and economic factors. As, in urban centers, people from upper strata of the society leave a considerable influence on the poorer and backward community, which help indirectly to imbibe personal hygienic factors in terms of socioeconomic development. Apart from that, public health programmes in terms of modern sanitation and immunization should be taken up regularly for improving the living conditions in slums.

Supply of Safe Drinking Water

Water is necessary for man's survival and well-being. Nature is required not just to meet psychological and domestic needs, but also for irrigation and food production, fire fighting, street cleansing, industries, hydro-electric power production, navigation, and waste-transportation. The quality required varies, with drinking water requiring the highest standards.

As we all know, drinking water can be contaminated through various activities. The first and foremost condition in supplying safe drinking water is the conditions of sewage disposal into water bodies should be agreed upon with the authorities responsible for the control and protection of water and also with sanitary and epidemiological services responsible for the protection of aquatic life.

We should keep in mind that surface water from lakes, streams and rivers is also a very good source of drinking water supply for rural communities. Simple filtration using the slow sand filter and chlorination will be adequate treatment to produce a potable water supply, provided that such surface water is not too turbid or highly coloured.

The issue of safe drinking water has been taken up as a prime necessity for betterment of life for any individual irrespective of his/her social, political or economic status. With people becoming more conscious the demand for 'safe drinking water supply for everyone' within a stipulated period has become the motto of UN.

Sewage

Under this term the used water from different sectors, i.e. domestic, trade and industrial, can be broadly called sewage. All these waste waters are collectively termed sewage. From the fecal waste component of domestic sewage with various pathogenic and non-pathogenic microorganisms to waste waters from trade and industrial premises is usually termed municipal sewage.

The discharge of sewage can pollute a river and other water courses. The extent and seriousness of such pollution will depend on the diluting and self-purifying capacity of the river, in relation to the volume of the sewage being discharged, as well as the amount of organic matter and any toxic constituents in such sewage. To safeguard the existing purity of the river and its beneficial use to communities downstream of the point of discharge, public health authorities require such sewage to be treated to the extent that the resultant effluent will comply with these sewage effluent standards requirement.

The objective of sewage treatment is to remove as much as practical the content of solids in the sewage, and to stabilize the effluent so that it will not unduly affect the quality of the receiving water, cause a nuisance, or be injurious to health.

The process of sewage treatment is carried out in two stages. The primary or first stage of treatment is mainly a physical process, and deals with the removal of the settleable solids. The secondary treatment consists of biological filter to treat domestic sewage.

To sum up, without proper sewage system it is impossible for any administration to provide safe drinking water either for urban or rural population. In most of the epidemics so far, human civilisation had encountered sewage problem which has been diagnosed as the chief criterion for the outbreak of water borne diseases. The developing nations of the world are facing this problem and cannot solve them because of economic constraints. So rich nations should help poorer nations to cope up with this problem.

Health Hazards in Agricultural Pest Control

Pesticides are chemicals that are used in order to protect crops. They are an integral part of intensive arable agriculture. They are partially responsible for the production of abundant food supplies, so that consumer food costs remain relatively low.

This, however, involves certain environmental risks, since most pesticides contain toxic materials. Most pesticides are synthetic organic compounds. The physical and chemical properties of these compounds vary widely. Hence, pesticides behave differently in the environment.

Pesticide behaviour is influenced by —

(i) **soil properties**, especially texture and organic matter content,

(ii) **application techniques**, i.e., foliar application versus surface applications or soil incorporation, and

(iii) **environmental conditions**, such as temperature, aeration and soil moisture.

Although used largely in the agricultural sector, pesticides sneak into air, water, food and, eventually, into the fetus. Their destructive nature is aggravated by their long staying power in the environment as well as inside our body fat.

Detrimental Effects of Pesticides on Human Health

To us, pesticides seem to be ordinary chemicals used in order to control pests and thereby increase food production. But, in reality, they are deadly killers. They deliver the ultimate flow by wrecking the human immune system :

(1) Pesticides suppress the human immune system.

(2) Organochlorines and organophosphates produce immunotoxicity. This reduces the animals' resistance to infections.

(3) Population exposed to pesticides suffer high rates of respiratory infection.

(4) Pesticides enhance the risk of cancer. They act directly as carcinogens or can also suppress the immune system.

The Green Revolution in India during the post-independence period saw a sudden rise in the use of pesticides. The policy-makers argued in favour of these hazardous chemicals since they saw no other alternative to feed a growing population. In spite of the detrimental effects of these pesticides, the government has chosen to turn a blind eye towards norms that would ban their usage. Researchers, politicians and policy makers should promote alternate agricultural methods so as to ensure the safety of the people.

Pest Management in Agriculture

Biological and Bio-Technological Control of Pests

This can be done in two ways —

(i) by using bacteria, virus and other pathogens which attack the pests, or,

(ii) by using predators or parasites or both.

A lot of work is yet to be done in this field, although the Indian Council of Agricultural Research has said that there has been remarkable success in some fields.

The most successful of these efforts was the total eradiction of prickly pear, a toxic plant, that had multiplied widely over the Indian countryside. It had been a great menace for many years.

The Indian branch of the Commonwealth Institute of Biological Control, situated in Bangalore, is trying to identify natural enemies of a few pests. The work is still at a very early stage.

Heavy Metal Toxicity

Toxic metals are dispersed in the biosphere mostly through industrial effluents, refuse burning, organic wastes, transport and power generation etc.

These metallic pollutants, in the long run, are washed out of the air by rain and brought onto land and waterways. Therefore, air is the major route for the contamination of the other components of the living environment.

For instance, the sources of the toxic metals that pollute air can be industrial smoke, since it contains copper, manganese, arsenic, nickel etc. When we inhale these elements at enhanced levels, they cause adverse physiological effects.

Plants such as mosses and lichens accumulate metals from the air since they are dependent on the atmosphere for their mineral supply. It has been found that plants near copper smelter plants have high levels of copper and zinc in them.

Environmental Pollution caused by Toxic metals — a cause of concern in India

(1) Automobile exhausts have been studied in Ahmedabad. They have revealed the presence of lead compounds in the surface soil along roadsides.

(2) The smoke released from motor-vehicle exhausts and domestic chimneys pose serious threat to the environment. Petrol, to which tetraethyl lead has been added, is a dangerous pollutant.

(3) During 1976, India produced almost four lack tonnes of caustic soda by mercury cell process. From this, an estimated 0.23 kg of mercury had been lost per tonne of caustic produced. Consequently, the effluents and emissions released from chlor-alkali industries, containing about 90.8 kg of mercury, led to the contamination of air and water.

(4) National Institute of Occupational Health, Ahmedabad, has collected baseline data related to the presence of metals in blood and urine among the Indian population

Twenty-six occupationally unexposed human volunteers from Ahmedabad were studied. The aim was to investigate whether their blood and urine contained lead, manganese, cobalt, nickel, zinc, copper, chromium, and cadmium.

The contents of most of these metals were more or less similar to values reported from foreign countries. However, the content of nickel in the blood was on the higher side for most.

(5) Bhabha Atomic Research Centre, Mumbai, has analysed the contents of toxic metals in various food samples in and around Mumbai.

Blood and urine samples of urbanites in Gujarat were also studied.

In general, it was observed that Nickel content in blood was quite high. Scientists say that this is supposed to be due to the consumption of vegetable ghee, or because of using cooking vessels of stainless steel.

Nickel not only produces systemic poisoning but is also carcinogenic in nature. Besides, the metal also causes skin diseases and ulcers.

From the mentioned cases, we can list down the various sources of toxic metals that are contaminating our environment. They are —

(i) organic wastes

(ii) sewage sludge

(iii) application of metal containing pesticides
(iv) seed dressings
(v) refuse burning
(vi) transport and power generation
(vii) non-permitted colours
(viii) metallic objects
(ix) paints and varnishes
(x) fuel ash
(xi) municipal compost
(xii) domestic rubbish
(xiii) use of stainless steel and electroplated utensils
(xiv) consumption of vegetable ghee, tea and spices.

The principal toxic metals, their sources and effects have been discussed below :

(1) **Manganese Poisoning**

India is the third largest producer of manganese ore. The country earns a considerable amount in foreign exchange through its export.

Manganese ores have various uses in industries. It is used in the manufacture of ferromanganese, varnishes, dry cell batteries, paints, inks, matches and fire-works. In ceramic industries, manganese ore is used as glass decoloriser.

Manganese is required by the human body as a trace element. But it shows harmful effects when in excess.

Manganese is a neurotoxin, i.e., it affects the central nervous system. It exerts toxic action on the brain and on other organs, such as liver, kidney and testes.

A number of families in a Japanese village, consuming well water, were reported to be suffering from manganese poisoning. Even cereals and legumes were found to contain this metal in an alarming amount.

Lead Poisoning

The most common source of lead pollution is the combination of petrol to which either tetraethyl or tetramethyl lead has been added.

The sources of exposure to lead poisoning are —

(i) **Food :** Regulations should be introduced to limit the lead content in canned foods. Lead reaches the foods from the soldered seams of cans. Cow's milk, soft drinks and beer are other sources of lead.

(ii) **Drinking Water :** Concentration of lead in drinking water increases if the water is distributed through lead pipes.

(iii) **Ambient Air :** Atmospheric lead comes from gasolene fuelled automobile emissions.

Lead poisoning in water has been reported from Lucknow and Kanpur in India.

Mercury Poisoning

When inhabitants of Minamata town, Japan, consumed fish from the Minamata Bay, they were reported to be suffering from mercury poisoning. This was because the fish contained methyl mercury that had been discharged from the adjoining factories.

Sources of mercury are —

(i) industrial effluents that contaminate the water-bodies,

(ii) fish from these contaminated water near chloralkali and paper manufacturing industries,

(iii) milk of cows and buffaloes grazing on land on the banks of contaminated rivers, such as the Kalu river that supplies water to the Mumbai region.

Mercury poisoning affects the nervous system, causing depression, anxiety, loss of concentration and tremors.

Cadmium Poisoning

Cadmium is a non-essential element. It is highly toxic to man and several other organisms.

Let us note some facts about the metal —

(i) Cadmium always occurs in nature in combination with zinc. Up to 1% of cadmium may be contained in commercial zincs that is used in galvanizing food utensils.

(ii) Cadmium level is found to be higher in smokers than in non-smokers.

(iii) Cadmium poisoning has attained the status of a formidable health hazard in industrialised nations.

(iv) Cadmium can reach our body through the consumption of vegetables sprayed with fertilisers containing the metal.

The most serious illness due to cadmium toxicity is the Ital-Ital disease. This affected Japan during the post World War II (1939-45) period. The metal causes chronic bronchitis, hypertension, cardiovascular diseases and testicular damage.

Vanadium Poisoning

Burning of fossil fuels releases vanadium air. The metal affects the productivity of plants and crops.

Arsenic Poisoning

Arsenic poisoning has been reported in the Gangetic West Bengal and Mumbai. Arsenic compounds are absorbed through skin.

Arsenic toxicity causes vomiting, nausea, diarrhea, severe irritation of nose and throat, skin eruption, inflammation, abdominal pain. In extreme cases, it may even prove fatal.

Chromium Poisoning

Chromium is used in manufacturing industries of jet engines, steel, paints, tool, photography, electric cells, matches, rubber goods etc. From these, the metal reaches human and animal bodies.

Chromium toxicity causes cancer, nephritis, ulcers and affects the central nervous system. It destroys the soil fertility and fish fauna.

Iron Poisoning

It is released from steel and other industries. Excess of iron causes rapid increase in respiration, pulse rates, congestion of blood vessels, vomiting, headache, drowsiness etc. Very high doses cause paralysis, low blood pressure, diarrhea, lung irritation and bone defects.

QUESTIONS FOR EXAMINATION

A. Essay-Type Questions

1. Define public health with the help of the following statement — "The terms Environment and Public Health are interdependent because both are determined by the interplay and integration of the two ecological universes."
   Ans. Pp. 124-125
2. Write in short description about the controlling factors which are playing determining role in public health.
   Ans. Pp. 124-126
3. The attainment of a healthy environment is becoming more and more complex — Discuss.
   Ans. Pp. 124-126
4. Describe the major water borne diseases.
   Ans. Pp. 125-127
5. Do you think 'environmental pollution' is responsible for air borne diseases ? If so, discuss briefly the reasons responsible for it.
   Ans. Pp. 127-128
6. "Plague was one of the most dangerous and dreaded airborne disease of nineteenth and early twentieth century" — Elucidate the statement.
   Ans. Pp. 127-128
7. How health conciousness in urban sphere has helped to prevent communicable diseases in a more effective measure than rural sector ? Explain with suitable examples.
   Ans. Pp. 129-130
8. Describe the detrimental effects of pesticides on human health.
   Ans. Pp. 131-133
9. Discuss about the heavy metal toxicity and human health.
   Ans. Pp. 132-134
10. Discuss about environmental pollution caused by Toxic metals.
    Ans. Pp. 132-133

B. Short Answer-Type Questions

1. What is public health ?
   Ans. Page 124
2. Define health ?
   Ans. Page 124
3. What is airborne diseases ?
   Ans. Page 127
4. What is waterborne diseases ?
   Ans. Page 125
5. What is foodborne diseases ?
   Ans. Page 128

6. What is sanitation ?

   Ans. Page 125

7. What do you mean by safe drinking water ?

   Ans. Page 130

8. What is sewage ?

   Ans. Page 130

9. What is health hazard ?

   Ans. Page 131

10. How do pesticides affect human health ?

    Ans. Page 131

11. What is Biological or Bio-technological control of pests ?

    Ans. Page 131

12. How many toxic metals are there ? Name them.

    Ans. Page 132

13. Name few heavy metals which have effect on human health.

    Ans. Page 132

14. What is manganese poisoning ?

    Ans. Page 133

15. Where is arsenic contamination in ground water ?

    Ans. Page 134

16. What is human health ?

    Ans. Page 124

Chapter 9

WASTE MANAGEMENT

INTRODUCTION

Everyone is familiar with wastes, especially those generated in municipalities, such as food wastes and rubbish, abandoned vehicles, demolition and construction of building wastes, street sweepings and garden wastes. These wastes are included in agricultural, industrial, mineral and domestic sources.

Treatment of Waste Water

Waste water is defined as a combination of domestic and industrial waste water, with or without rain runoff. Domestic waste water is sewage only and does not include rain runoff. Therefore, waste water is a complex mixture of natural inorganic and organic materials mixed with man-made substances. It contains everything discharged to the sewer, including materials washed from roads, railways and roofs, and, of course, where the sewer is damaged, ground water will also gain entry. In the broadest sense, waste water can be split into domestic (sanitary) waste water, also known as sewage, industrial waste water and, finally, municipal waste water which is a mixture of both.

The principal objectives of waste water treatment are —

(i) to convert the waste materials present in waste water into stable oxidized end products. It can be safely disposed off to inland water without any adverse ecological effects;

(ii) to protect human health in the society;

(iii) to recover and recycle the valuable components of waste water;

(iv) to ensure waste water is effectively disposed off on a regular and reliable basis;

(v) to provide an economic method of disposal.

Waste Water Characteristics

According to their characteristics, waste water can be distinguished into two categories : (a) domestic waste water and (b) industrial waste water.

(a) **Domestic Waste Water Characteristics :** The characteristics of waste water are physical, chemical and microbiological components (total solids, temperature, pH, colour, odour, carbohydrates, proteins, fats, BOD, heavy metals, sulphur, bacteria, algae, virus etc.). In domestic waste water specific toxic and hazardous compounds may exist, i.e. phenols and toxic organics.

(b) **Industrial Waste Water Characteristics :** Each industry is individual. It is not possible to enumerate wastes from all industry types as many wastes are specific to particular industries. Industrial waste water vary considerably in their nature and toxicity.

Waste Water Treatment Processes

Urban waste water is primarily organic in content. A significant number of industries including pharmaceuticals, chemical and food processing industries have high organic waste loads, so that the main treatment processes are geared towards organic removal. In a typical treatment plant, the waste water is directed through a series of physical, chemical and biological processes, each with a specific waste load reduction work.

The processes include the following stages —

(a) Pre-treatment

(b) Primary treatment

(c) Secondary treatment

(d) Tertiary treatment.

(a) **Pre-treatment of Waste Water :** Pre-treatment is the process or sum of processes that is the conventional method of waste water treatment. Through this system, the removal and disintegration of gross solids, the removal of grit and the separation of storm water are accomplished. Oil and grease are also removed at this stage of treatment. The stages of waste water pre-treatment process are shown here :

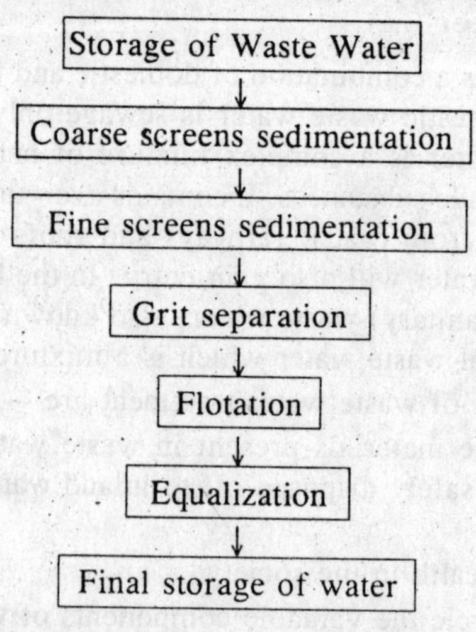

Fig. 23. Basic Waste Water Treatment Process

(b) **Primary Treatment of Waste Water :** Primary treatment is often called sedimentation, clarification or settling system. This is the unit process where the waste water is allowed to settle for a period in a settling tank or reservoir. The waste water is passed through a specially constructed sedimentation tank at such a velocity that the fine solids settle out of suspension by gravity.

The benefits of primary waste water treatment are —

(i) Regulation of suspended solids

(ii) Reduction in BOD

(iii) Reduction in the amount of waste activated sludge

(iv) Removal of floating material

(v) Finally, partial equalization of flow rates and organic load.

(c) **Secondary Treatment of Waste Water :** After primary treatment the settled waste water enters a specially designed reactor where it is mixed or exposed to a dense microbial population or microorganisms under aerobic conditions.

The secondary waste water treatment systems are categorized as —

(i) Suspended growth systems;

(ii) Attached growth systems;

(iii) Dual process systems.

(i) **Suspended growth systems :** It is defined as those aerobic processes that achieve a high microorganism concentration through the recycle of biological solids.

(ii) **Attached growth systems :** It allows a microbial layer to grow on the surface of the media while exposed to the atmosphere from where it draws its oxygen. The microbial layer is sprayed with the waste water.

(iii) **Dual process systems :** It utilizes two-stage arrangements of fixed film and suspended growth processes with the principal objective of achieving very high quality effluent standards.

(d) **Tertiary Treatment of Waste Water :** The principal methods are —

(i) Prolonged settlement in lagoons, irrigation in grassland or via percolation areas (for land treatment).

(ii) Straining through a fine mesh or filtration through sand or gravel.

Solid Waste Management

Solid waste management is concerned with the generation, onsite storage, collection, transfer and transport, processing and recovery, and disposal of solid wastes from a technological and modern society. Today, solid waste management is a multidisciplinary activity that is based on engineering principles but also involves economics, urban and regional planning, and the social sciences and environmental science, among other fields.

Sources of Solid Waste

Sources of solid wastes are related to land use pattern, density of population and the economic standard of the people in a particular area or zone or locality. Although any number of source classifications can be developed, the following categories have been found useful : (i) residential (ii) commercial, (iii) agricultural, (iv) municipal, (v) industrial, (vi) open areas and (vii) treatment plants. According to the World Health Organisation (WHO), the source and types of solid waste are classified in tabular form :

Table : Sources and Type of Solid Wastes

Sources	Facilities	Types of Waste
1. Domestic	Single family dwellings, multifamily dwellings, low, medium and high-rise apartments	Food, paper, packaging, glass, metals, ashes, bulky household waste, hazardous household wastes.
2. Commercial	Shops, restaurants, markets, offices, buildings, hotels, institutions.	Food, paper, packaging, glass, metals, ashes, bulky household wastes, hazardous household wastes.
3. Industrial	Fabrication, light and heavy manufacturing, refineries, chemical plants, mining, power generation.	Industrial process wastes, metals, lumber, plastic, oil, hazardous wastes.
4. Construction and demolition	Buildings, houses, etc.	Soil, concrete, timber, steel, plastics, glass, vegetation.

Table : Physical Composition of Solid Wastes

General Composition	Typical Composition	Detailed Composition
Organic	Food putrefaction	Food, vegetable
	Paper and cardboard	Paper, cardboard
	Plastics	Polyethylene terephthalate (PETE) **High-density** Polyethylene (HDPF) Polyvinyl chloride (PVC) **Low-density** Polyethylene (LDPE) Polypropylene (PP) Polystyrene (PS) Other multilayer plastics
	Clothing/fabrics	Textiles Carpets Rubber Leather
	Yard waste	Garden Trimmings
	Wood	Wood
	Miscellaneous organics	Bone
Inorganic	Metals	Tin cans Ferrous metals Aluminium Non-ferrous metals
	Glass	Colourless Coloured
	Dirt, ash, etc.	Dirt, screenings Ashes Stone Bricks
	Unclassified	Bulky items

Solid Waste Management

Solid waste management has four aspects —

(1) Public Health Aspect

(2) Legal Aspect

(3) Environmental Aspect

(4) Integrated management of solid waste.

(1) Public Health aspects of solid waste management

Solid waste may consists of —

(i) Human pathogens — handkerchiefs, diapers, contaminated food and surgical dressings

(ii) Animal pathogens — waste from pets

(iii) Soil pathogens — garden waste

Suitable conditions must exist for a person to be at risk from solid waste. These ae —

(i) There should be an infectious dose of the pathogens.

(ii) The pathogens should have a transmission route to the person, i.e. aerosol, fecal-oral route, hand to mouth etc.

(iii) The person must not have immunity to the pathogen.

The pathogens should be checked from invading the human host by the following methods —

(i) Good hygiene and dietary habits must be followed.

(ii) Those involved regularly with solid waste must be vaccinated for pathogenic diseases.

(iii) Specific waste storage and handling techniques must be introduced. The wastes most amenable to disease transmission must be separated at source. Less manual handling and more automated storage, collection and sorting is desirable.

(2) Legal aspects of solid waste

The Directive of Environmental Assessment and the proposed Directive on Landfill are important directives on solid waste in the Urban Centres.

Strict waste acceptance criteria and procedures are set out for :

(i) Waste acceptance

(ii) Chemical, physical and biological waste properties

(iii) Suitability of wastes

(iv) Waste loading rates

(v) Water, leachate and gas control

(vi) Water balance and groundwater protection.

The objectives of waste directives are :

(i) to promote clean technologies

(ii) to use landfill only as a last resort

(iii) to reduce overall packing quantities for landfilling and thereby reduce the volumes of municipal solid waste.

(3) Environmental aspects of solid waste

Although landfill is the most common route of solid waste disposal, it is undesirable and alternatives must be pursued :

(i) Landfill site and dump sites, if not properly operated, cause soil and groundwater contamination.

(ii) Landfill causes litter, scavengers, fires, rat infestations and a terrible odour.

(iii) Landfilling in moist climates produces enormous quantities of leachate which are toxic.

(iv) Landfilling in dry climate causes localized air pollution problems.

(4) Integrated management of solid waste

The following figure shows the hierarchy in waste management policy :

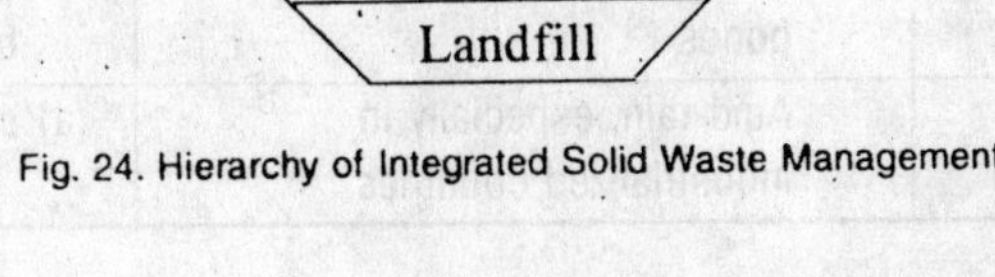

Fig. 24. Hierarchy of Integrated Solid Waste Management

The priorities in a waste management policy are :

(i) to reduce the amount of waste

(ii) to manufacture products with minimal waste

(iii) to promote good practice of waste monitoring

(iv) to identify areas for improvement by regular "waste audits" by various producers and consumers

(v) to reuse, reprocess and remanufacture products.

Water Pollution Management

Definition of Water Pollution

Water pollution may be defined as any physical change in the natural water by the addition of any foreign material that adversely affects human and aquatic life, directly or indirectly, in the short run or in the long run.

Water is considered to be polluted when it is contaminated with :

(i) suspended impurities, such as sand, mud, clay and organic matter;

(ii) dissolved gases like CO_2, NH_3, N_2, H_2S;

(iii) dissolved minerals like calcium, sodium and magnesium salts;

(iv) isotopes or radiologically active substances; and

(v) microorganisms like bacteria, viruses, protozoas and worms.

The pollution of water alters the physical properties of water, such as colour, odour, turbidity and temperature. The presence of dissolved or suspended chemical pollutants can make the water acidic or saline.

Sources of Water Pollution

The principal reasons behind water pollution are the problems like population increase, agricultural and industrial waste generation, sewerage disposal, radioactive waste generation, etc.

The sources of water pollution can be of two types :

A. Natural Sources

B. Man-made or Anthropogenic sources.

Table A. Natural Sources of Water Pollution

Class of Pollutants	Sources	Effects
Dust	(a) soil erosion (b) volcanic eruption (c) landslides (d) storms (e) earthquakes	Suspended particulate matter in water causes health hazards and epidemics
Gases	(a) volcanic eruption (b) dead and decaying organic matter	(a) acid rain (b) advance effect on aquatic life
Organic matter	decaying bodies of plants and animals in swamps or deep ponds	(a) introduces microorganisms in the water and affects human health and aquatic life
Rain Water	Acid rain, especially in industrialized countries	(a) eliminates aquatic life

Table B. Anthropogenic Sources of Water Pollution

Class of Pollutants	Sources	Effects
Pathogens	(a) animal wastes (b) human sewage	Outbreak of water borne diseases, such as dysentery, cholera, hepatitis, typhoid
Organic wastes	(a) human and domestic sewage (b) animal and plant waste (c) wastes from agro-based industries	(a) depletion of dissolved O_2 (b) death of aquatic organisms (c) foul smell in the water
Inorganic chemicals and minerals	(a) agricultural runoff (b) domestic sewage (c) animal wastes (d) wastes from petrochemical, fertilizer and similar other industries (e) mining activities.	(a) eutrophication (b) disruption in the aquatic ecosystem (c) high nitrate concentration in water
Heat	Cooling water from industrial and power generating installation	solubility of O_2 in water decreases
Radioactivity	Nuclear plants	cancer and genetic defects in humans

QUESTIONS FOR EXAMINATION

A. Essay-Type Questions

1. Discuss about waste water treatment.
   Ans. Pp. 137-139
2. Analyse the different characteristics of waste water.
   Ans. Pp. 137-139
3. Describe the waste water treatment processes.
   Ans. Pp. 138-139
4. Discuss the sources of solid waste in the urban centres.
   Ans. Pp. 139-140
5. How do you describe solid waste management ?
   Ans. Pp. 140-142
6. Describe the different sources of water pollution.
   Ans. Pp. 142-143

B. Short Answer-Type Questions

1. What is waste ?
   Ans. Page 137
2. How many types of wastes are there ?
   Ans. Page 137
3. What is the process of pre-treatment of waste ?
   Ans. Page 138
4. What is BOD ?
   Ans. Page 138
5. Define waste management.
   Ans. Page 140
6. How many sources of solid waste are there ?
   Ans. Page 140
7. What is the legal aspects of solid waste ?
   Ans. Page 141
8. What is water pollution ?
   Ans. Page 142
9. Define water pollution.
   Ans. Page 142
10. How many sources of water pollution are there ?
    Ans. Page 142
11. What are the effects of water pollution ?
    Ans. Page 142

Chapter 10

ENVIRONMENTAL POLITICS

History of Environmental Institution and Instruments

INTRODUCTION

There are more than one thousand recognised **Environmental Institutions** in the world. Among them only **ten International** organising Institutions have been discussed :

(1) **ACASTD : Advisory Committee on the Application of Science and Technology to Development** (UN) — functions mainly to the member nations regarding the development of Science and Technology in relation to environment.

(2) **ASEAN : Association of South East Asian Nations** — mainly functions for the group of South East Asian countries from political, economic and social point of view.

(3) **ASDB : Asian Development Bank** — It functions mainly for the Asian countries in the form of giving loans, and economic assistance for social, economic and humanitarian developments.

(4) **AGRIS : International Information System for the Agricultural Science and Technology (FAO)** — established for the improvement of agricultural processes all over the world with more emphasis on research and prevention of agricultural diseases.

(5) **CEC : Commission of the European Communities** — It was formed on the basis of agreements participated by most of the European nations for safeguarding economic and social interests.

(6) **CIOMS : Council for International Organisation of Medical Science** — mainly functions in order to prevent epidemics, public health and communicable diseases.

(7) **ECB : Environment Coordination Board** — The programmes relating to ecology, environment and public health are coordinated through this organisation of the UN among the member nations.

(8) **GATT : General Agreement on Trade & Tariff** — an international body which functions for the world wide trade that is export and import duties/tariff to be levied among the member nations.

(9) **GRID : Global Resource Information Database** — formed for collecting information on the resources situated at different countries.

(10) **IOI : International Ocean Institute** — Oceans comprise of 72% of global land mass, so it is mandatory for UN to study ocean as the centre of resources etc.

At the national level, there are nearly one hundred government recognised or under the control of Science and Technology deptt. organisations or institutions which have worked very hard after the independence to make themselves at par with their international counterparts. Among them only eleven have been discussed.

(1) **MSI : Meteorological Survey of India** — functions as the sole organisation for different kinds of weather predictions, researches in collaboration with its international counterpart.

(2) **GSI : Geological Survey of India** — one of the oldest and premier institutions founded by Britishers in the 18th century which is responsible for carrying out extensive survey of mineral resources in India, South Asia & S. E. Asia. Always works in collaboration with International bodies and its counterparts in other countries.

(3) **B.S.I : Botanical Survey of India** — functions as premier organisation in the field of research, medicinal contributions etc.

(4) **Z.S.I. : Zoological Survey of India** — has contributed a lot for protecting wild life, setting up national parks and ecological safeguarding of mankind.

(5) **A.S.I. : Anthropological Survey of India** — another oldest institution of British India of 18th century which has worked relentlessly for aborigines, tribes and backward people of India.

(6) **BARC : Bhabha Atomic Research Centre** — first Atomic Research Centre of independent India with lot of contributions and development for Atomic Energy.

(7) **IITs : Indian Institute of Technologies** — established with a view to carry out and impart technological knowhow in the rapidly developing technological scenario all over the world.

(8) **I.I.S. (Bangalore) : Indian Institute of Science** — one of the premier Swadeshi Scientific Institutions of India founded by Prof. C. V. Raman for working on the pure sciences.

(9) **C.S.I.R. : Council of Scientific and Industrial Research** — set up after independence as the parent body for monitoring the research works done by different regional laboratories and scientific organisations. They all work under the umbrella of CSIR.

(10) **I.C.A.R. : Indian Council of Agricultural Research** — Another important research and training organisation which brought revolutions in the form of "Green Revolution" in Punjab, Haryana. Carries out specialised research for agricultural seeds crops, fertilisers etc.

(11) **ENVIS** : Realising the importance of Environmental Information, the Government of India, in December 1982, established an **Environmental Information System** (ENVIS) as a plan program. The focus of ENVIS since inception has been on providing environmental information to decision makers, policy planners, scientists and engineers, research workers etc. all over the country.

Environmental Politics at the National and State Level

Introduction

The history of protection of environment in relation to Central Government has been enumerated under the different Acts undertaken by the Central Government. According to these Acts the Central Government shall have the power to take all such measures as deemed necessary or expedient for the purpose of protecting and improving the quality of the environment and preventing, controlling and alerting environmental pollution.

Some of the power given to the Central Government may include measures with respect to all or any particular matter.

Firstly, there should be coordination among the different State Governments, offices and other authorities.

Secondly, there should be wide range program for the prevention, control and abatement of environmental pollution at the national level for planning and execution.

Thirdly, there should be uniform standards in terms of quality in relation to the environment and its various aspects.

Fourthly, in order to control the various toxic discharges from different industries standards should be laid down for emission or discharge of environmental pollutants provided that different standards for emission of discharge may be laid down from different sources having regard to the quality or composition of the emission or discharge of environmental pollutants from such sources.

Fifthly, restriction of areas in which any industries, operations or processes or class of industries operations or processes shall not be carried out or shall be carried out subject to certain safeguards.

Sixthly, procedures and safeguards to be laid down for the prevention of accidents which may cause environmental pollution and remedial measures for such accidents.

Seventhly, procedures and safeguards laid down for the handling of hazardous substances.

Eighthly, manufacturing processes, materials and substances should be examined which are likely to cause environmental pollution.

Ninthly, carrying out and sponsoring investigations and research relating to problems of environmental pollutions.

Tenthly, inspection of any premises, plant, equipment, machinery, manufacturing or other processes, materials or substances and giving, by order, of such directions to such authorities, officers or persons as it may consider necessary to take steps for the prevention, control and abetment of environmental pollution.

Eleventhly, to give recognition or establish laboratories and institutes to carry out the functions entrusted to such environmental laboratories and institutes.

Twelfthly, collection and dissemination of information in respect of matters relating to environmental pollution.

Thirteenthly, the preparation of manuals, codes, guides, relating to the prevention, control and abatement of environmental pollution.

Lastly, such other matters as the Central Government deems necessary or expedient for the purpose of securing the effective implementation, control of and improvement of environment.

In order to carry out the aforesaid objects the Central Government has the necessary provisions with regard to appointment of officers and their powers and functions as they think fit and functions according to the directions of the Central Government.

The rules to regulate the environmental pollution by the Central Government may provide for all or any of the following matters :

(a) the standard of quality of air, water or soil for various areas and purposes.

(b) the maximum allowable limits of concentration of various environmental pollutants including noise for different areas.

(c) the procedures and safeguards for the handling of hazardous substances.

(d) the prohibition and restrictions on the handling of hazardous substances in different areas.

(e) the prohibition and restrictions on the location of industries and the carrying on of processes and operations in different areas.

(f) the procedures and safeguards for the prevention of accidents which may cause environmental pollution and for providing the remedial measures for such accidents.

The functions of the Central Board shall be to promote cleanliness of streams and wells in different areas of the state. However, the Central Board may perform all or any of the following functions :

(1) advice of the Central Government on any matter concerning the prevention and control of water pollution.

(2) Coordinate the activities of the State Board and resolve disputes among them.

(3) Provide technical assistance and guidance to the State Boards, carry out and sponsor investigations, research relating to problems of water pollution and prevention, control or abatement of water pollution.

(4) Plan and organise the training of persons engaged or to be engaged in programs for the prevention, control or abatement of water pollution and prevention on such terms and conditions as the Central Government may specify.

(5) Organise through mass media a comprehensive programme regarding the prevention and control of water pollution.

(6) Collect, compile, and publish technical and statistical data relating to water pollution and the measures devised for its effective prevention and control. Also preparation of manuals, codes or guides relating to treatment and disposal of sewage and trade effluents and disseminate information connected therewith.

The functions of State Board are more or less same in comparison to the Central Board except in few reservations :

Firstly, a comprehensive programme for the prevention, control or abetment of pollution of streams and wells in the state should be planned and thereof to execute.

Secondly, to advise the State Governments on any matter concerning the prevention, control or abatement of water pollution.

Thirdly, to advise the State Governments in order to laying down or modifying annual effluent standards for the sewage and trade effluents and for the quality of receiving waters (not being in an inter-state stream) resulting from the discharge of effluents and to classify waters of the state.

Fourthly, to involve economical and reliable methods of treatment of sewage and trade effluents having regard to the peculiar conditions of soils, climate and water resources of different reasons and, more specially, the prevailing flow characteristics of water in streams and wells which render it impossible to attain even the minimum degree of dilution.

Fifthly, To collaborate with the Central Board in organising the training of persons engaged or to be engaged in programmes relating to prevention, control or abatement of water pollution and to organise mass education programmes relating there to.

Sixthly, to advise the State Government with respect to the location of any industry — the carrying on which is likely to pollute a stream or well.

However, any direction to perform the functions of any State Board given to the Central Board in respect of any area would not preclude the Board from performing such functions in any other area in the State.

Human Rights Issues Relating to Environment

What is Human Rights ?

Man is born free with equal dignity, rights and moral claims which are inalienable and inherent in all human beings by virtue of their humanity alone. The claims are articulated and formulated in what we today called **human rights** and have been translated into legal rights, established according to the law-creating processes of societies — both national and international. The basis of these legal rights is the consent of the governed, that is the consent of the subjects of the rights.

The Human Rights Law

In order to draw up an International Bill of Human Rights, defining the human rights and freedoms referred to in the Charter, as charged upon the Commission on Human Rights, established in 1945, which is a subsidiary body of the Economic & Social Council (ECOSOC) — a principal organ of UN. A major step in drafting the International Bill of Human Rights was realised on 10th December 1948, when the U.N. General Assembly adopted the 'Universal Declaration of Human Rights' as a common standard of achievement for all peoples and nations.

The International Bill of Human Rights

On 16th Dec. 1966, the United Nations General Assembly adopted two Covenants — the International Covenant on Economic, Social and Cultural Rights (ICESR) and the International Covenant on Civil and Political Rights (ICCPR) and an Optimal Protocol to the ICCPR, allowing for complaints to be made by individuals on violations of their rights embodied in the covenant. The adoption of these two covenants endorsed the General Assembly resolution of 1950 that "that the enjoyment of civil and political rights and economic, social and cultural rights are interconnected and interdependent."

The International Covenant on Economic, Social and Cultural Rights (ICESCR)

Social security, an adequate standard of living including adequate food, clothing and housing, protection of the family, the highest attainable standards of physical and mental health, education and participation in cultural life are recognised by the Covenant. None of these rights protected under the Covenant can be suspended.

The International Human Rights Law for Child Protection

The Committee on the Rights of the Child, established under the convention and comprising the independent experts, examines periodic reports submitted by State Parties on the implementation of the convention. Which came into force on 2nd September 1990 less than one year after it had been adopted by the United Nations General Assembly. The United Nations International Children's (Emergency) Fund (UNICEF), which plays an important role in promoting the convention which may recommend to the General Assembly that studies on specific issues relating to the rights of the child should be undertaken by the Secretary General in reference to the children in armed conflict were the subject of a recent study. Apart from that "A special Rapporteur appointed by the Commission on Human Rights, is investigating the sale of children, child prostitution, and child pornography, taking into account the fact that these practices are being increasingly internationalized." Also, an African Charter on the Rights and Welfare of the child adopted by the Organisation of African Unity will enter into force after it has been ratified by fifteen member states.

The United Nation Educational, Scientific and Cultural Organisation (UNESCO)

Its competence extends to the rights relating to education, science (including social science) and culture and communication, which includes freedom of opinion and expression and freedom of the press.

According to the Universal Declaration of Human Rights by the United Nations which have been written as Articles are mostly civil and political rights and concern the freedom and personal security of individuals.

Accordingly, the **Article 25** has specially mentioned that "Everyone has the right to a standard of living adequate for the health and well-being of himself and of his family including food, clothing, housing and medical care and necessary social services." Also included are "Motherhood and childhood are entitled to special care and assistance."

Apart from that, Article 27 has also specifically mentioned "the protection of the moral and material interests resulting from any scientific, literary or artistic production of which he is the author."

To sum up, it can be said that human rights were the basic rights any human being enjoyed from the early civilisations. But at times from the historical anecdotes it is found human rights had been violated by the rulers for sake of establishing supremacy. After the Second World War (1939-45) people in general felt the necessity to form an International body called "United Nations," and, thus, the necessity of 'Human Rights' — which are basically legal, social and political by nature — came into existence. It is undoubtedly of special achievement that "Human Rights in Relation to Environment" has come a long way to establish its present position.

Women Commission

The International Covenant on Economic, Social and Cultural Rights (ICESCR) in India, as also **The National Commission for Women** was constituted vide the National Commission for Women Act, 1990, dated 30th August 1990 (No. 20 of 1990). It consists of a Chairperson, committed to the cause of women, 5 members and a member-secretary.

Functions of the Commission

Firstly, to investigate and examine all matters relating to the safeguards provided for women under the constitution and other laws.

Secondly, present to the Central Government annually and, at such other times, as the commission may deem fit, reports upon the working of those safeguards.

Thirdly, make in such reports recommendations for the effective implementation of those safeguards for improving the conditions of women by the Union or any State.

Fourthly, review from time to time, the existing provisions of the constitution and other laws affecting women and recommend amendments thereto so as to suggest remedial legislature measures to meet any lacunae, inadequacies or shortcomings in such legislations.

Fifthly, take up the cases of violation of the provisions of the constitution and of other laws relating to women with the appropriate authorities.

Sixthly, look into complaints and take suo moto notice of matters relating to deprivation of women's rights, non-implementation of laws enacting to provide protection to women, and noncompliance of policy decisions, guidelines or instructions aimed at mitigating hardships and ensuring welfare and relief to women.

Seventhly, call for special studies or investigations into specific problems or situations arising out of discrimination and atrocities against women and identify the constraints so as to recommend strategies for their removal.

Eighthly, undertake promotional and educational research so as to suggest ways for ensuring due representation of women in all spheres and identify factors responsible for impeding this advancement.

Ninthly, participate and advise on the planning process of socio-economic development of women.

Tenthly, evaluate the progress of the development of women under the Union and any state.

Eleventhly, inspect or cause to be inspected a jail, remand home, women's institution or other place of custody where women are kept as prisoners or otherwise, and take up with the concerned authorities for remedial action, if necessary.

Twelfthly, fund litigation involving issues affecting a large body of women.

Thirteenthly, to make periodical reports to the Government on any matter pertaining to women and, in particular, various difficulties under which women toil.

Fourteenthly, any other matter which may be referred to it by the Central Government.

Powers of the Commission

The Commission shall have all the powers of a civil court trying a suit and, in particular, in respect of the following matters —

(i) summoning and enforcing the attendance of any person from any part of India and examining him on oath,

(ii) requiring the discovery and production of any document,

(iii) receiving evidence on affidavits,

(iv) requisitioning any public record or copy thereof from any court or office,

(v) issuing commissions for the examination of witnesses and documents, and

(vi) any other matter which may be prescribed.

The Fourth World Conference on Women was held in Beijing (China) from September 4-15, 1995 on the theme **"Equality, Development and Peace"**. The Indian delegation not only played a leading role in drafting the Declaration and Platform for Action but also earned the distinction of being the first to endorse the Beijing Declaration and Platform for Action without any reservation.

The Beijeing Declaration can be summed up as —

(1) Determination to advance, to develop, acknowledge, recognise and to dedicate the goals of equality, development, peace, voices, status and to unreservedly addressing the constraint, obstacles and thus enhancing further the advancement and empowerment of women all over the world.

(2) To ensure the full implementation of human rights of women and of the girl child as inalienable, integral and indivisible part of all human rights and fundamental freedoms.

(3) That women's empowerment and their full participation on the basis of equality in all spheres of society, including participation in the decision making process and to power are fundamentals for the achievement of equality, development and peace.

(4) Women's rights are human rights.

Regarding the **"Platform for Action"** which was taken up in the Beijing Conference the foremost importance was given to promote and protect the human rights of women, through the full implementation of all human rights instruments, especially the convention on the elimination of all forms of discrimination against women.

To ensure equality and non-discrimination under the law and in practice. To achieve legal literacy. It is further pointed out that women engaged in the defence of human rights must be protected. Governments have a duty to guarantee the full enjoyment of all rights set out in the Universal Declaration of Human Rights, the International Covenant on Civil and Political Rights and the International Covenant on Economic, Social and Cultural Rights by women working peacefully in a personal or organisational capacity for the promotion and protection of human rights. Non-governmental organisations, women's organisations and feminist groups have played a catalytic role in the promotion of the human rights of women through grassroot activities, net working and advocacy and need encouragement, support and access to information from Governments in order to carry out these activities.

Women's Participation in different works related to Environment

Introduction : It is a widely accepted fact in India that both women and environmental issues have been neglected in the developmental process over the last several years. Along with articulation and growing perception of this neglect is the perception of the link between the two, that is of gender perspectives within environmental concerns. It has arisen primarily on two accounts, i.e. to be seen as the ecological consciousness of women, and the disproportionate impact of environmental degradation on them.

It is now a well-established fact that women play a predominant role in activities relating to natural resources and that the degradation of these resources, in turn, has a disproportionate effect on women is fairly well established by now.

The diversity among women, between rural and urban women, and between different classes of rural women, presents all woman being clubbed together. Apart from these, there are problems which have common characteristics and shared by all women but at the same time significant differences in the priorities, consciousness and roles of women across classes, and regions. Therefore, the problems unleashed by the processes of development do not affect all women in an equal manner, even in the same regional or cultural context.

(a) **Urban Environment and Women Participation**

Under this heading which deals with the middle, higher and lower classes from socio-economic point of view demonstrate no particular consciousness of ecological issues, at least no more or less than urban men, which leads one to believe that there are no gender differentials in inherent awareness of or no concern for environmental issues, at least among members of these classes.

With the progress in civilisation the urban women were the first to get the fruits of civilisation and, with industrial revolution, the prospects of the participation of women in different fields of works have brightened.

Let's classify the women in different categories — (i) Teachers, (ii) Industrial workers (**Specially designated jobs**), (iii) Nurses, (iv) Office assistants, (v) Bureaucrats, (vi) Company secretarial jobs, (vii) Doctors, (viii) Engineers, (ix) Midwives and health assistants, (x) Domestic help, (xi) Sales women, (xii) Housewives.

It is no doubt a step towards development reflected from the different categories mentioned above about the women of urban sector and their participation which is linked to environment. It needs special mention about those categories specially linked to higher education and upwardly mobile women of the society who enjoy the fruits of environmental benefits and exploit environment to its maximum point like water, natural resources for their personal comfort and well being compared to those women who are socially downwardly mobile due to lack of socio-economic power. So one has to be very careful regarding this all-pervasive differences between stratas of the society.

(b) **Rural Environment and Women's Participation**

The close association between women and natural resources is valid primarily in a rural context, and especially among women of less affluent families. For such women, the association which over generations have required them to provide food, water, fuel, fodder and income come from the surrounding base have existed in association with environment. Fulfilling these roles has given them a special understanding of natural resources and led then to adopt a more sensitive attitude towards them. It is noteworthy that this consciousness is different from that of rural men's as also from that of rural women of affluent households who do not typically carry out such roles.

With the progress of civilisation the scope of work for rural women have been less compared to its urban counterpart. In spite of the practical constraints in relation to socio-economic factors, today's rural women are also engaging themselves in different types of works with their limited qualifications and other kinds of hardships. They may be categorised under (i) Agricultural labour, (ii) Trader, (iii) Shopkeepers, (iv) Teachers, (v) Village level workers, (vi) Women workers (**VLWWs**), (vii) Domestic help, (viii) Midwives, (ix) Health workers, (x) Housewives.

(c) **Women's Consciousness of the Environment**

It is not something inherent, i.e. thus, conservative approach is arising out of their being women as is often propagated. We can find it rooted in their roles and work tasks, which lead them to interact extensively with natural resources for survival. Apart from that, women's existence remains circumscribed by the domestic sphere in relation to their options, motivations and perceptions almost totally defined and coloured by their domestic roles. It is more clearly seen in cases where women's exposure to cash economics or to the dynamics of system external to their domestic sphere has been significant. In such cases, women's priorities reflect different attitudes and association with the environment. Similarly, where the survival of their households do not depend on biomass resources, they lack the skill in managing such resources. It is, thus, the specific tasks that poor women perform and the knowledge base and skills that build up as a consequence of performing such tasks over several years that give rise to the special concerns they share on ecological issues and the understanding they demonstrate in managing natural resources. Similarly, these women feel the impact of environmental degradation because they interact with it for survival.

(d) **Relationship between Women and the Environment**

There is a need to look at the two in tandem. This arises not surely because women are perceived as victims of environmental destruction, but despite the traditional roles played by women in the management of natural resources and the knowledge they possess based on which different roles are carried out. But now they have been completely marginalised from the processes that seek to formulate strategies for the use and management of resources. More significantly, in the process of this marginalisation, women have further lost status and power, by losing access to resources as well as control over their labour and knowledge.

(e) **The special difficulties that women face in their extraordinary work burden or lack of access to health care**

It is really regrettable that this problem faced by women is located in the sexual division of labour marked by a double work burden (**at home and outside**). The problem lies in the specific nature of tasks they do, and the unequal distribution of resources like food within the household, which stems from women's inferior status in the household and from a lack of control over cash and productive resources like land.

To sum up, for women's participation in different works related to environment the first issue to be taken care of is that the both women and environmental issues have been neglected in the developmental process for a long period.

Secondly, people now are realising that women play a predominant role in activities related to natural resources.

Thirdly, there is a lot of difference from socio-political and economic points of view among urban and rural women which is preventing them to be clubbed together.

Fourthly, the rural women are more conscious about environmental degradation and try to preserve ecological balance compared to urban women who exploit environmental resources for personal benefits.

Fifthly, The scope of work has been expanded both for urban and rural women after advancements in science and technology but environmental exploitation has increased to an alarming state.

Finally, Women's consciousness towards environment needs further study to be taken up in great details. Otherwise, the environmental consciousness among women of all categories cannot be imbibed. Which, in the long run, will hamper human civilisation to the extent of unforeseen devastations.

Let's conclude by saying that unless people from all stratas, socio-economic groups, socio-cultural levels, governmental levels do not come up and take up this issue at a top priority level, civilisation will be in jeopardy in near future.

Green Bench

What is the "Green Bench" ?

The **"Green Bench"** was formed as per the directive of the Hon'ble Supreme Court of India, to take up all kinds of ecological and environment related matters. Each High Court in India has to, and has indeed, set up a **"Green Bench"**. All cases that are related to environment are adjudicated by the Green Bench.

Why is it called the "Green Bench" ?

In the cause-list of the High Court, it is mentioned as the **"Environment and Pollution Bench"**. However, since it was formed to save the greeneries, especially in the urban areas, and also to maintain the equilibrium of the eco-system, it was popularly known as the **"Green Bench"**. Cases include senseless destruction of greeneries, contaminating and filling up of water bodies, sound and odour pollution and all other activities that degrade our environment.

Why was the "Green Bench" formed ?

Howrah Ganatantrik Nagarik Samiti filed a writ petition under Article 32 of the Constitution of India before the Hon'ble Supreme Court of India, regarding various environmental and pollution related hazards in and around Howrah. Mr. Subhas Dutta, the Secretary, used to argue the case in person in the Hon'ble Supreme Court. The matter was heard several times before the Hon'ble Supreme Court of India. Finally, a division bench of the Hon'ble Supreme Court, presided over by Hon'ble Justice Kuldeep Singh, directed the Hon'ble Chief Justice of Calcutta High Court to form a bench for taking up environment and pollution matters. The Chief Justice of Calcutta High Court also complied with the direction and formed the Green Bench.

When was the Green Bench formed ?

The Green Bench was formed in 1996. The first sitting of the Green Bench in the Calcutta High Court was on 17th June 1996. At that time, the Bench consisted of Hon'ble Justice Umesh Chandra Banerjee and Hon'ble Justice Ronojit Kumar Mitra.

Calcutta High Court had the first Green Bench in India as per the direction of the Hon'ble Supreme Court.

How many Judges are there in the Green Bench ?

The Green Bench is a Division Bench consisting of two Hon'ble Judges. At present (2001), the Green Bench of the Calcutta High Court is presided over by Hon'ble Chief Justice Ashok Kumar Mathur and Hon'ble Justice Barin Ghosh.

The construction of an underground aquarium at Victoria Square, Camac Street : A struggle to protect the precious water body

Bengal Janakalyan Sanskriti Utthan Trust, jointly with the Calcutta Municipal Corporation, took up a project to construct an underground aquarium, using the waterbody at Victoria Square. The same kind of aquarium is already in Singapore and New York.

But "People United for Better Living In Calcutta" (PUBLIC), who works for the cause of environment and pollution control, filed a writ petition before the Green Bench of the Hon'ble High Court of Calcutta, challenging the proposed project on the ground of change and conversion of the water body.

It is to be noted under the 1994 Amendment of Inland Fisheries Act that filling up and changing the nature and character of water body measuring more than 5 cottahs, and which contains water for six months in a calendar year, is banned in West Bengal, and it is also a punishable offence. Taking the shelter of that Act, the case was filed. The matter was heard for many days before the Green Bench.

Ultimately, the Hon'ble High Court allowed the project after making some modifications and framing some guidelines for the proposed project. It was also observed that the Project was not contradictory to the mentioned Act. Therefore, there is no chance of filling up the pond or changing the nature and character of the water since the pond is required for the underground aquarium.

Environmental Movements for Environmental Protection

The term **Environmental Protection** is closely linked to environmental movement because in the recent period of human history there is strikingly high rate of resource utilisation. Ever-expanding and intensifying agricultural and industrial production has, in turn, generated increasing demands on the world's total stock and flow of resources. Apart from that, the increasing dependence on modern technologies on the resources of nature through quick spread of energy and intensive production technologies mean lesser dependence on nature and natural resources. But these demands are particularly generated from the industrially advanced countries in the North and the industrial enclaves in the developing countries in the South. Regarding these the conflicts become visible when the resource and energy-intensive industrial technologies are challenged by the communities whose survival depends on the conservation of the resources threatened by destruction and over-exploitation.

In India, the movements with regard to environmental issues are emerging from the conflicts over natural resources and the people's right to survival are spreading in Indian sub-continent where most of the natural resources are already being utilised to provide the basic needs for survival to a large population. Therefore, the introduction of resource and energy-intensive production technologies under such conditions has resulted in economic growth only for a small minority. Thus the deteriorating condition of natural resources of any country has, in the recent past, created environmental movements of various levels. In India, the environmental consciousness of the elite can be said to have started from the Stockholm Conference on Environment held in 1972, but the ecological sensitivity of the rural masses has been in their culture and consciousness.

All of the People's environmental movements have come as response to their survival base as a demand for the conservation of very vital resources that are still remaining and sustaining the people of any country. The most important people's environmental movements in India in the last few decades have taken place around the issue of the conservation of these essential natural resources.

(a) Chipko Movement for Environmental Protection

This movement which started with the Himalayan area of the State of UP, and later spread in other mountain areas like the Western Ghats, the Aravallis and the Vindhyas. The Britishers introduced the concept of modern forest management in relation to ecological significance and local use value. It is a movement "of those people who are living in and around the forest that sustain their lives". All the economic activities connected with the livelihood of these people are based on forest resources, which play a very vital role in the stabilization of the soil and water systems and, thus, maintain fertility of the land. Therefore, the non-conversion of the mixed natural forests to monoculture of commercial species is the motto of this movement.

(b) **Some other Movements for Environmental Protection**

There are people's movements going on in diverse areas of the country against the big dams like **Tehri** in the north, **Sersi** in the south, **Koel-karo** on the east, **Inchampalli** in Central India. These movements are against the destruction of forests, agricultural lands, the resources of the forests, the destruction of the life support system through the introduction of water-logging, salinity etc.

(i) **Two Environmental Movements in Karnataka — Samaj Parivartan Samudaya (SPS)**

It has been actively associated with the two people's movements, viz, the one against pollution of Tungabhadra river and air by major two industries. The movement against pollution of Tungabhadra river began in 1983 with formation of Village Environmental Committees in all affected villages with priority for women, fisherfolk, shepherds etc. who are most affected. The other movement against air pollution by major harmful industries grew steadily from padyatra in the affected village, the environmental camps, talks with different bodies directly involved for this pollution etc.

(ii) **The Environmental Society of Chandigarh**

It is seen that the impact of mass media including radio, television and newspaper have impact for arousing awareness among the common people. With the regular highlighting of evils of **Environmental Pollution** and in creating an environmental awareness in the people the Environmental Society of Chandigarh has become landmark of this type of movement. Apart from this, there are several other non-governmental organisations who are working for the environmental conservation and protection. The society has established itself as one of the foremost in India and working actively educating the citizens about environmental protection and conservation.

To sum up precisely it is felt that people who are closely living within environment or along the environment have tried to protect environment or conserve it with their own adopted methods and techniques because forests give them socio-economic protection and livelihood. But with the onset of British rule in India (1757) the environmental degradation and deforestation started for their own commercial interests. After independence, with the onset of liberalisation in overall administration, people have started forming new resistance groups against any environmental pollution, deforestation for any commercial vandalism and clandestine use of natural resources including minerals. In this respect the role of women are becoming noteworthy.

QUESTIONS FOR EXAMINATION

A. Essay-Type Questions

1. Describe the different environmental institutions in the world.
   Ans. Pp. 145-147
2. Give a statement about the environmental politics at the National and State levels.
   Ans. Pp. 146-148
3. Write an essay on Human Rights issues.
   Ans. Pp. 148-150
4. Analyse about the women's commission and environment.
   Ans. Pp. 151-154
5. Discuss about women's participation in different works related to environment.
   Ans. Pp. 151-154
6. Explain about the "Green Bench".
   Ans. Pp. 154-155
7. Describe the environmental movement in India.
   Ans. Pp. 155-156
8. Discuss any two environmental movements in India.
   Ans. Pp. 155-156
9. Discuss the role of Women's Commission.
   Ans. Pp. 153-154

B. Short Answer-Type Questions

1. What is ENVIS ?
   Ans. Page 146
2. How was human rights law created ?
   Ans. Page 149
3. What is Women's Commission ?
   Ans. Page 150
4. What are the role of women on environment ?
   Ans. Page 151
5. What are the women's consciousness about environment ?
   Ans. Page 152
6. What are the relations between women and the environment ?
   Ans. Page 151
7. What is the **"Green Bench"** ?
   Ans. Page 154
8. Why is it called the **"Green Bench"** ?
   Ans. Page 154
9. Why was the **"Green Bench"** formed ?
   Ans. Page 154
10. When was the **"Green Bench"** formed ?
    Ans. Page 154

11. How many Judges are there on the **"Green Bench"** ?

    Ans. Page 154

12. What is the necessity of the environmental movement ?

    Ans. Page 155

13. What do you mean by Chipko Movement ?

    Ans. Page 155

14. When was the environmental society of Chandigarh formed ?

    Ans. Page 156

15. What is Human Rights ?

    Ans. Page 148

MODEL SHORT QUESTIONS AND ANSWERS

1. **What is throughput ?**

   Ans. If all the people we'll be adding to the earth try to be high consumers, we'd have to extract resources from the earth much faster and process them into products faster. Eventually, all that stuff will turn into waste, which we then throw back into nature. This processing and discarding of materials is called throughput.

2. **What is overshoot ?**

   Ans. If a swiftly growing society exceeds the carrying capacity of its natural systems, the population keeps growing for a while. The excess population is called overshoot.

3. **What is photosynthesis ?**

   Ans. Plants use chlorophyll to take energy from the sun, carbon from CO_2 in the air and water containing nutrients from their roots to make glucose ($C_6H_{12}O_6$). This process is called photosynthesis.

4. **What is meant by greenhouse effect ?**

   Ans. The surface temperature of our planet is very delicately balanced. If all the solar energy striking the earth were to remain here, the planet would be unlivable. Fortunately, most of the heat is radiated back to space and captures just enough heat to provide our normal surface temperature. We call this as greenhouse effect.

5. **What is global warming ?**

   Ans. Burning of fossil fuels adds heat directly to the atmosphere and also pollutes the air and adds to the greenhouse effect. As CO_2 builds up, the earth gets hotter and hotter. This is referred to as global warming.

6. **What is Entropy ?**

   Ans. Entropy is a process by which energy gets transformed and scattered.

7. **What is geothermal energy ?**

   Ans. In a few places, heat from the interior of the earth is close enough to the surface to allow people to tap into it and make it do work. That is called geothermal energy.

8. **Name a non-solar energy source ?**

   Ans. Tidal energy, nuclear power.

9. **What is ecology ?**

   Ans. Ecology is the study of the interactions between organisms and their environment.

10. **What is an eco-system ?**

Ans. Eco-system comprises the biotic community in conjunction with the associated complex of physical factors that characterize the physical environment.

11. **What is adaptation ?**

Ans. Any heritable trait, i.e. one which is capable of being transmitted to the next generation, be it behavioural, morphological or physiological which aids survival or reproduction in a particular environment is an adaptation to that environment.

12. **What do you mean by tolerance ?**

Ans. The degree of environmental variation that a species can cope with is that species' range of tolerance.

13. **What do you mean by pollution ?**

Ans. Presence of abnormally high concentrations of harmful substances in the environment.

14. **What is biosphere ?**

Ans. The part of the Earth's environment in which living organisms are found and with which they interact to produce a steady state system, effectively a whole planet eco-system. Sometimes it is termed 'ecosphere' to emphasize the interconnection of the living and non-living components.

15. **What do you understand by the term environmental science ?**

Ans. It is the study of environments. This may be interpreted fairly strictly as the physical environment or may include the biological environment of an organism; or, in its widest sense, it may also consider social, cultural and other aspects of the environment.

16. **Who are called producers ?**

Ans. In an ecosystem, an organism that is able to manufacture food from simple inorganic substances are called producers.

17. **Who are consumers ?**

Ans. In the widest sense, a heterotrophic organism that feeds on living or dead organic material.

18. **What is genetics ?**

Ans. It is the scientific study of genes and heredity.

19. **What is meant by bio-geochemical cycle ?**

Ans. The movement of chemical elements from organism to physical environment to organism in more or less circular pathways.

20. **What is biome ?**

Ans. A biological subdivision that reflects the ecological and physiognomic character of the vegetation. Biomes are the largest geographical biotic communities that is convenient to recognise.

21. **What is afforestation ?**

Ans. The establishment of forest by natural succession or by the planting of trees on land where they did not grow formerly.

22. **What is reforestation ?**

Ans. The establishment of a particular type of woodland by planting into an existing, different woodland type.

23. **What is agroforestry ?**

Ans. A system of mixed arable farming and forestry that has been practised for millenniums in many parts of the tropics, especially in rain-forest environments.

24. What is soil ?

Ans. The natural, unconsolidated, mineral and organic material occurring on the surface of the earth, it is a medium for the growth of plants.

25. What is an aerosol ?

Ans. A colloidal substance, either natural or man-made, that is suspended in the air because the small size (0.01-10μm) of its particles make then fall slowly.

26. What is forest ?

Ans. A plant formation that is composed of trees, the crowns of which touch, so forming a continuous canopy or the trees that make up a forested area.

27. What is meant by renewable resources ?

Ans. A resource produces as part of the functioning of natural systems at rates comparable with its rate of consumption.

28. What is meant by non-renewable resources ?

Ans. A resource that is concentrated or formed at a rate very much slower than its rate of consumption.

29. What is biomagnification ?

Ans. An increase in the concentration of a chemically stable substance along a food chain in extreme cases leading to physical ill-effects.

30. What is coagulation ?

Ans. The clumping together of colloidal particles to form a large mass; it may be caused by heating or by addition of ions that neutralise the electrical charge which stabilizes the colloid.

31. What is flocculation ?

Ans. A process in which clay and other soil particles adhere to form larger groupings or aggregates thereby coarsening the soil texture and making heavier soils easier to cultivate.

32. What is desalination ?

Ans. A series of processes whereby salt water is rendered potable.

33. What is desertification ?

Ans. The process of desert expansion or formation which may occur as a direct consequence of climatic change, as a result of poor land-use policy or owing to some complex interaction of factors.

34. What does CSMCSRI stand for ?

Ans. CSMCRI stands for Central Salt and Marine Chemicals Research Institute.

35. Where is CSMCRI situated ?

Ans. It is situated in Bhavnagar.

36. What is CITES ?

Ans. CITES stands for Convention of International Trade in Endangered Species.

37. What does ICSU and IUCN stand for ?

Ans. ICSU stands for International Council for Scientific Unions. IUCN stands for International Union for Conservation of Nature and Natural resources.

38. What does UNESCO and UNEP stand for ?

Ans. UNESCO stands for United Nations Educational, Scientific and Cultural Organisation.

UNEP stands for United Nations Environmental Programme.

39. **What is MAB ?**

Ans. MAB is Man and Biosphere Programme.

40. **What does BSI and ZSI stand for ?**

Ans. Botanical Survey of India and Zoological Survey of India stands for BSI and ZSI, respectively.

41. **What does DNES stand for ?**

Ans. DNES stands for Department of Non-conventional Energy Sources.

ESSENTIAL AND IMPORTANT TERMS

FOR OBJECTIVE AND SHORT QUESTIONS

ABIOTIC — Non-living, The part of the environment that is not biological; includes water, soil, climate, geology.

ACCLIMATISATION — Process by which an organism adjusts itself to new conditions, a new environment or a different climate.

ADAPTATION — The process by which an organism has evolved to fit itself into its way of life in terms of its behaviour, ecology, physiology etc.

ANGIOSPERMS — A division of the plant kingdom that are commonly called flowering plants. Their reproductive organs are found in flowers. The seeds are in a closed ovary or fruit.

AUTECOLOGY — The ecology of individual organisms and populations; includes physiological ecology, animal behaviour and population dynamics; usually involves the study of one or two species.

BENTHIC — Relating to on or near the bottom of water. Refer to organisms which live at the bottom of rivers, seas, oceans etc.

BIO-CLIMATIC — Microclimates with reference to fauna and flora.

BIO-CONTROL — Biological control, especially of pests.

BIO-DEGRADABLE — Refers to subtances that can be easily broken down by living organisms.

DIVERSITY — A portmanteau term; gained popularity in the late 1980s; describes all aspects of biological diversity, such as ecosystem complexity, species richness and genetic variation. The variety of life found at various levels of biological organisation.

BIO-GEO-CHEMICAL — Usually refers to cycles of chemical elements, such as hydrogen, oxygen, nitrogen etc. from organism to physical environment to organism (or through biotic and abiotic parts of ecosystems).

BIO-GEOGRAPHY — The study of the geographical distribution of organisms and the different habitats in which they occur, as well as the ecological relationships involved.

BIOLOGICAL COMMUNITY — Populations of different species living in the same geographical area, within which there are interactions between the different populations.

BIOLOGICAL CONSERVATION — An activity aiming to ensure the continued existence of all levels of biological diversity.

BIOLOGICAL OXYGEN DEMAND (BOD) BIOCHEMICAL OXYGEN DEMAND — An indication of the polluting capacity of an effluent, where microorganisms take up dissolved oxygen and cause pollution by decomposing the organic material present in the effluent; measured as the weight (mg) of oxygen used by one liter of sample effluent stored in darkness at 20°C temperature for 5 days.

BIOLOGICAL PRODUCTIVITY — The productivity of organisms and ecosystems; defind by primary, secondary and community productivities.

BIOMASS (STANDING CROP) — The total mass of all living organisms (includes producers, consumers and decomposers) or of a particular set (eg. a species), found either in an ecosystem or at a particular tropic level in a food-chain; usually expressed as dry weight; expressed more accurately as the carbon, nitrogen, or calorific content per unit area.

BIOME — A geographical region which is classified according to the major type or dominant vegetation and the main climate. For instance, the temperate biome refers to that particular geographical area which has a temperate climate and forests composed of mixed deciduous tree species.

BIOSPHERE — The part of the earth's environment (atmosphere, lithosphere, hydrosphere) in which living organisms are found.

BIOTA — A general term referring to all living organisms.

BIOTIC — Relating to living organism or life.

BIOTOPE — The smallest geographical unit of the biosphere, or of a habitat, that can be delineated according to its own characteristic biota.

BUFFER ZONE — An area or zone that assists in protecting a habitat from disturbance, damage or pollution. It is a man-made or natural area that is managed to protect the 'integrity' of that area.

CARRYING CAPACITY — The maximum population of a certain organism that can be sustained by a particular environment.

CHLOROFLUOROCARBON (CFC) — One in a range of compounds that are chemically inert and in which a chlorinated hydrocarbon is treated with hydrogen fluoride; used widely in fire extinguishers and also as refrigerants, aerosol propellants, solvents also used in manufacturing of foam plastics. CFCs are 'greenhouse' gases since they can absorb long-wave electromagnetic radiation. Due to their chemical stability, they survive in the atmosphere long enough to enter the stratosphere, where they undergo decomposition by ultraviolet radiation, thereby liberating chlorine that results in the thinning of the ozone layer.

CHLOROPHYLL — The green pigment present in plants that helps in photosynthesis by absorbing radiant energy from the sun.

CLIMAX COMMUNITY (CLIMAX VEGETATION) — The stable biological community that comes into being at the end of successional changes. The vegetation reaches a state of equilibrium with the environment.

COMMUNITY — (SEE BIOTIC COMMUNITY)

CONSERVATION — The continued existence of species, habitats and biological communities (protected from damage, disturbance and pollution) and the interactions between species and their environment. It implies biosphere management within certain social and economic constraints.

CRUSTACEA — A diverse subphylum of Arthropoda (a highly diverse phylum of joined-limbed animals); the animals have two pairs of antennae, one pain of mandibles, and two pairs of maxillae, e.g. lobsters, crabs, shrimps, barnacles, slaters, woodlice.

DECIDUOUS — Applied to these parts of animals or plants that are shed seasonally, such as deer antlers or leaves of certain plants.

DETRITUS — Litter that is formed from fragments of dead material, such as dung, corpses, leaf litter etc.

DISPERSAL — The nature or tendency of an organism to move away. It can happen either from its birth site (natal dispersal) or from its breeding site (breeding dispersal).

DISPERSION — The spatial pattern of distribution of different organisms.

ECOLOGICAL SUCCESSION — A process where the biological communities go through a sequence of changes, eventually leading to a climax community.

ECOLOGY — The study of the interrelationships between living organisms and their environment.

ECOSYSTEM — A term first used by A. G. Tansley (1935), encompassing the living communities (biological communities) and their physical environment and the processes operating therein, including the flow of energy through the system.

ECOTONE — Area or zone between two different types of vegetation communities.

EDAPHIC FACTORS — Pertaining to the soil and influenced by characteristics of the soil or the substratum.

ENVIRONMENT — All the surrounding that can be differentiated as the natural environment and artificial environment; the complete range of external conditions, physical and biological, surrounding an organism.

EPIPHYTE — A plant that grows on another plant-seeking physical support.

EVAPOTRANSPIRATION — A combined term used to express total loss of water from vegetation, soil and water bodies.

EVERGREEN — Refers to a tree or shrub that has persistent leaves.

FOOD CHAIN — The sequence of energy transfer from the primary producers (autotrophs), through a series of organisms that either eat or are eaten (assumed that each organism feeds on only one other type of organism). At each stage, considerable energy is lost as heat. There are two basic types of food-chain — the grazing food chain and the detrital food-chain.

FOOD-WEB — A diagrammatic representation of feeding relationships of organisms within an ecosystem. It is actually a series of interconnecting food-chains.

FOSSIL FUEL — Refers to organic material deposits that are dug from the ground (derived from the Latin *fossilis* from *foedere*, meaning 'to dig'). They can be burnt for fuel, chiefly coal, oil, gas. These are formed by alteration or decomposition of animal and plant remains, that occurred under pressure.

GEOGRAPHIC INFORMATION SYSTEM (GIS) — Computer-based information systems by which objects in the environment can be linked geographically to map features; usually computerised systems that can capture and store data that describe regions and conditions on the Earth's surface.

GRASSLAND — A natural biological community composed principally of different species of grasses. The various kinds of grassland communities may be classified on the basis of the climate, the geology of the area and the dominant grass species.

HABITAT — The typical locality of particular characteristics in which a population of a species lives.

MACRO-CLIMATE — The climate prevailing in a major geographical region.

MICRO-CLIMATE — The climate prevailing in a particular habitat; a climate affected by the local environment, such as topography, soil, vegetation etc.

NICHE (ECOLOGICAL NICHE) — The 'space' or 'ecological role' occupied by a particular species and the resources used by a species. The niche has many dimensions; each resource (food, time of feeding etc.) and each abiotic factor (temperature, salinity etc.) can be considered a dimension of the niche.

PARASITE — An organism (typically small) that lives in or on mother organism (host) to derive nourishment.

PLANKTON — Aquatic organism, usually without any locomotive organisms, that drift with water movements; PHYTOPLANKTONS (plants), ZOOPLANKTONS (animals).

POPULATION — A collection of individuals (animals or plants of the same species) in a defined geographical area.

RAIN FOREST — Tropical forest where annual rainfall exceeds 254 cms.

RIPARIAN — Referring to the edge of rivers or streams.

SCLEROPHYLLOUS— Hard leaved; leaves that are drought resistant.

SPECIES — A group of the same kind of organisms which reproduce amongst themselves and are usually reproductively isolated from other groups of organisms.

SUBSISTENCE FARMING — Growing crops that is just enough to feed the farmer and his family; common in developing countries.

SUBSOIL — Layer of soil present under the topsoil; contains little organic matter, chemical substances from the topsoil are leached into it.

SUBTROPICS — Area lying between the tropics and the temperate zones.

SUCCESSION — Series of stages through which a plant community reaches its final stable state (or climax).

SUCCULENT — Refers to plants having fleshy leaves or stems in which water is stored, such as cactus.

SWAMP — Area where the land is very wet, such as mangrove swamp (swamp covered with mangroves).

SYNECOLOGY — The study of whole plant and animal communities; includes the study of terrestrial ecosystems, biological aspects of oceanography, along with applied problems of human management and disturbed ecosystems.

TAIGA — Forest covered region situated between Arctic Tundra and the steppe.

TAXON (plural TAXA) — A population or a group of populations, given a distinguishing name and ranked in a definite category.

TAXONOMY — Way of scientific classification of organisms; word derived from *taxis* (Greek), meaning "arrange".

TEMPERATE — A midlatitude climate, neither very hot nor very cold; influenced from time to time by both polar and tropical air masses.

TERRESTRIAL — Referring to land.

TERRESTRIAL RADIATION — Long-wave electromagnetic radiation from the earth's surface and atmosphere.

TORRID ZONE — General climatic name given to the equatorial zone (between the northern and southern tropics).

TRANSPIRATION — Loss of water from a plant to the atmosphere, through its stomata of leavs and the lenticles of stems.

TROPHIC LEVEL — One of the steps or levels in the transfer of food or energy in a chain.

TUNDRA — Extremely cold Arctic and Alpine region, devoid of trees, but with grasses, mosses, lichens and low shrubs.

WET LAND — General term applied to open water habitats; permanently or seasonally waterlogged land areas supporting a characteristic soil and vegetation; they include swamps, bogs and marshes.

WILTING — Limpness due to loss of plant turbidity because of insufficient water content in plant tissue which is needed to hold the cells rigid.

XEROPHYTE — A plant that can grow even in extremely dry conditions; adapted with waxy leaves, water storage capacity, and leaves reduced to spines in order to minimise water loss through transpiration.

MULTIPLE CHOICE QUESTIONS
with
ANSWERS

MULTIPLE CHOICE QUESTIONS WITH ANSWERS

Chapter 1. FUNDAMENTALS OF ENVIRONMENT

A. Tick (√) the correct answer :

(i) Life is dependent on the Climate ☐ Water ☐ Environment ☐ .

(ii) The earliest life on the earth have been found about 3·5 billion (350 crore) ☐ 4·5 billion (450 crore) ☐ 5·5 billion (550 crore) years ago.

(iii) Most of the environmental problems are created by Man ☐ Animal ☐ Nature ☐ .

(iv) The population growth of Bacteria is double within 20 minutes ☐ 30 minutes ☐ 40 minutes ☐ .

(v) Chlorofluorocarbons (cFC_S) are largely used in Refrigerants ☐ Television ☐ Radio ☐ .

(vi) Coal and Petroleum are called non-renewable resources ☐ renewable resources ☐ .

(vii) The earth's environment is constant ☐ ever changing ☐ fluctuating ☐ .

(viii) Most of the oxygen in the atmosphere has come from water through the photosynthetic activities of green plants ☐ blue alge ☐ wild animal ☐ .

(ix) Alfred Lothar Wegener is a German ☐ Russian ☐ Italian ☐ meteorologist.

(x) The name of the ancient landscape is 'Pangaen' ☐ 'Peaguin' ☐ .

(xi) The world's highest mountain is the Himalayas ☐ Rocky ☐ Alps ☐ .

(xii) The Sahara desert of Africa was situated near the South Pole ☐ North Pole ☐ Equator ☐ .

(xiii) Cyclone and Typhoon is the natural ☐ man-made ☐ disasters.

(xiv) The Richter Scale ☐ Vinear Scale ☐ Linear Scale ☐ use for measuring the amplitude of seismic waves.

(xv) The Pacific Ring of fire is located in and around the Pacific Ocean ☐ Indian Ocean ☐ Atlantic Ocean ☐ .

(xvi) Bhopal gas disaster is on December 3, 1984 ☐ December 3, 1985 ☐ December 4, 1984 ☐.

(xvii) The nuclear plant accident occurred on April 28, 1986 ☐ April 25, 1986 ☐ April 27, 1986 ☐ at Chernobyl.

(xviii) In 1800 A.D. ☐ 1700 A.D. ☐ 1600 A.D. ☐ only 2·2% of population lived in European cities.

(xix) In 1800 A.D. only 2·2% ☐ 3·2% ☐ 4·2% ☐ of population lived in European cities.

(xx) In 1700 ☐ 1800 ☐ 1900 ☐ only 12 million cities in the world.

(xxi) In 1965 ☐ 1975 ☐ 1985 ☐ the total million cities are 230 in the world.

(xxii) The first Industrial Revolution was started in 1660 ☐ 1760 ☐ 1860 ☐.

(xxiii) The period of Renaissance was as early the 15th century ☐ 16th century ☐ 17th century ☐.

(xxiv) The United Nations Stockholm Conference on Environment was held in 1972 ☐ 1973 ☐ 1974 ☐.

ANSWERS

(i) Environment. **(ii)** 3·5 billion (350 crore). **(iii)** Man. **(iv)** 20 minutes. **(v)** Refrigerants. **(vi)** Non-renewable resources. **(vii)** Ever changing. **(viii)** Green plants. **(ix)** German meteorologist. **(x)** 'Pangaen'. **(xi)** Himalayas. **(xii)** The Equator. **(xiii)** Natural disasters. **(xiv)** Richter Scale. **(xv)** The Pacific Ocean. **(xvi)** December 3, 1984. **(xvii)** April 28, 1986. **(xviii)** 1800 A.D. **(xix)** 2·2%. **(xx)** 1900. **(xxi)** 1985. **(xxii)** 1760. **(xxiii)** The 16th century. **(xxiv)** 1972.

Chapter 2. NATURE AND NATURAL PROCESSES

A. Tick (√) the correct answer :

(i) We live on the earth's surface ☐ continents ☐ landmass ☐.

(ii) The Sun is the nearest star to the earth ☐ the Jupitor ☐ the Saturn ☐.

(iii) The Sun is only 150 million ☐ 160 million ☐ 170 million km. away from the earth.

(iv) The solar surface is called the photosphere ☐ photosynthesis ☐ protoplanets ☐.

(v) The earth's crust is rich in silica and aluminium called SiAl ☐ SiMa ☐ layer.

(vi) The earth's crust is rich in silica and magnesium called SiAl ☐ SiMa layer ☐ .

(vii) 78·08% ☐ 78·80% ☐ 78·00% ☐ nitrogen in the atmosphere.

(viii) 20·95% ☐ 20·90% ☐ 20·59% ☐ oxygen in the atmosphere.

(ix) The total mass of the atmosphere is approximately $5{\cdot}2 \times 10^2$ tonnes ☐ $5{\cdot}2 \times 10^{12}$ tonnes ☐ $5{\cdot}2 \times 10^{15}$ tonnes ☐ .

(x) The composition of constituent gases from the surface (upto 100 Km.) is called homosphere ☐ heterosphere ☐ .

(xi) The upper mantle is called Asthenosphere ☐ Mesosphere ☐ .

(xii) The lower mantle is called Asthenosphere ☐ Mesosphere ☐ .

(xiii) The earth's crust is rich in nickel and iron called NiFe ☐ Mg ☐ .

(xiv) The Igneous rock is called Primary ☐ Stratified rocks ☐ .

(xv) Sandstone is a Igneous ☐ Sedimentary ☐ Metamorphic ☐ rock.

(xvi) Limestone is a Igneous ☐ Sedimentary ☐ Metamorphic ☐ rock.

(xvii) Quartzite is a Igneous ☐ Metamorphic ☐ rock.

(xviii) Marble is a Igneous ☐ Metamorphic ☐ rock.

(xix) Hydrosphere on the glove covers nearly 351,059,200 sq. km. ☐ 361,059,200 sq. km. ☐ 361,060,200 sq. km. ☐ .

(xx) The Atlantic Ocean ☐ Indian Ocean ☐ Pacific Ocean ☐ is largest in area.

(xxi) The oceans exchange 300 billion ☐ 250 billion ☐ 200 billion ☐ tons of carbon dioxide with the atmosphere every year.

(xxii) The Earth Summit held at Rio de Janeiro in Brazil in June, 1992 ☐ July, 1992 ☐ August, 1992 ☐ .

(xxiii) The Inter Tropical Convergence Zone is called I.T.C.Z. ☐ I.T.C. ☐ .

(xxiv) Nitrogen cycle ☐ Rock cycle ☐ is one of the Bio-geochemical cycle.

ANSWERS

(i) The earth's surface. **(ii)** The earth. **(iii)** 150 million km. **(iv)** Photosphere. **(v)** SiAl. **(vi)** SiMa. **(vii)** 78·08%. **(viii)** 20·95%. **(ix)** $5{\cdot}2 \times 10^{15}$ tonnes. **(x)** Homosphere. **(xi)** Asthenosphere. **(xii)** Mesosphere. **(xiii)** NiFe. **(xiv)** Primary. **(xv)** Sedimentary. **(xvi)** Sedimentary. **(xvii)** Metamorphic. **(xviii)** Metàmorphic. **(xix)** 361,059,200 sq. km. **(xx)** The Pacific Ocean. **(xxi)** 200 billion. **(xxii)** June, 1992. **(xxiii)** I.T.C.Z. **(xxiv)** Nitrogen cycle.

Chapter 3. ECOSYSTEM

A. Tick (√) the correct answer :

(i) Mangrove forests are found in the Coastal areas ☐ Mountain areas ☐ Polar areas ☐.

(ii) Carbon is a inorganic substances ☐ organic substances ☐.

(iii) Carbohydrates is organic compounds ☐ inorganic compounds ☐.

(iv) Polar bear ☐ wolf ☐ red fox ☐ seen in the Tundra area.

(v) The Steppes is located in the southern Russia ☐ Africa ☐.

(vi) The Veld grassland is in Africa ☐ Australia ☐.

(vii) The Pampas grassland occur in South America ☐ Africa ☐.

(viii) Average salt content in marine water is 3·50% ☐ 3·05% ☐ 3·00% ☐ by weight.

(ix) India has lost 3·3 million ☐ 3·4 million ☐ 3·5 million ☐ hectares of forest lands in between 1952-1972.

(x) Chipko Movement was started in 1972 ☐ 1973 ☐ 1974 ☐.

(xi) Savana is one of the Tropical ☐ Equatorial ☐ Polar ☐ grassland.

ANSWERS

(i) The Coastal areas. **(ii)** Inorganic substances. **(iii)** Organic compounds. **(iv)** Polar bear. **(v)** Russia. **(vi)** Africa. **(vii)** South America. **(viii)** 3·50%. **(ix)** 3·4 million. **(x)** 1972. **(xi)** Tropical.

Chapter 4. POPULATION AND ENVIRONMENT

A. Tick (√) the correct answer :

(i) World population was 545 ☐ 535 ☐ 525 ☐ million in 1630.

(ii) World population was 5716 ☐ 5715 ☐ 5714 ☐ million in 1995.

(iii) The average annual availability of water per capita was 5236 ☐ 5235 ☐ 5230 ☐ cubic meters in 1951.

(iv) The average annual availability of water per capita was 2227 ☐ 2226 ☐ 2225 ☐ cubic meters in 1991.

ANSWERS

(i) 545 million. **(ii)** 5716 million. **(iii)** 5236 cubic meters. **(iv)** 2227 cubic meters.

Chapter 5. LAND AND WATER USE OF THE EARTH

A. Tick (√) the correct answer :

(i) The cropland is 45% ☐ 55% ☐ 65% ☐ in South Asia.

(ii) The cropland is 7·00% ☐ 8·00% ☐ 9·00% ☐ in sub-Saharan Africa.

(iii) Asia covers nearly 30 per cent ☐ 35 per cent ☐ 40 per cent ☐ land area in the world.

(iv) Australia covers nearly 5·5 per cent ☐ 5·6 per cent ☐ 5·7 per cent ☐ land area in the world.

(v) The forest land cover is only 0·01 ☐ 0·02 ☐ 0·03 ☐ hectare per capita in West Bengal.

(vi) Oceans and seas covers nearly 95 per cent ☐ 96 per cent ☐ 97 per cent ☐ of water on the earth's surface.

(vii) Saline water is 95 per cent ☐ 96 per cent ☐ 97 per cent ☐ on the earth's surface.

(viii) Precipitation on oceans are $3{\cdot}24 \times 10^{14}$ ☐ $3{\cdot}25 \times 10^{14}$ ☐ $3{\cdot}26 \times 10^{14}$ ☐ cubic meters per year.

ANSWERS

(i) 45%. **(ii)** 7·00%. **(iii)** 30 per cent. **(iv)** 5·7 per cent. **(v)** 0·01 hectare. **(vi)** 97 per cent. **(vii)** 97 per cent. **(viii)** $3{\cdot}24 \times 10^{14}$ meters per year.

Chapter 6. AIR POLLUTION

A. Tick (√) the correct answer :

(i) Most of the human being requires for breathing about 14 kg. ☐ 15 kg. ☐ 16 kg. ☐ of air everyday.

(ii) A man can survive without food for 5 weeks ☐ 4 weeks ☐ 3 weeks ☐.

(iii) A man can survive without water for 3 days ☐ 4 days ☐ 5 days ☐.

(iv) The average forest area should be 33·00% ☐ 34·00% ☐ 35·00% ☐ of the total land area of the country.

(v) The average global temperature has increased by 0·5°C-1·5°C ☐ 0·5°C-1·15°C ☐ 0·5°C-2·00°C ☐ during the last 100 years.

(vi) The sea-level has rised near about 0·10 meter ☐ 0·12 meter ☐ 0·15 meter ☐ during the last 100 years.

(vii) The green house effect is about 10-12% ☐ 10-15% ☐ 10-20% ☐ by the CFCs.

(viii) One molecule of Ozone O_3 ☐ O_2 ☐.

(ix) The intensity level of sound is 130 decibel ☐ 140 decibel ☐ 150 decibel ☐ from Jet-plane during take-off time.

(x) The Intensity level of sound is 35 ☐ 45 ☐ 55 ☐ decibel from a Radio.

(xi) Ammonia is a odour ☐ noise ☐ pollutant.

ANSWERS

(i) 14 kg. **(ii)** 3 weeks. **(iii)** 5 days. **(iv)** 33·00%. **(v)** 0·5°C-1·5°C. **(vi)** 0·15 meter. **(vii)** 10-12%. **(viii)** O_3. **(ix)** 150 decibel. **(x)** 45 decibel. **(xi)** Odour.

Chapter 7. ENERGY SOURCE

A. Tick (√) the correct answer :

(i) Coal is a Renewable energy resource ☐ Non-renewable energy resource ☐.

(ii) Tidal power is a Renewable energy resource ☐ Non-renewable energy resource ☐.

(iii) Biomass is a Renewable energy resource ☐ Non-renewable energy resource ☐.

(iv) Hydro-electricity is a Fund resource ☐ Flow resource ☐.

(v) Geo-thermal energy is a Conventional resource ☐ Non-conventional resource ☐.

(vi) Tidal power is a Conventional energy resource ☐ Non-conventional energy resource ☐.

(vii) Outside the atmospheric layer the average intensity of solar energy is 1·2 Kilowatt per square meter (1·2 Kw/m^2) ☐ 1·3 Kilowatt per square meter (1·3 Kw/m^2) ☐ 1·4 Kilowatt per square meter (1·4 Kw/m^2) ☐.

(viii) The net amount of solar energy on the earth's surface is about 0·7 Kw/m^2 (0·7 Kilowatt per square meter) ☐ 0·8 Kw/m^2 (0·8 Kilowatt per square meter) ☐ 0·9 Kw/m^2 (0·9 Kilowatt per square meter) ☐.

(ix) The ultraviolet radiation is less than 300 nm ☐ less than 400 nm ☐ less than 500 nm ☐.

(x) The visible radiation is 400 to 550 nm ☐ 400 to 650 nm ☐ 400 to 750 nm ☐.

(xi) The infra-red radiation is 750 to 1500 nm ☐ 750 to 2000 nm ☐ 750 to 2500 nm ☐.

(xii) The 'Dynamo' was discovered by Michael Faraday ☐ James Watt ☐ Eli Whitney ☐.

(xiii) A large number of Nuclear Power Stations have been established in the year 1945 ☐ 1950 ☐ 1955 ☐.

(xiv) Bio-gas or Gubar gas is a Renewable source of energy ☐ Non-renewable source of energy ☐.

(xv) The first Geothermal energy generation plant was started at Hawaii ☐ Tokyo ☐ Osaka ☐.

(xvi) Kalapakkam is a Hydel power station ☐ Nuclear power station ☐ Thermal power station ☐.

ANSWERS

(i) Non-renewable energy resource. **(ii)** Renewable energy resource. **(iii)** Renewable energy resource. **(iv)** Flow resource. **(v)** Non-conventional resource. **(vi)** Non-conventional energy resource. **(vii)** 1·2 Kilowatt per square meter (1·2 Kw/m^2). **(viii)** 0·9 Kw/m^2 (0·9 Kilowatt per square meter). **(ix)** Less than 400 nm. **(x)** 400 to 750 nm. **(xi)** 750 to 2500 nm. **(xii)** Michael Faraday. **(xiii)** 1950. **(xiv)** Renewable source of energy. **(xv)** Hawaii. **(xvi)** Nuclear power station.

Chapter 8. ENVIRONMENT AND PUBLIC HEALTH

A. Tick (√) the correct answer :

(i) Human tolarable limit of noise is 50 decible ☐ 60 decible ☐ 70 decible ☐.

(ii) Hepatitis is a Virus infection disease ☐ Bacteria infection disease ☐.

(iii) Cholera is a Virus infection disease ☐ Food borne disease ☐.

(iv) Chicken pox is an air borne disease ☐ water borne disease ☐ Food borne disease ☐.

(v) Leprosy disease may transmitted through air ☐ water ☐ food ☐.

(vi) Human malaria is transmitted through male Anopheles mosquito ☐ female Anopheles mosquito ☐.

(vii) Kalazar is transmitted through Sand fly ☐ Fly ☐ House fly ☐.

(viii) Arsenic is available in ground water ☐ pond water ☐ rain water ☐.

(ix) According to WHO, the permissible limit of arsenic in water is 0·03 mg. per litre ☐ 0·04 mg. per litre ☐ 0·05 mg. per litre ☐.

(x) Berrilium is used in thermal power plants ☐ atomic power plants ☐.

ANSWERS

(i) 60 decible. **(ii)** Virus infection disease. **(iii)** Food borne disease. **(iv)** Air borne disease. **(v)** Air. **(vi)** Female Anopheles mosquito. **(vii)** Sand fly. **(viii)** Ground water. **(ix)** 0·05 mg. per litre. **(x)** Atomic power plants.

Chapter 9. WASTE MANAGEMENT

A. Tick (√) the correct answer :

(i) Distiled water P^H is 6·00 ☐ 7·00 ☐ 8·00 ☐.

(ii) Detergent is one of the sources of Air pollution ☐ Water pollution ☐.

(iii) Biochemical Oxygen Demand is called BOD ☐ BD ☐ DO ☐.

(iv) Chemical Oxygen Demand is called COD ☐ BOD ☐ CD ☐.

(v) The dust particle size varies from 0·1 to 0·75 micron ☐ 0·1 to 0·65 micron ☐ 0·1 to 0·55 micron ☐.

(vi) Smoke particle size varies from 0·5 to 1·00 micron ☐ 0·5 to 2·00 micron ☐ 0·5 to 3·00 micron ☐.

(vii) Fumes particle size varies from 0·03 to 0·3 micron ☐ 0·02 to 0·3 micron ☐ 0·01 to 0·3 micron ☐.

(viii) Mercury is present in Petroleum ☐ Coal ☐ Iron ☐.

(ix) Polychlorinated Dibenzo-dioxins is called PCDD ☐ PCD ☐ PCDF ☐.

ANSWERS

(i) 7·00. **(ii)** Water pollution. **(iii)** BOD. **(iv)** COD. **(v)** 0·1 to 0·75 micron. **(vi)** 0·5 to 1·00 micron. **(vii)** 0·03 to 0·3 micron. **(viii)** Coal. **(ix)** PCDD.

Chapter 10. ENVIRONMENTAL POLITICS

A. Tick (√) the correct answer :

(i) Green Bench was established in the Allahabad High Court ☐ Calcutta High Court ☐ Suprime Court ☐ .

(ii) Green Bench has been working since June, 1996 ☐ July, 1996 ☐ August, 1996 ☐ .

(iii) The Forest Act in India was enacted in 1972 ☐ 1982 ☐ 1993 ☐ .

(iv) The Atomic Energy Act in India was enacted in 1952 ☐ 1962 ☐ 1972 ☐ .

(v) The Wildlife Protection Act in India was enacted in 1952 ☐ 1962 ☐ 1972 ☐ .

(vi) The Water Prevention and Control of Pollution Act in India was enacted in 1957 ☐ 1967 ☐ 1977 ☐ .

(vii) The Forest Conservation Act in India was enacted in 1960 ☐ 1970 ☐ 1980 ☐ .

(viii) The Air Prevention and Control of Pollution Act in India was enacted in 1961 ☐ 1971 ☐ 1981 ☐ .

(ix) The Environmental Protection Act in India was enacted in 1966 ☐ 1976 ☐ 1986 ☐ .

(x) The National Environment Tribunal Act in India was enacted in 1975 ☐ 1985 ☐ 1995 ☐ .

ANSWERS

(i) Calcutta High Court. **(ii)** June, 1996. **(iii)** 1972. **(iv)** 1962. **(v)** 1972. **(vi)** 1977. **(vii)** 1980. **(viii)** 1981. **(ix)** 1986. **(x)** 1995.